Descent into Darkness

JAMES J. ZATKO

Descent

THE DESTRUCTION OF THE

into

ROMAN CATHOLIC CHURCH IN

Darkness

RUSSIA, 1917–1923

—

The University of Notre Dame Press

1965

PREFACE

THE PURPOSE of this study is to tell in a scholarly way the history of the Roman Catholic Church in Russia during the Bolshevik Revolution. It is based upon materials gathered from United States sources—for instance, the Library of Congress, the Hoover Library at Stanford, and the Archives of the Polish Roman Catholic Union in Chicago, Illinois—and in Poland. While some of this material has been used, much of it has never been previously consulted, especially the materials from the library of Monsignor B. Ussas, Warsaw, Poland. This research would have been impossible without three fellowships from the Ford Foundation and one fellowship from the University of Notre Dame. To these excellent institutions the author expresses his deepest gratitude.

Special thanks are due to Professor Stephen Kertesz, Professor of International Relations and Chairman of the Committee on International Relations at the University of Notre Dame, and to Miss Emily Schossberger, the director of the University of Notre Dame Press. Their steady and personal interest helped this book see the light of day.

There is no particular dedication in this book, but the author humbly offers it in homage to the kind relatives and good friends, here and abroad, who encouraged him, endured with him, and supported him during the grievous times that every scholar knows.

James J. Zatko

July 16, 1964
Feast of Our Lady of Mount Carmel

CONTENTS

X

ABBREVIATIONS

AAS   *Acta Apostolicae Sedis*

BA   *Budkiewicz Archive*

CA   *Cieplak Archive*

DPR   *Documenta Pontificum Romanorum Historiam Ucrainae Illustrantia*

KP   *Kurjer Polski*

KU   *Komunikaty Urzędowe Sekretarjatu Arcybiskupa Metropolity Mohylowskiego*

KW   *Kurjer Warszawski*

NAD,RS   National Archives, Document Division, Russian Section, Record Group 59, Department of State, Washington, D.C., Decimal File (1910–1929)

OR   *Osservatore Romano*

OZ   *Obvinitelnoe Zakliuchenie*

US *Foreign Relations*
      Papers relating to the Foreign Relations of the United States, 1923

ZZVP   *Zhurnal Zasedaniia Vremennogo Pravitelstva*

I

The Historical Background

Christianity in Russia has a history almost as old as the history of the Russian state. The first certain information we have comes from the time when Prince Igor of Kiev concluded a treaty with the Byzantine Empire in 944. Moreover, contacts with the Western Church occurred with surprising frequency, in the light of later events: from the monk Adalbert in the time of Olga to the embassies during the reign of Vladimir, who converted Russia to Christianity.

The Mongol conquest produced effects of the greatest importance in the ecclesiastical history of the areas now a part of Russia. While the eastern principalities fell under the Mongol rule, the western were gradually absorbed into the rising Grand Duchy of Lithuania. When the Grand Duchy of Lithuania united with the Kingdom of Poland, the western principalities were opened to Catholic and Western influences, whose history can be traced from the Council of Constance to the Union of Florence, the Union of Brest, and the Synod of Zamość.

However, the conflict between the Polish-Lithuanian Commonwealth and the Grand Duchy of Moscow in the sixteenth and seventeenth centuries gained momentum, until in the eighteenth century it became clear who the victor was. All this finally issued in the Partitions of Poland. For the Catholics of the area, Byzantine and Latin, this had fateful consequences.

The Partition of Poland

According to the First Partition Treaty, signed in St. Petersburg on August 5, 1772, Russia received the palatinates of Witebsk and Mścisław, part of those of Połock and Mińsk, as well as the remainder of Polish Livonia, the Duchy of Curland. Of the 1,300,000 inhabitants acquired thus by Russia, there were 900,000 Catholics, of whom 100,000 followed the Latin rite while 800,000 were Uniate or Greek Catholics.

The First Partition in 1772, with this influx of Catholics into the Russian state, brought in its wake many problems for the Catholics of these lands—not the least being the disruption of diocesan territories, both Latin and Greek Catholic. Within the lands annexed by Russia, there was no resident Latin bishop at all. The situation of the Greek Catholics, however, was not quite so unfortunate, for within the lands there was the archdiocese of Połock with Jason Smogorzewski (1780–1788) as the incumbent. Yet there were legal complications even for the Greek Catholics, because the episcopal title of Kiev—the mother of all the Russian and Ruthenian churches—and the title of Smoleńsk had been preserved only in the Commonwealth; and the Greek Catholic archbishop of Lwów, Leo Szeptycki (1749–1779), bore also the ancient and honored title "The Metropolitan of Kiev" from the year 1762. Practical jurisdiction, however, had been in the hands of the archbishop of Połock.

Complicated as the religious problem was, Catherine II (1762–1796) had also to undertake the political task of integrating the Catholics—Roman and Greek—into the Russian governmental structure. Peter I (1682–1725), by eliminating the patriarchate, had effectively subordinated the Russian Orthodox Church to the civil authority; its position would serve as a model for the organization of the Catholic Church. The initial steps in this direction had already been taken.

One of Peter I's creations that seemed destined to play an important role in the history of the Catholic Church in Russia was the College of Justice for Livonia, Estonia, and Finland—a branch of the Central College of Justice. This College of Justice for Livonia,

Estonia, and Finland was to be the governing body for the Protestants of the Baltic lands acquired by Peter in the Treaty of Nystad in 1721 after the Great Northern War, and to act as the court of second instance in all temporal and spiritual affairs after the local Protestant consistory. The senate of the Empire was to be the court of last instance. Thus, the Baltic College of Justice functioned as a central consistory for all Lutheran and Reformed churches in Livonia, Estonia, and Finland. In 1734, Empress Ann (1730–1740) extended the authority of the Baltic College over the Protestants of the whole Empire.

The original occasion for Catherine's intervention in Catholic affairs of pre-Partition times was the strife raging among the various national groups within the Catholic body in St. Petersburg—composed as it was of Germans, French, Italians, and Poles. The Germans especially looked askance upon the Italian missionaries sent by the Congregation of the Propaganda, missionaries unable to speak anything but Italian. Complaints sent to the Propaganda led to no solution, for the Congregation delayed and temporized. Finally, the Germans took their complaints to Catherine II. On November 6, 1766, she subordinated the Catholic parish of St. Petersburg to the College of Justice of Livonia, Estonia, and Finland, at the same time ordering the College to prepare a charter for the congregation at St. Petersburg. An *ukaz* of February 12, 1769, announced a basic law, consisting of eleven sections and fifty-one articles, prescribing the administrative procedures not only for the church in St. Petersburg but also for the Moscow congregation, and later for the Catholic churches of the Empire.

According to the regulation, the majority from the four nationalities elected the superior of the mission, a right which belonged to the Catholics because they had built the church. The elections, preceded by a mass and sermon, were to be held in the church. A member of the Baltic College and a secretary supervised the election. The secretary was obliged to inform the College of Foreign Affairs of the result with the purpose of obtaining the approval of the proper ecclesiastical authorities, undoubtedly Rome. The faithful also elected eight representatives, two from each nationality; each national group was responsible for the nomination of four candidates. Then the College of Justice confirmed the elected representatives, who held office for three years and were responsible for the administration of church temporalities. Together with the superior they took the inventory of church goods; they also administered the finances and supervised the church school for the Catholic children.

The *ukaz* also regulated the acquisition and permanence of the clerical staff. The College of Foreign Affairs served as the necessary intermediary in securing clergy from beyond the imperial frontiers. Every newly-arrived religious priest had to present himself to the College of Justice with his personal documents. The number of Reformed Franciscans in St. Petersburg was raised from four to six, and they were obliged to serve the Catholics of Kronstadt, Riga, and Reval. The *ukaz* also raised the number of Capuchins permitted to work in Moscow from two to three. All could remain in Russia for eight years. Nor were these priests to call themselves "missionaries"; and proselytizing was severely forbidden. The German Catholic colonies on the Volga remained under the care of Reformed Franciscans until 1803, when Alexander I replaced the Franciscans with Jesuits. In 1803 there were about 9,751 Catholics on the Volga.

After the Partition, an *ukaz* of December 14, 1772, gave authority to the future Roman Catholic bishop of Russia over all monasteries, churches, and clergy and obliged him, as well as the Greek Catholic Archbishop Smogorzewski of Połock, to follow exactly the Regulation of 1769 in the government of his church. Both bishops were to be assisted by consistories of two or three assessors rather than by a cathedral chapter.

The *ukaz* forbade the clergy of both rites to proselytize among the Orthodox; required an imperial *placet* for papal and curial documents; and in administrative affairs made the College of Justice the first instance of appeal, while the senate was the second.

This administrative structure was crowned by the founding of a bishopric in Belorussia. On October 1, 1773, Stanislas Siestrzencewicz-Bohusz (1731–1826) was consecrated in Wilno as the bishop of Mallo *in partibus,* to serve as vicar general of Bishop Ignatius Massalski (1762–1794) for the territories of the Wilno diocese lost in the First Partition. Soon after, on November 22, 1773, Catherine made Siestrzencewicz the bishop of Belorussia, with residence in Mohylew. Finally, he was ordered to obey the Regulation of 1769 in administering the Catholic Church in Russia.

These activities of the Russian imperial government had not passed unnoticed or unprotested in Rome. Already, in 1769, the Apostolic See had decided to send a visitator to Russia, to undo or correct the damage done by papal temporizing; but the events that led immediately to a diplomatic exchange between Rome and St. Petersburg were related to the Greek Catholics of the Empire. Metropolitan Szeptycki, the Greek Catholic archbishop of Lwów, died in 1779. Thereupon the king of Poland, Stanislas August Poniatowski (1764–1795), that weak but well-intentioned monarch, decided that Archbishop Smogorzewski of Połock should succeed to the metropolitan see, and that Maximillian Ryłło, the bishop of Chełm—a see destined to figure prominently and tragically in Greek Catholic history—was to occupy the archdiocesan see of Połock, a see sanctified by the relics of Andrew Bobola. The nuncio in Warsaw, Andrea Archetti (1776–1788), and Catherine II approved these changes; but, meanwhile, Bishop Ryłło had accepted from Empress Maria Theresa (1740–1780) the see of Przemyśl, now under Austrian occupation, for he was none too anxious to go to Catherine's Russia as archbishop. Catherine, therefore, felt personally insulted, or pretended to feel so; hence, she would not agree to Archetti's nomination of the superior general of the Basilians, Porphyrius Waszyński, to the archdiocesan dignity. In fact, she preferred to leave the see vacant. This situation threatened to become disastrous for the Greek Catholics, for episcopal liturgical and juridical functions ceased—thus threatening to disorganize Greek Catholic life, religious and social.

Catherine determined to profit by this unhappy situation of the Greek Catholics. In the diplomatic exchanges she raised her demands, until the price for concessions to the Greek Catholics included three conditions: Siestrzencewicz was to become the archbishop of all Roman Catholics in Russia; he was to have the use of the *pallium*, a sign of metropolitan dignity; and he was to have a coadjutor chosen by Catherine herself.

Pius VI (1775–1799) in a letter of October 27, 1781, accepted the idea of an archbishop of Mohylew, the use of the *pallium* by the archbishop, and a coadjutor, but he objected to the appointment of Siestrzencewicz as the archbishop. Catherine, however, countered with an *ukaz* of January 17, 1782, in which she established an arch-diocese of Mohylew, whose extent included all of Russia and whose incumbent was to be none other than Siestrzencewicz. To crown her ecclesiastical venture, Catherine named Canon John Benisławski, of Polish descent and formerly a Jesuit, the archbishop's coad-jutor. Two days later she wrote to inform the pope.

The papal court again applied the technique of delay, but Cath-erine threatened dire measures unless she had her way. The nuncio in Warsaw, Archetti, rang the alarm in Rome and counseled even-tual acceptance of the *fait accompli*, but only after negotiations had been spun out to all possible lengths. Alarmed by the nuncio's report, Pius VI, addressing a letter to Catherine, pointed out that his own conditions had been quite reasonable: reparation of papal honor by a bishop who had offended it, and a Greek Catholic bishop for the Catholics of that rite. He himself had been more than willing to meet the requirements of the empress: to send a nuncio to St. Petersburg in order to establish an archbishopric, to invest the archbishop with the *pallium*, and to consecrate Canon Benisławski. Thus had the empress triumphantly outmaneuvered the papal diplomats.

The curial diplomats now turned to the problem of sending a minister to the imperial court. The instructions were finally drawn up and sent to Archetti on May 10, 1783. Archetti passed through Wilno, Riga, Dorpat, Narva, and finally on July 4, 1783, after a journey of twenty days, arrived in St. Petersburg. There Archetti created the new archdiocese of Mohylew on April 26, 1783, and on January 18, 1784, the feast of St. Peter at Rome, granted the arch-bishop the honor of the *pallium* in the church of St. Catherine. Canon Benisławski was consecrated titular bishop of Gadara *in partibus* on January 28, 1784, but even though he was named coadjutor, this did not give him the right of succession.

With all these efforts Archetti succeeded in establishing canon-ically the Roman Catholic Church in Russia: an archbishop was at the head of the organization, a cathedral chapter existed to advise the bishop, a coadjutor was named and consecrated, and both a cathedral and seminary were in being. All this, nevertheless, left unsolved the problem of the Greek Catholics, of whom there were about 900,000. That the problem would be difficult to solve is suggested by the hostile attitude Catherine took toward the Greek Catholics. The very success of the Byzantine-Slavonic Catholic Church within the Polish-Lithuanian Commonwealth made it suspect in Russian eyes; hence, Archetti's accomplishment in organizing the Byzantine rite Catholics of Russia is the more substantial.

The chief effort here was directed to procuring imperial consent to the appointment of a new archbishop of Połock, and in this Archetti succeeded. Archbishop Siestrzencewicz recommended for the see the Basilian Heraclius Lisowski as a man devoted to the Union. Although Archetti was urging the nomination of Lisowski as early as September 29, 1783, Lisowski was not consecrated until April 7, 1784.

This, in sum, was the settlement that the Roman Catholic Church was able to make with the imperial government of Catherine II; in general, it represented an acceptance by the papacy of what Catherine achieved by her autocratic power, except for Archetti's success in providing an incumbent for the see of Połock. The value of the work done by Archetti should not be underestimated, as he laid the groundwork for an organized Roman Catholic life in Russia by establishing the hierarchy. In naming Lisowski the archbishop of Połock he also enabled the Slavonic rite Catholics to continue a hierarchical existence—thus, perhaps, prolonging for some time the life of that much persecuted body in Russia. After Archetti left St. Petersburg on June 2, 1784, he was appointed cardinal, both as a compliment to Catherine and as a reward for successfully carrying through a difficult task.

Indeed, Archetti's arrangement might have been the permanent settlement of the organizational question for Roman Catholics. Unfortunately for Poland, however, Catherine's appetite for land continued.

In the Second and Third Partitions both Poland and the Catholic Church once again suffered serious losses. In the Second Partition, approved by the "mute Diet" on September 2 and 3, 1793, Russia annexed the Ukraine and half of Lithuania, that is, 96,525 square miles and 3,100,000 inhabitants; in the Third Partition in 1795, Russia acquired Lithuania to the line of the Niemen, Wołyń, and the land of Chełm up to the Bug River, an area of 56,239 square miles. These acquisitions, besides bringing into the Empire a very large number of Catholics, involved serious canonical problems; however, Catherine's attitude and conduct did not facilitate a solution.

The lands seized in the Second and Third Partitions embraced six dioceses of the Latin rite and four of the Byzantine-Slavonic. The Latin ones were:

1 The diocese of Livonia, to which were attached some of the churches of Curland;
2 The diocese of Samogitia, which corresponded to the provinces of Samogitia and formed a part of the *guberniia* of Lithuania;
3 The diocese of Wilno, which embraced most of Lithuania and the palatinate of Mińsk;
4 The diocese of Łuck, which embraced a large piece of Lithuania and a part of Wołyń;
5 The diocese of Kiev, whose bishop resided at Żytomierz, and which included almost all of Wołyń and a part of Podole;
6 The diocese of Kamieniec-Podolski, which covered part of the palatinate of Bracław and extended into Galicia.

Overlapping these Latin dioceses were four Byzantine-Slavonic bishoprics:

1 The diocese of Kiev and Halicz, whose bishop bore the title of metropolitan and whose jurisdiction extended over all Lithuania;
2 The diocese of Brest-Litowsk and Włodzimierz-Wołyński, partly in Lithuania and partly in Wołyń;
3 The diocese of Pińsk and Turów, within the province of Mińsk up to the approaches of the Prypeć River;
4 The diocese of Łuck and Ostróg in Wołyń.

Thus, with the archdiocese of Mohylew and that of Połock, there was a total of twelve dioceses in Russia after the Third Partition.

Moreover, the relations of the archbishops of Mohylew and Połock to the bishops of the new lands had to be determined. Catherine, therefore, proceeded to "rearrange" the ecclesiastical organization. Since the see of Wilno was vacant, Catherine suppressed the title, and the bishop of Livonia, John Kossakowski, took possession of the see without having the title. She suppressed the Latin dioceses of Łuck, Kiev, and Kamieniec-Podolski but by her own autocratic power also established the dioceses of Pińsk and Łotyszów. She even appointed the incumbents: Monsignor Caspar Cieciszewski, the former bishop of Kiev, was assigned to Pińsk, while Monsignor Anthony Sierakowski, only a titular bishop, was named for the other see. Monsignor Sierakowski administered the diocese of Wołyń in spite of the protests of its canonical incumbent, Bishop John Dembowski.

If such was the fate of the Latin diocesan organization, the fate of the Byzantine Slavonic Catholics could hardly be any better. These Catholics had already been warned of what was in store for them: in 1780 Orthodox pastors were nominated for Eastern rite Catholic parishes; in 1794 it was declared a crime to belong to the Eastern rite church; and in the last two years of Catherine's reign, 1794–1796, 2,600 parishes had been closed, as well as 50 monasteries. During Catherine's "enlightened reign" about 1,000,000 Byzantine Slavonic Catholics joined the Orthodox church; in fact, ever since the Second Partition every fierce pressure was used—moral and physical force, as well as police activity—to bring these Catholics into the Orthodox fold. After the Third Partition, when "conversion" was pressed with renewed energy, the Greek Catholic metropolitan, Theodosius Rostocki (1788–1805), bishop of Kiev and Halicz, went to St. Petersburg to protest, but he was merely forbidden to return to his see. Finally, in September, 1795, Catherine abolished the metropolitan see and its three other Byzantine-Slavonic dioceses, allowing only the archbishopric of Połock to exist and to serve these millions of Eastern rite Catholics incorporated into the Russian Empire. This archdiocese, almost infinite in extent and impossible to administer, was probably made so deliberately, in order that Eastern Catholicism would die of neglect. Persuasion, prison, exile, and death formed the techniques of religious propaganda. In order to strip the Byzantine-Slavonic Church of its economic power, Catherine plundered the monastic and episcopal properties to enrich her favorites and their families. For a while, however, the Church was spared, because, by a kindly providence, Catherine died in November, 1796.

Paul I (1796–1801)

Catherine was succeeded by Paul I and, as in other matters, he began to make changes in the governmental structure and policy insofar as they affected Catholics. On February 26, 1797, an imperial *ukaz* had instituted in the College of Justice a separate department for Roman Catholic affairs, to which matrimonial cases as well as disciplinary clerical cases were to be sent as the court of second instance. The final court of appeal was to be the senate. The Roman Catholic department was to consist of six members—three clerical and three lay—under the chairmanship of General Łobarzewski, and the official language was to be Russian. After protests by Archbishop Siestrzencewicz, motivated perhaps by his resentment of having his own authority circumscribed, Paul, by an *ukaz* of February 6, 1798, and another of February 15, 1798, separated the department for Roman Catholic affairs entirely from the College of Justice and made the archbishop its president. Besides Archbishop Siestrzencewicz the department consisted of a vice-president, three clerical members, three lay members, a procurator, and two secretaries.

The complications in the Catholic Church in Russia, originating largely because of Catherine's independent action, required the intervention of papal authority. Even before the death of Catherine, as early as February 3, 1796, Cardinal Ignazio Busca, the papal secretary of state, had expressed to Lorenzo Litta (1794–1796), the nuncio at Warsaw, Pius VI's desire to send a minister to the court of St. Petersburg and had ordered him to open negotiations to this end. By March 22, 1796, Catherine had agreed in principle to a diplomatic mission from Rome to St. Petersburg; and her death did not prevent the consummation of an agreement, for Paul I also agreed to the papal mission. Archbishop Lorenzo Litta, who had arrived as nuncio in Warsaw on March 24, 1794, was chosen the nuncio to the imperial court at St. Petersburg. The objective of his mission was to organize the Catholic Church in the former Polish territories, to install bishops where they were needed and, above all, to protect the Byzantine-Slavonic Catholics who were most in danger.

Thanks to Archbishop Litta's skill as a diplomat, during his stay in St. Petersburg he was able to reconstitute the Latin and Byzantine-Slavonic Catholic hierarchies. By virtue of an *ukaz* of April 28, 1798, the Latin hierarchy was headed by the archbishop of Mohylew, whose metropolitanate included the dioceses of Wilno, Samogitia, Łuck, Kamieniec-Podolski, and the new diocese of Mińsk. Each bishop, besides receiving an auxiliary, was also given a consistory to aid him. An appeal from the consistory's judgments could be made to the department of Roman Catholic affairs, then to the senate, and finally to the emperor. This arrangement, undoubtedly, circumscribed the authority of the bishops and allowed for the interference of a lay, and non-Catholic, authority in ecclesiastical matters. The archbishop was allowed to reside in Mohylew, St. Petersburg, or in Kiev, and he had three auxiliaries: one at Mohylew, one at Połock, and one at Kiev.

The emperor also re-established the Byzantine-Slavonic Catholic hierarchy. The archdiocese of Połock, under Archbishop Lisowski, remained; and it was to minister to the Catholics of Belorussia. The diocese of Mińsk, whose ordinary was to be Bishop Arsenius Głoniewski, included the *guberniias* of Lithuania and Mińsk. Finally, the bishop of Łuck was to be Stephen Lewiński.

On July 27, 1798, Archbishop Litta gave these imperial arrangements their canonical legitimization by publishing the Acts that systematized the ecclesiastical situation in Russia. The nuncio did not, however, grant to the archbishop of Mohylew the authority he desired over the Byzantine-Slavonic Catholic bishops of Russia, for the nuncio wished to preserve their independence.

Although Archbishop Litta was forced to leave Russia on April 29, 1799, mainly because of his involvement in the unfortunate, and somewhat ludicrous, affair of the Knights of Malta, the work he accomplished in reorganizing the hierarchy was not inconsiderable, for it endured basically in the form he gave it until its destruction by the Bolsheviks in the twentieth century. While due credit must be given to the nuncio for his diplomatic skill, Paul I—so often represented as tyrannical and unfair—must be commended for having made a fair settlement with the Latin and Eastern rite Catholics of Russia, as fair indeed as both groups were to see for many a day.

Alexander I (1801–1825)

With Alexander I, successor of Emperor Paul, a new spirit entered into government circles—rumors of reform, constitutionalism, tolerance. But all these tendencies collided with Alexander's determination to preserve intact his autocratic power within Russia.

Since Alexander was so much interested in problems of political reform, it is not surprising that he undertook to reform the relations of the Roman Catholic Church with the government. On July 16, 1801, he appointed a special committee to examine the decrees of Catherine II since the year 1795 and those of Paul I from 1798 to 1800, and then to recommend a basic law for the religious affairs of the Empire. For the Catholics this was to mean that in administrative matters they were to be free of every foreign influence. On August 13, 1801, the committee presented to the imperial senate a project for the administration of the Roman Catholic Church. After corrections by the senate, Alexander approved the plan with an *ukaz* of November 13, 1801.

The decree itself abolished the department of Roman Catholic affairs and created the Roman Catholic College, a department of government, which preserved the old Petrine terminology, even when Alexander was abolishing other colleges or boards in favor of ministries.

The first article described the College as an ecclesiastical court, made up of lay and clerical personnel, to deal with matters in consonance with civil law. Enigmatically, the article provided that purely spiritual matters, dogmatic or canonical, should remain within jurisdiction of the consistories, and finally within the jurisdiction of the chief consistory or Ecclesiastical College. This article is hardly a model of clarity.

Article Two prescribed the structure of the College. The leading member was, of course, the archbishop of Mohylew; the other members were one bishop and one mitred prelate. The College nominated two candidates for each post, the choice to be made by the senate. Beyond this it was also to have six assessors, elected for three years by the chapters of the Latin dioceses from among the canons or the prelates.

The third article instructed the College to proceed according to the laws of the Church, but at the same time to respect the imperial decrees, and, by virtue of its oath of fidelity, to protect the autocratic power and the interests of the monarchy.

According to the fourth article, complaints against bishops or appeals from the decisions of the diocesan consistories were to be sent to the College. In matrimonial cases—whether of divorce or nullity—requiring two concurring judgments, after one diocese had submitted its judgment the College was to send the case to the consistory of another diocese. If the first and second decisions concurred, then the decision was final; but if the two judgments differed, then the College itself would make the final and binding decision.

In the fifth article the relations of religious with their superiors were regulated. Religious were permitted to have provincials, but these provincials were forbidden to have dealings with superiors general or any other authorities beyond the frontiers of Russia.

The sixth article forbade bishops to hold a benefice in their own or in another diocese; nor could anyone hold more than one parish. The College and the senate presented for imperial confirmation candidates for abbots, suffragan bishops and mitred prelates.

The immovable property and capital funds of monasteries and churches were to be preserved in their entirety and without damage, the same as government property, according to Article Seven. Buildings and foundations belonging to monasteries, destined for use as seminaries, schools, or orphanages, were to be used for that purpose. These buildings, as well as homes in which ecclesiastical persons lived, were free from any attachment.

The last article obliged the Ecclesiastical College to obtain exhaustive information from diocesan bishops on monasteries, churches, the clergy, ecclesiastical and clerical property, and any important events. The College must decide problems and affairs in accordance with canon law, the present decree, and the imperial laws.

Besides the archbishop, bishop, mitred prelate, and the six assessors, the College was to have a procurator, two secretaries, one interpreter, one executor, and several clerks. The College's budget was 18,500 rubles.

From a canonical viewpoint, Alexander's decree was just as offensive as the arrangements of Catherine and Paul; for by drawing an extremely fine distinction between the spiritual and temporal, it enabled the government to interfere in exclusively ecclesiastical problems, e.g., matrimonial cases, relations between bishops and religious orders, and monastic elections. Moreover, since the Roman Catholic Ecclesiastical College was the exclusive product of civil authority, the Roman Catholic central authority could not countenance it. Finally, the Ecclesiastical College usurped authority over the Byzantine-Slavonic Catholics, who were made subject to it, even though they had no representative in it. Eventually, a Greek Catholic department was established.

The responsibility of the College was vast, even if only the number of Latin Catholics be considered. In 1801 there were in Russia six dioceses, including the archdiocese of Mohylew; 1,710 secular priests of Latin rite; 3,094 male religious in 318 monasteries and religious houses; 569 religious women who lived in 80 convents; and 1,639,854 faithful over fourteen years of age. There were 845 churches.

By the time of Alexander's death (1825), the basic organization of the Church had been set. Beyond the basic hierarchical organization, the Ecclesiastical College—that institution destined to be a sign of contradiction in relations with Rome until the second half of the century—had been established. Until the 1870's, the College remained the chief instrument of imperial government and control over the Catholic Church. In the Roman Catholic Church, great harm had been done to it by its own archbishop who consistently displayed his willingness to subject the Church to governmental control; and in his attitude toward the Eastern rite Catholics, convinced though he may have been that the ultimate policy of the Russian government was absorption of that church into the Orthodox, he showed imprudence in his efforts to win control over that imperilled church and succeeded only in alienating its chief hierarch.

A year after the Decembrist disturbances, Archbishop Siestrzencewicz died (December 1, 1826), ending a stormy, but in many ways distinguished, career. A man of high intelligence, he was a prelate of the Enlightenment and a member of: the St. Petersburg Academy of Sciences; the Warsaw Society of the Friends of Science, honored by the universities of Cracow, Wilno, and Moscow; the St. Petersburg Academy of Medicine, as well as the London Agricultural Society. He was also something of an authority on the archeology of the Crimea. Besides these scientific pursuits, the archbishop showed himself beneficent and generous. At his own expense he built the church of St. Stanislas in St. Petersburg and another in Małatycze. He established scholarship funds for fifteen Belorussian boys, and four for girls.

For all his personal accomplishments, however, from the viewpoint of the Catholic Church and its center in Rome his policy proved to be unfortunate. His subjection to the civil authority and his ambition for the cardinalate or even a patriarchate of sorts caused him to follow a course that did not conform to the canonical regulations of his church or to the desires of the papacy—a papacy which was in straitened circumstances during the Napoleonic times. He was, in short, typical of the humane, but vain and worldly, bishop of the Polish Enlightenment.

Nicholas I (1825–1855)

Under Nicholas I the policy of Catherine I, in guarding the autocracy and preserving the territorial acquisitions from Poland by extending Orthodoxy in those lands, received an added impetus from the developing nationalism of Nicholas' reign. His attack on Catholicism was an indirect attack on the Polish character of the Borderlands. By destroying the religious support of national feeling and by eliminating the social and economic base of religious strength in the Borderlands, Nicholas hoped to integrate the peoples into a Russified and unified state—at whose head stood the Orthodox autocrat, head of both Church and State. The likeliest element for the process of assimilation was the Greek Catholic Church, whose liturgical rites were quite similar to those of the Orthodox churches, except in certain usages where Roman Catholic influence had remained strong—as in the building of multialtared churches and the ringing of bells during mass. These "Latinisms," as they are sometimes contemptuously called, were approved by the Synod of Zamość in 1720, which looked upon them as developments, legitimate and desirable, resulting from a lively cultural contact with the Latin rite within the boundaries of the Polish-Lithuanian Commonwealth. It was, therefore, against the Byzantine-Slavonic Catholic Church that Nicholas directed his destructive action.

Since the Basilians were so numerous and powerful, it is no wonder that Nicholas' first blow should strike that cradle of bishops. Through his *ukaz* of October 9, 1827, Nicholas forbade the Basilians to accept new candidates from among Latin Catholics. Although the Ecclesiastical College had already in Alexander's reign forbidden the Basilians to accept Latin Catholics as candidates, the Eastern rite Catholic Bishop Josaphat Bułhak had requested this ban to be lifted; and it had been lifted at a meeting of both departments, so that the Basilians again supplemented their ranks with Latins. Indeed, the bishops themselves admitted that unless the Basilian ranks were strengthened with candidates from the Latins, it would prove impossible to continue the Order's extensive works.

The final steps toward Nicholas' destruction of that church began on January 1, 1837, when he ordered the overprocurator of the Holy Synod to assume control of Greek Catholic ecclesiastical affairs with the same rights and privileges that the minister of the interior had formerly exercised over that unhappy church. This was only a temporary measure, for on March 17, 1839, Nicholas subjected the Greek Catholic Ecclesiastical College to the Orthodox Holy Synod.

To consummate this work, only the consent of the church's hierarchy and clergy would suffice, but Metropolitan Bułhak remained loyal to the Catholic Church until his death in the late autumn of

1838. Freed then from the moral force of the metropolitan's loyalty, four clerics published their transfer to the Orthodox Church on February 12, 1839. The Act of Połock proclaimed that the Union of Brest was but the result of astute policy by the "one-time" Commonwealth of Poland and of the pressure of the Latin clergy, who would not endure the Russian nationality. The clergy who signed the act declared themselves an indivisible part of the Russian nation and rejoiced to call themselves Russians.

By an *ukaz* of June 23, 1839, the emperor crowned the years of effort by finally incorporating the Byzantine-Slavonic Catholic Church into the Eastern Orthodox All-Russian Church, thus underscoring the nationalist character of the whole process. From that time on, the Eastern rite of the Catholic Church ceased to exist in the Russian Empire, except for Chełm in the Kingdom of Poland, and the Catholic Church lost more than 1,500,000 members.

The finishing touch to the organizational unification of the onetime Byzantine-Slavonic Catholic Church came in 1843 and again in 1847. In 1843, the Ecclesiastical College of Belorussia and Lithuania was then declared suppressed; and in 1847 the archives of the "Greek Catholic" College and those of the metropolitans were incorporated into the archives of the Holy Synod. Thus, the last traces of the Byzantine-Slavonic rite disappeared so to speak, and a stillness settled over the surface; but beneath the surface are the long decades marked by martyrdom and acts of unsung heroism— the end of which is not yet in sight.

Important for the future of the Latin church was the destruction of monasteries that went on in Russian territories. As early as 1832 the orders had been subjected to episcopal rule; but when the government discovered that the bishops were protecting the orders, Nicholas' *ukaz* of December 16, 1842, was even then restricting the activity of religious to purely religious duties within the church.

The government waged a much more effective campaign against the religious orders by the simple process of confiscating and closing the monasteries and convents. At the time of Arezzo's mission to Russia in 1803–1804, there were 323 Latin monasteries in the Catholic archdiocese and dioceses, not counting the 83 monasteries of the Basilians of the Greek Catholic church. By 1847 only 72 monasteries for men remained. Of the 40 women's convents for Latin nuns only 34 still existed in 1846.

Irrespective of the Concordat of 1847, the monasteries of the Dominicans, Franciscans, Bernardines, Carmelites, Trinitarians, Piarists, and Marian Sisters were confiscated in 1850. In that same year a convent of Benedictine nuns was closed. So the march went on—in spite of petitions, negotiations, and agreements.

A more sophisticated attempt to win control over the Latin church by negotiation suggested itself during the tenure of that subservient prelate, Martin Łaski, whom the government expected to co-operate in its plans. The Russian government, therefore, advised its representative in Rome, Count Charles Nesselrode, to study the situation, especially in view of the accession of a new pope, Pius IX (1846–1878). Nesselrode's conversations with Cardinal Luigi Lambruschini and Cardinal Giovanni Corboli-Bussi resulted in a memorandum which he presented to the government and to it was added a document, the work of Cardinal Corboli, which detailed the position of the Holy See. To study and investigate the situation, Nicholas convoked a special committee, composed of the minister of the interior, Leo Aleksevich Perovskii; Count Charles Nesselrode; Count Alexis Orlov; Count Paul Kiselev; Count Sergei Uvarov; Count Dmitrii Bludov, and Privy Councillor Turkul, the state secretary for Polish affairs. The committee met seven times: March 27, April 10–13, April 28, and July 13, 1846. The result of all these discussions was the decision to open negotiations with the Holy See in order to conclude a concordat. Negotiations, protracted over a year, achieved this much desired result and led to expectations that the position of the Church would be eased somewhat in Orthodox Russia. The concordat—signed in Rome on August 3, 1847, by Cardinal Lambruschini on behalf of the Holy See and by Count Bludov and A. Butenev on behalf of the Russian government—regulated several important problems. A new delimitation of diocesan boundaries was effected, which brought the ecclesiastical divisions into line with the civil administration. The archdiocese of Mohylew was divided into seven dioceses, the new one being the diocese of Kherson. The diocese of Wilno included, according to the concordat, the *guberniias* of Wilno and Grodno; that of Samogitia the *guberniias* of Kowno and Curland; that of Mińsk the *guberniias* of Mińsk, that of Łuck-Żytomierz the *guberniias* of Kiev and Wołyń; that of Kamieniec-Podolski the *guberniia* of Podole; that of Kherson the *guberniias* of Astrakhan, Bessarabia, Kherson, Ekaterinoslav, Saratov, Taurida, and the Caucasus; that of Mohylew the other *guberniias* of the Empire—Finland, Turkestan, and Siberia. The new diocese of Kherson was to have an auxiliary residing in Saratov, where the seminary would also be located. The Catholics of Armenian rite would be subject to the bishops of Kherson and Kamieniec-Podolski until Armenian bishops were appointed.

In the administrative structure, the Church achieved some improvement. The bishop was to be recognized as the only judge and adminstrator in the diocese, although the consistory would be permitted to consider certain matters; and the seminaries were to become completely dependent on the bishops, who after consulting with the government had the final say over candidates and the appointment and removal of professors. The archbishop of Mohylew remained in supreme charge of the Theological Academy in St. Petersburg, and he named the rector, the inspector, and the professors of the Academy after consulting with the government and obtaining the opinion of the Academy's senate.

The bishops were to name pastors after coming to an understanding with the government. Moreover, churches could be freely restored, or even new ones built, whether from the funds of societies or individuals.

One of the provisions of the concordat that was soon filled was the erection af a new diocese, even though the title of the diocese was changed. In place of the diocese of Kherson, envisioned by the concordat, the diocese of Tiraspol with residence at Saratov was established in 1848. Its head was to be one of the bishops of the province of Mohylew, and his jurisdiction included the *guberniias* of Saratov, Samara, Kherson, Ekaterinoslav, Taurida, and Bessarabia, an area of 462,504 square miles. The origin of the Catholic settlements in the region goes back to the policy of Catherine II, who invited foreign settlers to fill and populate the regions along the Black Sea and the Volga. In her decree of July 22, 1763, the empress guaranteed the free exercise of religion, allowing the settlers to build churches with bell towers; but the construction of monasteries was forbidden. The first bishop of Tiraspol was Ferdinand Kahn, a

Dominican, who was installed in 1850; his auxiliary was Bishop Vincent Lipski. The new diocese represented a real patchwork of nationalities: Russians, Poles, Armenians, Kirghiz, Circassians, Ossetins, Daghestanis, Germans, French, and Italian.

In spite of the very substantial agreement, serious problems remained unsettled, as indicated by Pius IX in a secret consistory of July 3, 1848. These included: freedom of communication with the Holy See; return of confiscated church and monastic property; the removal of the government secretary in the diocesan consistory, where he acted as a government spy; revocation of the law which forbade priests to bless mixed marriages; freedom of ecclesiastical courts in matrimonial cases; reform of the laws determining the conditions for entry into religious orders; removal of the *ukaz* forbidding religious to conduct schools; the restoration of the office of provincial for religious orders; revocation of the law which forbade conversion to Catholicism; and terminating the persecution of Eastern rite Catholics. Indeed, the condition of the Byzantine-Slavonic Church had not even been considered in the concordat. Still, Pius IX did not forget their plight, for in a letter to the archbishop of Mohylew and his suffragans he reminded them that Eastern rite Catholics were subject to the care and jurisdiction of the Latin bishop in whose diocese they happened to be. The bishop, he wrote, was bound to provide, if possible, priests who would care for the faithful according to their own rite; and he also ordered them to minister industriously and with alacrity to their spiritual needs, as well as do all they could to preserve the dignity of the Eastern rite. Thus did Pius react to the prohibitions of the tsar, who attempted to prevent the Latin clergy from helping the Byzantine-Slavonic Catholics. But, unfortunately, the efforts of the pope found little support in the archbishops of Mohylew at this period, except for the extraordinary figures Monsignor Felix Szczyt and Archbishop Ignatius Gołowiński (1851–1855).

Alexander II (1855–1881)

With the military defeat of the 1863 Polish rebellion, vengeance fell heavily on the Catholics both in Poland and in the northwestern provinces of Russia. In the northwest, Michael Muravev, the governor of Lithuania, distinguished himself by his fanatical cruelty, while in Poland the tsar himself undertook the repression. Alexander's interference with the hierarchical organization knew no bounds. In 1865 the diocese of Kamieniec-Podolski was abolished and in 1869 the diocese of Mińsk suffered the same fate. Between 1831 and 1863 in the Mińsk *guberniia* alone, 146 churches and chapels were closed. These aggressions did not go unanswered; for as early as October 2, 1866, Pius IX in a consistory of cardinals described the sufferings of the Catholic Church in Poland and Russia. In the same allocution he announced an imminent exposition of the persecution in Russia. Alexander was not slow to react; by an *ukaz* of November 22, 1866, he unilaterally revoked the Concordat of 1847 and declared relations broken between Russia and the papacy.

According to the imperial *ukaz* of May 10, 1867, the affairs of all Roman Catholics, clerical and lay, requiring the decision of the Holy See, were to be sent to the Ecclesiastical College. The Roman Catholics of Poland were included in this prescription. All the bishops of the Kingdom and Empire, including the archbishop of Mohylew, were obliged to have recourse to the Ecclesiastical College. The archdiocese was under the rule of an administrator, Bishop Joseph Staniewski (1863–1871).

If the Ecclesiastical College decided that the matter must indeed be submitted to the pope, then the president of the college would proceed to contact the pope in the most convenient manner.

After the decision had been made by the pope and returned to the president of the College, the president must submit all the documents in the case to the minister of internal affairs; and only after he had judged that there was nothing in the decision contrary to the laws of the Empire, would the decision be executed.

Clerics named to the metropolitanate or to a bishopric were obliged to proceed in the same way in order to obtain canonical establishment by the pope; and diocesan ordinaries had to use the same procedure to obtain approval of suffragans.

No act, brief, bull, instruction, or papal decision had any legal effect within the Empire or the Kingdom, unless it had been processed in the manner prescribed by law. Ignoring this law would make an individual liable to legal penalties.

The purpose of the decree was to hobble the Catholic Church in Russia and Poland as much as possible. It more effectively subjected the church of Poland to the Russian government in St. Petersburg, thus eliminating its separate organization as a reminder of an independent national existence. Finally, the decree contained within it the elements of a completely schismatic church, for the connection maintained with Rome was of the most tenuous kind. That it should provoke a decisive conflict on the problem of the Ecclesiastical College was not to be doubted; for Pius IX was cut from other cloth than was Gregory XVI.

On October 17, 1867, Pius IX issued an encyclical, *Levate*, wherein he formally and solemnly condemned the Ecclesiastical College, and he also forbade the bishops to take part in its activities. When news of the pope's stand finally reached them, Bishops Kasper Borowski, Zygmunt Feliński, Anthony Fijałkowski, Stanislas Krasiński, Ladislas Lubeński, and Vincent Popiel were exiled because of their attitude toward the condemned institution; but Bishop Staniewski continued to preside over the College.

The strong reaction of the papacy, the resistance of a few heroic bishops, and the unpleasant impression created in the foreign press persuaded the Russian government to come to an understanding with the pope. From the papal viewpoint negotiations issued successfully: vacant bishoprics were filled in Poland, the exiles were returned, and Bishop Fijałkowski became the archbishop of Mohylew (1872–1883). In agreement with the papacy, on March 9, 1873, Alexander II transferred the chapter and consistory of Mohylew to St. Petersburg and ordered a cathedral to be built there.

The negotiations also dealt with the question of the Ecclesiastical College, the Roman authorities demanding either the abolition of the institution or its reform according to canon law. In 1873 the Russian government declared that it was prepared to reform the College and remove from its structure all that the Holy See found objectionable. The College was to lose all judicial power and become a purely administrative body. A congregation of cardinals meeting in Rome on December 15, 1873, agreed that, with reform in the sense suggested, the College could be tolerated; but in order to clarify its "administrative" function, the cardinals insisted on removing from the jurisdiction of the College any spiritual matters as well as any ecclesiastical disciplinary action. On December 19 the pope confirmed the cardinals' decision, and finally the Holy Office also added its approval on August 26, 1874.

For the Russian government, Alexander's *ukaz* of February 18, 1875, announced that the College had ceased to be the intermediary between Catholics in Russia and the Holy See, and that its jurisdiction in matrimonial cases had ceased. With this the College ceased to be an uncanonical institution, and the bishops were permitted to take part in its activities. In spite of occasional transgressions beyond the limits of its competence, the College continued to exist until 1917; however, it declined in importance once it had been limited only to administrative matters, and the matrimonial and disciplinary actions had been removed from its jurisdiction. Its last reorganization in 1901 is testimony to its decline in importance.

As difficult as relations between Catholics and the government usually were, the Russian government did not hesitate to attack church services. The minister of internal affairs, P. A. Timashev, in a circular of January 20, 1868, requested the Ecclesiastical College to sound out the diocesan authorities for their views on the introduction of the Russian language into the supplementary services; but ecclesiastical administrators rejected the idea and the College added that if any language were to replace Polish, it must be Latin. The College based its rejection of Russian for church services on (1) the bulls of Pius V, Clement VIII, Paul V, and Urban VIII, which under the gravest penalties had enjoined the very words of the ritual to be used; (2) on the Church's principle that there should be no innovations; and (3) on the fact that the use of the Russian language would create the impression that a change of religious allegiance was contemplated.

In spite of the College's negative attitude, the tsar, by an *ukaz* of December 25, 1869, permitted the use of Russian where the needs and desires of the faithful required it; then Timashev ordered the College to transmit this decree to the diocesan authorities that were to be responsible for its implementation.

So strong was the resistance—both locally and in Rome—to this move, that in 1877 the newly restored diplomatic relations were once again broken off; and although there were continual negotiations even until 1882, full diplomatic relations were not restored. Nor did the Russian government relent in its drive to introduce Russian into the supplementary Catholic service. Indeed, it afforded only an excuse to continue the persecution that had really been unabated from 1863, and a struggle raged over the problem of language. Archbishop Alexander Gintowt (1883–1889) resisted, weakened, resisted, and occasionally gave way; on May 13, 1884, he categorically forbade the clergy to introduce Russian. The archbishop tried to negotiate, reason and persuade, but to no avail; and by 1884 there were thirty-four vacant pastorates, in which the Russian language had been introduced. Threatened with the closing of churches if he did not fill the pastoral positions with clergy willing to follow governmental policy, the archbishop felt he had to give way. Even so, he managed to outmaneuver the government somewhat for he sent excellent priests to the Mińsk *guberniia*, whom he ordered to minister also to the Russified parishes, just as they administered their own pastorates which had not submitted to the new ritual. However, the government soon saw through this maneuver and began to close the churches. The governor of the Mińsk *guberniia*, Prince Turbetskoi, closed eighteen churches.

The Edict of Toleration, 1905

Even though the edict of toleration appeared only in April 1905, the pressure of events had already produced some adjustments in the government's attitude toward the Church. Archbishop Boleslas Kłopotowski hardly assumed control of the archdiocese of Mohylew when he received from Cardinal Mariano Rampolla, the papal secretary of state, an important letter informing him that in virtue of an agreement between the Apostolic See and the imperial Russian government on April 2, 1897, the archbishop was to fill the parochial pastorates in the diocese of Mińsk, left vacant because of the conflict over the use of the Russian language in the church services. The condition attached was that these priests should administer the sacraments and exercise their ministry in church using only Latin. The cardinal assured the metropolitan that he had no reason to fear opposition from the government; but if difficulties arose, the Apostolic See would undertake to settle them. A letter from the pope in 1902 further clarified the line of conduct to be followed: first of all, the pastors of the parishes in dispute were to abstain from preaching any sermons at all, until a new settlement could be reached; secondly, lest the faithful be deprived of religious instruction, the pastors should assemble the people in church other than the time of liturgical services and explain the catechism in the language to which the Catholics of the area were accustomed.

However, with the breath of revolution abroad in the land, the decree of religious toleration finally appeared on April 17, 1905. Besides religious toleration, the law declared that anyone could leave the Orthodox Church without loss of rights and without penalties. The law also provided that should parents change from one faith to another, their children under fourteen years of age would also adopt the new faith; but if one of the parents remained in the old faith, the younger children were also to stay in the original faith. On the other hand, children of fourteen years or over were not to leave their faith until the age of twenty-one, even should their parents do so.

Among the most striking effects of the edict of toleration was that it opened the gates for a return of many so-called schismatics, namely Byzantine-Slavonic, who had preserved their Catholic allegiance since 1839, or in Chełm since 1875. This marvelous work of preservation owed much to the courage of the clergy, and after 1875 to the work of the Jesuits from beyond the frontiers of the Russian Empire who penetrated that empire in disguise, as merchants for instance, and ministered secretly to the Catholics; but above all, this rush into the Catholic Church testified to the courage and perseverance of the people, some of whom had preserved their faith and refused to enter the Orthodox Church, being thus without ministrations of priests for over twenty years. As to the numbers that returned to the Church, even Orthodox sources admitted that between 1905 and 1909 a total of 233,000 persons left the Orthodox faith to join the Catholic Church.

The edict also opened the way for episcopal visitations in all the dioceses. The most spectacular visitation was the journey of Bishop John Cieplak through all of Siberia to Sakhalin, where he visited the Catholic settlements peopled by those who had been attracted to promises of land in Siberia.

Another extraordinary development in the history of the Catholic Church which the edict permitted was the organization of a Russian Catholic Church, not a resurrection of the Union of Brest but a new creation—a truly Russian Catholic Church of Eastern rite. As early as 1896, Father Alexis Zerchaninov, a priest in the Orthodox Church, recognized the Catholic Church as the true church, and for his convictions spent the years 1898 to 1901 in prison. Some Orthodox priests followed him openly into Catholicism, while others, having secretly acceded to the Catholic Church, continued to function in the Orthodox Church. After the edict of toleration, Father Zerchaninov opened a small chapel in St. Petersburg in 1908. In the year 1910, Pius X placed these new Eastern rite Catholics under the jurisdiction of Metropolitan Andrew Szeptycki, the Ukranian Catholic archbishop of Lwów; those who secretly remained in the Orthodox Church were under the jurisdiction of the Latin archbishop of Mohylew. Moreover, the great reforming minister, Peter Stolypin (1863–1911), gave legal recognition to this church on April 17, 1911.

Under the favorable atmosphere of this early springtime of Catholicism in Russia, literary activities began. Father John Dejbner, active in the Russian Eastern Rite Catholic Church, began in 1910 to publish an excellent journal, *Slovo Istiny (The Word of Truth)*, drawing on the ideology of Soloviev. Father Anthony Około-Kułak, destined for distinguished service to the Catholic Church in Russia during its most turbulent times, published in Russia *Vera i Zhizn (Faith and Life)*, a journal with an apologistic and ascetic character. Father John Urban, a Jesuit, published a scholarly-type monthly, *Katolicheskoe Obozrenie (The Catholic Review)*, but only a few numbers appeared. Although its circulation was not great, its quality was excellent. However, that there were problems is seen from the career of Edward Ropp, who had become bishop of Wilno in 1903. He was many-sided in his activities: he supported the Catholic press, defended priests who were persecuted by the government, and he opposed socialism. On February 7, 1906, he also founded the Constitutional Catholic Party, whose program demanded freedom of communication between bishops and the Holy See; diocesan rule according to canon law; recognition of ecclesiastical courts; introduction of religious orders, brotherhoods and religious societies; adequate salaries for the clergy; suppression of the Ecclesiastical College; a free hand for the bishops in educating their clergy; and exemption of Catholics from taxes for the support of the Orthodox Church. So great was Wilno's confidence in its bishop that the electorate sent him to the *duma* as its deputy. But his activity eventually led to his exile by administrative sentence on October 5, 1907. His most serious "offenses" in the government's eyes were first of all, his organization of the Catholic Constitutional Party; secondly, his ignoring of the Russification policy of the tsarist government; thirdly, his signing with forty-nine other *duma* delegates of a declaration on freedom of conscience and religion; and lastly, his nationalist activity in "Polonizing" the Lithuanians and Belorussians in the northwestern regions of Russia. For these "crimes" he spent ten years in exile until his recall by the Provisional Government.[1]

With the beginning of the world war in 1914, great changes were in store for Europe—changes little suspected by the leaders of nations as they embarked on what for many proved their last adventure. For the Catholic Church, an era was coming to an end. Having been a carrier of Western European ideas, it had accomplished a historic task, for whatever disasters or whatever successes were in store for it, the Catholic Church in Russia had become too large to be easily wiped out, even though its hierarchy should disappear. This meant, too, that whatever government should appear in Russia, it would have to deal with a Western-oriented institution, whose supreme head was beyond the reach of the government. Whether this boded good or ill remained to be seen.

Socially, the most significant change in the structure of the Catholic Church was that it had ceased to be an exclusively Polish institution, even though it remained as yet predominantly so. This

---

[1] Jan Wasilewski, *Arcybiskupi i administratorowie archidyecezji mohylowskiej* (Pińsk, 1930), pp. 178–180.

meant that the Church could no longer be condemned as a foreign body, because it had become a part of Russian society, whether through its members who belonged to the Latin rite or those who belonged to the newly organized Russian Catholic Church of the Byzantine rite.

Other changes, less blessed, had also been wrought in the nine-teenth-century history of the Catholic Church. Numerically, its strength had not increased. The government had practically annihilated Catholic monastic institutions and monastic life. The Byzantine Slavonic Catholics did not have an organized existence in Russia since 1839, and the same 200,000 that returned to the Catholic Church in 1905 were a tragic reminder of the glory that had departed. For Catholics, the sheer physical means of worship had been destroyed, as hundreds of churches had been closed. Thus in this weakened state, the Catholic Church had to face the future.

What this future was to be, mercifully no one knew. The war, of course, prevented the quiet work of restoration, so desperately needed. Nor was there to be time for the Church to undertake the much needed social work among the Russian people; neither was there to be time for developing closer relations with the Orthodox Church—with that ultimate objective, the union of churches, in view. Indeed, with the Provisional Government in power after the revolution of 1917, there came a ray of hope that it might be so, but it proved only a false dawn.

II

The Catholic Church and the Provisional Government

The outbreak of the February revolution in 1917 found the Romanov dynasty isolated from the populace of the Empire. Even those who had benefited from Romanov rule, such as the Russian Orthodox Church, failed to rally to the dynasty; and those who had suffered serious persecution at its hands were even less likely to spring to its defense. The Holy Synod of the Russian Orthodox Church adopted a cautious attitude toward the revolution. It felt that the revolution should give the Orthodox Church autonomy in internal affairs but should at the same time preserve for it its dominant or favored position as the church of the majority of the Russian people. The church courts, the church's legislation on marriage and divorce, its records, its holydays, and its schools were to remain untouched and be recognized by the government. The church authorities also felt that compulsory religious instruction should be retained in schools and that government subsidies for the church should be continued. The only areas of disagreement between the Provisional Government and the Orthodox Church proved to be the problem of parochial schools, which the government hoped to nationalize, and the problem of compulsory religious instruction in nonreligious schools.[1]

[1] John S. Curtiss, *The Russian Church and the Soviet State, 1917–1950* (Boston, 1953), pp. 14 and 18–19. A well-documented work, but somewhat naive about Bolshevik intentions toward the churches.

The Catholics greeted the February revolution with greater hopes than did the Orthodox, for the Provisional Government soon gave them reason to think that a better day was dawning. On March 15, 1917, the Provisional Government took a decisive step in Russian-Polish relations, which naturally included the question of the relations between the government and the Catholic Church in the archdiocese of Mohylew. What it did was to set up the Commission for the Liquidation of the Affairs of the Polish Kingdom, whose chairman was to be appointed by the commission. Part of the commission's membership was to consist of representatives from the ministries of internal affairs, foreign affairs, war, education, and justice. But it was also to include representatives of the leading Polish organizations in Russia. The commission's task, as the government defined it, was to ascertain the location and condition of government properties and communal institutions in the Kingdom of Poland; to prescribe the manner in which they were to be preserved and transferred to the Polish state; to indicate the procedure for liquidating government institutions functioning in the Kingdom of Poland; to determine the mutual relations between the Russian government and the Roman Catholic Church in Russia as represented by the archbishop of Mohylew and to solve the problem of Polish soldiers in the Russian army and of Polish prisoners of war. The government also authorized the commission to invite other government ministries and nongovernmental groups to such meetings that might involve their interests. It appointed as chairman of the commission Alexander Lednicki, a distinguished Pole and St. Petersburg lawyer, who enjoyed the confidence of both parties at this time. It was the chairman's responsibility to report to the government on the commission's work.[2]

As the Provisional Government had outlined the commission's structure and duties in general terms only, the commission itself had to settle most of the details of its organization and work. According to the original plan it was to consist of twenty-six members, thirteen of whom were to represent the Russian government,

[2] ZZVP, I, Nos. 19–22, pp. 1–2; Nos. 49–51, pp. 1–2. This important but neglected source is in the Hoover Library at Stanford University, Stanford, California. See also KP, May 11, 1917; KW, April 16, 1917.

while thirteen Poles were to act for the Polish population in Russia. The government departments which were finally represented in the commission included internal affairs, foreign affairs, education, war and navy, justice, agriculture, commerce and industry, finance, communications, the Holy Synod, the accounting commission, the legal department, and the commissariat of the former ministry of the imperial court. The wide representation of government departments illustrates the complexity of Polish problems in wartime Russia. On the other hand, of the thirteen Polish members provided only ten served on the commission when it first started its work. They were Bishop Ropp as representative of the Roman Catholic Church; I. Szebeko and J. Mrozowski as representatives of the Central Committee of the Landed Gentry; A. Babiański and W. Rawicz-Szczerbo as representatives of the Polish society for aid to war victims; A. Wierzchlejewski as representative of the Polish committee in Moscow; J. Zdziechowski as representative of the agricultural credit society; and S. Światopełk-Czetwertyński as representative of the central agricultural society.[3]

It was no easy matter to determine the competence of the commission in detail. A report by W. Grabski with a supplement by Mrozowski, which attempted to set out the rights of the commission with some precision, was discussed on May 20 and 27 and June 7, 1917, and was accepted by the commission with insignificant changes. It laid down that as the commission was an organ of the central government, it should submit to the government its resolutions on matters concerned with government institutions functioning in the Kingdom of Poland and with the preservation of government properties until they could be turned over to the future Polish state. If the government approved these resolutions, such approval would render them decisive and final. In order to locate and establish the condition of government properties, the commission was to do preparatory and investigative work, collecting and organizing data to facilitate a decision whether the properties were subject to return to the Polish state. It interpreted the term "properties of government

[3] *Sprawozdanie z działalności Komisji Likwidacyjnej do Spraw Królestwa Polskiego za czas od 15-go marca do 1-go sierpnia, 1917 r.* (Petrograd, 1917), pp. 2–3; *KW*, May 30, 1917. This report of the liquidation commission (an extremely rare item) is also in the Hoover Library, Stanford, California.

institutions of the Kingdom of Poland" as meaning all assets and obligations originating in or connected with the Kingdom of Poland, all immovable as well as movable property belonging to government institutions functioning within the Kingdom, and all sums deriving from the financial settlement by the Russian treasury with the future Polish state. Similarly it interpreted the term "property of communal institutions of the Kingdom of Poland" in such a way as to cover the properties of communes, towns, philanthropic organizations and other juridical persons with a public character. As the commission had been deputed to "define the manner of preserving and directing government and communal institutions of the Kingdom of Poland until they are turned over to the Polish state" the report pointed out that it would need to create its own administrative staff for these properties. It also laid down that when determining the way in which Russian government institutions functioning in the Kingdom were to be abolished, the commission should treat each institution in detail, specifying its term and the means to be used to deal with it.[4]

The commission, which faced an enormous task, tried to proceed with its work in an orderly fashion. From the outset it recognized the following seven important fields of activity: affairs connected with the former ministry of the court and appanages; affairs of the Catholic Church; affairs of military and civilian prisoners; affairs of municipal economy and institutions of public benevolence; land and peasant affairs; the staffs of institutions which were abolished; and questions of finance. The business arising from these many and varied problems laid a considerable burden of work on the commission, because the many Poles scattered throughout Russia, especially by the war, turned to the commission for advice and help. The policy of the chairman demanded that no letter or request should remain unanswered, and the volume of correspondence and business is suggested by the fact that on July 26, 1917, no less than 2,459 items were received by the commission and 2,379 sent out.[5]

[4] *Sprawozdanie z działalności* . . . , pp. 4–5; *KW*, June 22, 1917. The Polish press followed events in Russia as closely as the war and revolution permitted.
[5] *Sprawozdanie z działalności* . . . , pp. 6 and 7–9; *KW*, June 22, 1917; D. Kolpinskij, "Początki katolicyzmu wschodniego obrządku w Rosji," *Kościół katolicki w Rosji: Materiały do jego historji i organizacji* (Warsaw, 1932), p. 32.

With the establishment of the Provisional Government, freedom, it seemed, had arrived for the Russian people and the many nationalities and religious groups that composed the heterogeneous Russian Empire. While the national problem plagued and dogged the Provisional Government, the government made an excellent agreement with the Roman Catholic Church. Undoubtedly, the arrangements with the Catholic Church provided for more freedom than the Church knew almost anywhere else in the modern world.

Within this atmosphere of freedom, as early as March 3, 1917, the Roman Catholic clergy in St. Petersburg began to hold meetings in which the new political and social developments in Russia were discussed and studied. In fact, in these meetings there began serious efforts to organize a Christian Democratic movement in the Russian Empire.

On March 3, 1917, Bishop John Cieplak, the administrator of the archdiocese of Mohylew, presided over a meeting of forty-six Roman Catholic clergy who gathered in order to discuss the serious problems that now faced the Roman Catholic Church in the revolutionary political situation. The bishop felt very strongly that the

In order to cope with the problems involved in these critical areas, the commission separated into twelve sections. Section I concerned itself with matters under the administration of the commissariat of the ministry of the court and appanages; its head was Alexander Lednicki himself. Section II dealt with the problems of the Catholic Church; its chairman was S. Kotlyarevsky, and its members Bishop Edward Ropp, A. Kartashev, S. Światopełk-Czetwertyński, W. Grabski, and J. Mikhaylovsky. The Roman, Armenian and Russian Catholic interests formed the subject matter of the section's deliberations. Besides the section's members, the following bishops were invited to meetings: Cieplak, Dubowski, Godlewski and Kessler, and Exarch Leonid Fedorov. The chairman of Section III, which was concerned with the problem of military and civilian prisoners, was A. Babiański. Section IV on the municipal economy and institutions of public benevolence was presided over by J. Mrozowski. Land problems fell within the purview of Section V, whose chairman was J. Zdziechowski. Section VI occupied itself with the evacuated personnel of the liquidated government institutions; its chairman was M. Shchukin. Section VII, the financial and control section, was under the chairmanship of W. Grabski. Section VIII, the legal section, was presided over by P. Gussakovsky. Section IX treated the problem of public instruction; here again Lednicki was the chairman. Among the interested persons invited by this section was Bishop Cieplak, who represented the Church's interest in education. Section X included in its sphere the problems of judicial and administrative institutions; once again, Lednicki acted as chairman. Section XI, which dealt with commerce and industry, had as its chairman, W. Rawicz-Szczerbo. Finally, roads and communications came under Section XII, whose chairman was M. Shchukin.

social and political position of the Catholic Church, which the
dominant Russian Orthodox government had considered as "alien"
and hostile, demanded a social and political organization whose
object would be to unite all Catholics in order to prevent developments hostile to the Catholic Church. The Church must be freed
from its position of inferiority and must be given freedom of opportunity within the Russian Empire, no matter what the final form of
that empire.[6]

The clergy generally agreed that some form of organization was
needed, but they disagreed on the type of organization. While some
believed that a political organization was required by the political
events, others spoke sharply against direct political action and suggested associations of workers and the faithful after the model of
the *Volksverein* in Germany. Father Alexander Wójcicki, later a
professor at the Catholic University of Lublin and the leading
theorist of Christian Democracy in St. Petersburg, had followed the
work of Christian Democracy in Belgium, France and Italy.

Explaining to the assembled clerics the principles of Christian
Democracy, Father Wójcicki declared that it must be based on the
moral law and the essential dignity of the human person; that it
must defend the right of private property; that it demand a just
wage for labor; and that it must work for a just government. To
carry out these principles a party organization was necessary; but
the party must be dedicated to progressive and evolutionary action,
not to revolution. Father Wójcicki pointed out that the Catholic
organizations in Germany and Belgium had begun as efforts in the
social field, but successful social action required them to take
political action as well.

Others like Father Anthony Malecki argued that the clergy should
use either the existing religious organizations and confraternities,
e.g., the Society of St. Vincent de Paul, or form electoral committees of parishioners who were to inform the local population about
the issues involved in the elections. Father S. Maciejewicz emphatically declared that a political program had to be drawn up before
any attempt was made to organize a party or committees; accord-

[6] General Meeting of the St. Petersburg Clergy, March 3, 1917. These minutes
were made available to the author by Monsignor Bronislas Ussas, a priest of the
archdiocese of Mohylew, now resident in Warsaw.

ingly, Father Zygmunt Łoziński, later appointed bishop of Mińsk, proposed that Father Wójcicki prepare a statement on the nature and program of Christian Democracy. Father I. Radziszewski, rector of the Theological Academy and later the rector of the Catholic University of Lublin, stressed the importance of disseminating political and social information among the clergy and laity and the importance of cooperation between the clergy and laity in social and political matters. Finally, the assembly voted to form a committee to prepare a political program.[7]

This Organizing Committee, presided over by Father Radziszewski, met on March 10, 1917, to begin the difficult task of drawing up a political program and deciding a few thorny questions. The most important of these problems was whether priests should belong to political parties and engage directly in political activity. Fathers Maciejewicz and Lankajtis, members of the committee, felt that before all else a political program must be drawn up and that all action should be primarily political. Father Wójcicki, on the other hand, argued convincingly that clergy should not engage in purely political activity. Monsignor Constantine Budkiewicz, pastor of the magnificent St. Catherine's church in St. Petersburg, and later victim of Bolshevik persecution, emphasized that political activity by the clergy might prove detrimental to the Church and might well divide the clergy and laity at such critical period. All this notwithstanding, Father Lankajtis stated that political action was absolutely necessary, but this did not mean that the individual priests were to join political parties. What he meant was that the clergy must assume some sort of direction of Catholic political activity. With this Father Radziszewski agreed. Father Fabian Abrantowicz, also a member of the committee, then suggested that this might be done by means of a pastoral on social and political matters.

After this extensive discussion, the committee agreed that priests were not to join political parties but they were to use their influence on Catholics to promote the interests of the Church. Among other decisions, the committee approved the project of publishing pamphlets and brochures which were to represent the Catholic view-

[7] *Ibid.*, March 3, 1917.

point on social and political questions. To achieve this goal, it would be best for the Catholics to own their own printing press. As a supplement to this project, Father Maciejewicz suggested the forming of a central committee which would send reliable men to organize parochial committees whose task it would then be to explain the Catholic position locally. Returning to his favorite theme, Father Maciejewicz once more declared that only a program will provide a center around which committees can be formed; accordingly, the committee requested Father Wójcicki to draw up such a program.[8]

At the second meeting of the Organizing Committee, March 13, 1917, Father Wójcicki offered his political program, which he hoped the Catholics would present to the Provisional Government at the Constituent Assembly. He placed freedom of religion at the head of the program. As to education, he proposed that religious instruction be given in all schools and that both private and free schools be recognized by the government. In the social realm there were proposals for the protection of the workers, an eight-hour day, the freedom to strike, and insurance for the workers. To crown the labor legislation, there was to be a ministry of labor. Holy days were to be recognized as days of rest. The program also included equal rights for women; free choice of a civil or religious marriage; regulation of divorces; and the protection of private property, which did envisage some land reform but the details were never spelled out. The committee accepted this program with the addition of Father Maciejewicz's suggestion that equality of rights for *all* and the removal of existing restrictions on rights be included.[9]

This political program was presented on March 15, 1917, to the general meeting of the St. Petersburg clergy, who accepted it as a basis on which to unite all the Catholics of Russia behind Christian Democracy. To make this program known and to acquaint the faithful with the Church's teaching on social and political issues, Father John Wasilewski suggested the purchase of a printing press; but Father Lankajtis added the caution that the newspaper ought to be geared to the workers not to the *dewotki!* Bishop Cieplak, still the administrator of the archdiocese, asked whether it might not be wise

[8] First Meeting of the Organizing Committee, March 10, 1917.
[9] Second Meeting of the Organizing Committee, March 13, 1917.

to organize within the archdiocesan headquarters a central committee for social and political matters; this proposal was not acted upon until the next meeting.[10]

After the political program had been drawn up, there arose the need for actual organization to put flesh on the dry bones. On March 22, 1917, when the clergy met again, Bishop Cieplak moved the creation of a central committee to function at archdiocesan headquarters and to co-ordinate all the political and social activity of the archdiocese. In connection with this motion, the question was raised whether the bishop-administrator should appoint the members of the committee or whether they ought to be elected. The clergy decided that there should be such a committee and that five priests and several laymen should be elected to serve on it. Father Radziszewski became the chairman of the committee, of which, of course, Father Wójcicki was also a member. The names of the laymen on the central committee are not known; it is not even certain they were elected at all for only ten clerical members are listed as attending the meetings.[11]

This central committee, which met for the second time only on October 12, 1917 (owing perhaps to the disturbances of the summer and the negotiations with the Provisional Government), adopted as its official title "The Social Council in Assistance upon the Ordinary of the Archdiocese of Mohylew."[12] The Social Council, as it was henceforth known, was soon involved in a disagreement with the Christian Democracy in Moscow. Father Lutosławski, leader of the Christian Democrats in Moscow, had in fact given the movement there a national Democratic direction. The Moscow Christian Democrats had asked for admission as a *koło*—that is, as an affiliated group of the Board of St. Petersburg Clubs.[13] Although the Moscow Christian Democrats were persuaded of their errors, the problem was not

[10] General Meeting of the St. Petersburg Clergy, March 15, 1917.

[11] *Ibid.*, March 22, 1917. According to these minutes, the members of the Central Committee (later the Social Council) were these priests: Radziszewski, Wójcicki, Abrantowicz, Reklajtis, and Tarsun; candidate members were Chwiecko, Rancan, and Łoziński. However, the minutes of May 18, 25, 1917, list the following as members: Radziszewski, Budkiewicz, Chwiecko, Iwicki, Maciejewicz, Rancan, Reklajtis, Świrski, and Wójcicki. Bishop Cieplak had reorganized the original group because it had proved ineffective: "Rada słabo funkcjonowała."

[12] Meeting of the Social Council, October 12, 1917.

[13] *Ibid.*, October 12, 1917; also meeting of October 17 or 18, 1917.

truly solved because a decision would have to be made as to the ultimate character of the Christian Democratic groups.

Other obstacles fell into the path of the Christian Democratic movement. Father Anthony Ursz, the Catholic pastor in Dźwińsk, had tried to organize a group there, but the low educational level and lack of an educated personnel for leadership kept the movement very weak.[14]

Father John Sokołowski, pastor in Horodok, province of Mińsk, declared that in Horodok there simply was no foundation for a Christian Democratic organization; the only organization he had was the Confraternity of the Living Rosary which, he said, at least did not arouse national antagonism.[15] Father Ignatius Łapszyc reported the same from Samara. However, letters from Orsza and Krasnojarsk to the Social Council clearly indicate considerable success; and the pastor from Krasnojarsk asked for literature to be made available to his organization.[16] Father Henry Budrys of Wieliż wrote that he had successfully organized a Christian Democratic Club that had 700 members.[17] According to Father Paul Kaziunas, a District Council for the Witebsk territory was active in trying to unite in preparation for the Constituent Assembly; but he complained of a lack of materials and asked for direction.[18]

That some organization was actually carried through is quite clear, but the extent of it is very difficult to judge. However, the reports to the Social Council illustrate the widespread attention that Christian Democracy was actually getting in Russia. However, the reports also suggest that many of the clergy, either misunderstanding the meaning of social action or opposing political and social action, devoted their time to strictly religious organization, e.g., the Confraternity of the Living Rosary. The Social Council actually discussed such questions as whether entry of names into the records of religious confraternities was a requisite for gaining indulgences attached to membership in the confraternities.[19] At times this gave the proceedings an unreal and remote air.

In the meantime, the task of regulating the relations between the Roman Catholic Church and the Russian government fell to the

[14] *Ibid.*, November 23, 1917.   [15] *Ibid.*, November 23, 1917.
[16] *Ibid.*, November 23, 1917.   [17] *Ibid.*, December 6, 1917.
[18] *Ibid.*, November 23, 1917.   [19] *Ibid.*, December 6, 1917.

second section of the Liquidation Commission which was presided over by Bishop Ropp. Since the Provisional Government had abolished all religious and national restrictions, the second section assumed that the scope of its work included the elimination of restrictions imposed by the former tsarist government on the Roman Catholic Church and Catholics in Russia and the removal of all misunderstandings between the Catholic Church and the Russian government. But it really regarded as its primary task the abrogation of all connections between the Russian government and the Catholic Church in both the Kingdom of Poland and Russia proper.

The investigative and preparatory work of the second section proceeded expeditiously, for the problems involved were well known to the members and consultants invited to the discussions—for example, Bishop Cieplak and Bishop Ropp, who knew from clerical meetings what views the clergy held on these matters. The materials needed were also easily obtainable. Hence, the discussions proceeded quickly and it was possible to submit resolutions to the plenum of the commission with very little delay. The section addressed itself to a whole variety of problems. The plenum of the commission had already discussed the government's unilateral removal of priests from parishes, and the second section undertook to draft a guarantee that in the future the appointment of priests to parishes would depend entirely on the ecclesiastical authorities, who would merely inform the civil authorities of the nominations made. Tsarist legislation on mixed marriages also came under study. This legislation laid down that mixed marriages solemnized only before a Catholic priest could not be recognized as valid unions, and that children of mixed marriages belonged to the Orthodox confession, a position which created much hardship for the Catholic parties in mixed marriages. Another problem which the second section tackled was the problem of Catholic churches seized by the tsarist government. Here it decided that as the reasons for the seizure had been political, the churches affected should be restored to the Catholics. But at the same time, it agreed that for the moment the decision should not be put into effect if Orthodox services were really conducted in any of the churches concerned. Related matters which were also dealt with included the placing of memorials

in churches, inscriptions on wayside crucifixes, and religious pro-
cessions, all of which the imperial government had kept under
close control. In the educational field, the section had to face the
problems involved in religious instruction for Catholic pupils and
students, an issue which, surprising though it may seem, was connected with nationality. In the past, it had been the director of the
gymnasium who had determined a pupil's nationality; and this
decision was important because it also determined the choice of
language in which pupils received their religious instruction. The
right of the Roman Catholic authorities to supervise religious instruction in schools had also to be studied and, if possible, guaranteed.
Another matter which the second section took up was the right to
establish monasteries and convents freely. But the representatives
of the government departments asked that a final decision should
be postponed until the government's general policy had been
announced.[20]

After the second section had discussed the various problems, it
brought its resolutions before the commission which very soon
accepted a number of them, including some which were important.
On May 5, 1917, a plenary session of the commission approved a
resolution which revoked the imperial decrees of June 5, 1866, and
July 15, 1869, suppressing the Kamieniec-Podolski and Mińsk dioceses, and a decree of April 16, 1883, placing the diocese of Mińsk
under the administration of the archbishop of Mohylew. The suppression of these dioceses was canonically invalid, and hence they
continued to exist in the eyes of the Church, even though Wilno had
assumed administration of the diocese of Kamieniec-Podolski,
Mohylew of Mińsk.[21] The vigorous action taken by Catholics in
the dioceses suggested that the suppression was by no means a
dead issue; for example, the Catholics of Mińsk lost no time after
the February revolution in asserting themselves and seeking the
resurrection of their diocese. On April 8, 1917, they held a meeting
in the Mińsk theater under the chairmanship of the head of the
city, Stanislas Chrzątkowski, and were told that Bishop Cieplak,
administrator of the archdiocese of Mohylew and the diocese of

---

[20] *Sprawozdanie z działalności* . . . , pp. 14–15.
[21] *Dziennik Petrogradzki,* May 16, 1917 (a very rare copy of the St. Petersburg Polish Daily); *Sprawozdanie z działalności* . . . , pp. 24–25.

Mińsk, had energetically begun to revive the diocese, and that Prince Lvov, president of the council of ministers, had promised all possible government assistance. A thousand signatures were called for to indicate that the Catholics of the diocese supported the project, and the meeting voted a declaration thanking the Provisional Government for decreeing religious freedom and toleration, and also asking it to restore the diocese of Mińsk. The resolutions adopted were sent to Bishop Cieplak by means of a delegation and he, in his turn, raised the matter with the Provisional Government.[22]

As far as official circles were concerned, the initiative for the restoration of the Mińsk and Kamieniec-Podolski dioceses came from the Liquidation Commission, which had sent the government its own resolution on the matter. On May 21 the government for its part voted to revoke the suppression decrees as well as the decree of April 16, 1883, which united the Catholic church in Mińsk with the archdiocese of Mohylew.[23] Pope Benedict XV appointed as the new bishop of Mińsk Father Łoziński, formerly a professor at the Theological Academy in St. Petersburg, but his consecration did not take place until August 1918. In 1917 the diocese of Mińsk had about 292,000 Catholics and 82 churches.[24] In 1919 the pope also appointed Father Peter Mańkowski as bishop of the diocese of Kamieniec-Podolski, in the re-establishment of which Bishop I. Dubowski of Łuck-Żytomierz had specially interested himself. In 1913 it included about 101 churches, and 312,102 Catholics.[25]

Other problems which hampered Catholic life in Russia also clamored for attention. For instance, on May 13, 1917, a plenary session of the commission dealt with the enforced registration of conversions to Roman Catholicism from the Orthodox faith, based on the requirements of Russian law. Until the government could prepare a final law of its own on religious toleration and freedom, the commission recommended a temporary arrangement with two main provisions. First, any person over fourteen who left the Orthodox communion to join the Catholic Church was to make an oral or written statement before the appropriate civilian official,

---

[22] *KW*, May 15, 1917.   [23] *ZZVP*, I, No. 86, pp. 64–65.
[24] Jan Wasilewski, *Arcybiskupi i administratorowie archidyecezji mohylowskiej* (Pińsk, 1930), p. 185; *Polska*, August 11, 1918.
[25] *Polska*, December 1, 1918.

who in turn was to inform the ecclesiastical authorities concerned. Second, if one of the parents belonged to the Roman Catholic Church and the other parent left the Orthodox Church to join the Catholic Church, their children under fourteen were considered members of the Catholic Church, provided the ecclesiastical authorities deemed them as such.

The commission's concern with conversion from Orthodoxy to Catholicism was intended to relieve the minds of many perplexed people as quickly as possible, for no one knew just when the expected decree on freedom of conscience would be issued. Earlier, the decree on religious toleration of April 17, 1905, had been interpreted in a restrictive sense by a circular of the minister of internal affairs dated August 18, 1905, which was the product of government fears induced by mass conversions to Catholicism after the decree's publication. Under it the prospective convert had to announce himself to the government authorities, and they informed the authorities of the Orthodox Church. He was then subjected to a thirty-day "admonition," and only if it proved ineffective would the government regard him as a Catholic. It was because of the limitations on toleration under the 1905 decree that a new decree was considered necessary.

On May 20, 1917, the commission approved the regulation proposed by its second section for the building, enlargement, and renovation of Catholic churches. The general regulations on public building and buildings naturally had to be observed; but in the future the furnishing of Roman Catholic domestic chapels and movable altars as well as the manner of services were to be subject to the decision of the Roman Catholic authorities alone. Collections for the building, along with enlarging and renovating of Catholic churches and chapels, were also to be dependent on the consent of the Catholic ecclesiastical authorities. New parishes were to be established by the diocesan authorities, but the local authorities had to be informed. At the meeting of May 20 the commission also agreed to revoke the following article of the law on foreign confessions: "In cases where the activity of persons belonging to the Roman Catholic Church appears injurious from the point of view of government order or the peaceful course of religious life among the local population, the minister of internal affairs must communicate with the appropriate Roman Catholic diocesan authorities to take suitable measures to halt the injurious activity of the persons concerned. If the diocesan authorities fail to take such measures, or if the minister of internal affairs considers the measures to be insufficient, the minister is to inform the appropriate diocesan authorities that the clerical person in question be removed from his office; the diocesan authorities must then take the necessary steps to execute the above demand.[26] This law had enabled the government to insist on the removal of priests on purely political grounds; and although it was originally directed against the Catholic clergy, it had been extended during the war to cover Protestant pastors and clergy as well.

As the commission's work was essentially preparatory, its resolutions had to be submitted to and approved by the Russian Provisional Government in order to become law. The basis for its activity was the Provisional Government's recognition of an independent Poland as part of the future European settlement, which was given on March 16, 1917. The Provisional Government had also entrusted the commission with the task of establishing regular relations between the Roman Catholic Church in Russia and the Russian state. The result was that the government faithfully implemented the recommendations which the commission submitted to it.

The government first of all undertook the task of restoration by undoing the more drastic acts of the defunct tsarist government. On May 9, 1917, it freed Wilno's Bishop Ropp (1851–1939) from the sentence of exile imposed by an imperial decree of October 1, 1907, and restored him to his office and his diocese.[27]

The return of Bishop Ropp from exile provided the beginnings of a solution for another problem, namely, the vacancy in the archdiocese of Mohylew, which was under the care of an administrator, Bishop Cieplak, that distinguished cleric and leader.[28] At the instance of the Ministry of Internal Affairs, the government instructed its minister of foreign affairs on May 20, 1917, to enter into diplomatic contacts with the Roman Curia in order to have

[26] *Sprawozdanie z działalności* . . . , pp. 24–25; *KW*, July 1, 1917.
[27] *ŻZVP*, I, No. 73, p. 10.   [28] Wasilewski, *op. cit.*, pp. 178–180.

Bishop Ropp nominated archbishop of Mohylew and metropolitan of the Roman Catholic Church in Russia. On July 25, 1917, Pope Benedict XV made the nomination,[29] and on December 2, 1917, the archbishop formally took up his new office, showing the energy and zest of a much younger man in both the religious and political fields. He had already helped to draw up the basic law to regulate Church-State relations in the new Russia and had served as a member of the Liquidation Commission. In the political sphere he organized the Christian Democratic Party, which began to show surprising strength in the districts along the Neva river. He also divided Siberia and central Russia into deaneries in order to facilitate the administration of his huge archdiocese, which was perhaps the largest in the world.

In national affairs the archbishop was a thorough Pole in both sentiment and outlook. But in ecclesiastical matters he was a strong opponent of nationalism and partisanship and would have no "privileged" language or rite in his church. He was anxious that the church should not become the arena of nationalist conflicts, and his co-operation with the Russian Synod of Catholic Clergy of the Eastern Rite, which met in St. Petersburg under the presidency of Metropolitan Szeptycki, indicated his wide tolerance and friendliness towards the Eastern church. Once he became archbishop of Mohylew, he assisted the clergy of the Eastern rite in every way. For example, he ordained deacons for the Eastern church and supported it by material means, since he saw in it possibilities for successful Catholic activity in Russia. But the Bolshevik revolution put an end to these seemingly substantial dreams.[30]

When Bishop Ropp was elevated to the archbishopric of Mohylew, the question arose as to the now vacant see of Wilno. On July 29, the minister of internal affairs, S. Kotlyarevsky, proposed to the Provisional Government the name of Bishop Cieplak, administrator of the archdiocese of Mohylew. Earlier Father Cieplak had completed his higher studies at the Theological Academy in St. Peters-

[29] *Ibid.*, p. 180; ZZVP, I, No. 84, p. 3; *Ministerstvo vnutrennikh del. proyekty i predpolozheniya ministerstva*, July 29, 1917, No. 3879, p. 1. The papal documents were published in the first issue of the archdiocesan paper, *Kronika archidyecezji mohylowskiej*, January 1918.
[30] Wasilewski, *op. cit.*, pp. 181–182; ZZVP, II, No. 148, pp. 9–10.

burg and had served as a professor of dogmatic theology from 1882 till 1908. From 1904 to 1907 he had also represented the Kielce diocese in the Ecclesiastical College in St. Petersburg. He was subsequently made an auxiliary bishop of Archbishop Apolinary Wnukowski of Mohylew and had carried out the first episcopal visitation of Siberia, which was part of the archdiocese. When Archbishop Vincent Kluczyński resigned from the archiepiscopal office in 1914, Bishop Cieplak ruled the archdiocese as administrator until the appointment of Archbishop Ropp. In view of his past services the Provisional Government had asked the Holy See to grant him the personal rank of an archbishop; and the Ministry of Internal Affairs now urged the Provisional Government to approach the Vatican again for the nomination of Bishop Cieplak to the see of Wilno.[31] The Bolshevik coup of November 1917 frustrated the idea. But Archbishop Ropp subsequently asked the Holy See to make Bishop Cieplak a titular archbishop, which it did by naming him titular archbishop of Ochrid.[32]

Even after the restoration of its dioceses and bishops, the Catholic Church still had claims on the government arising from the seizure of some of its churches during the nineteenth and early twentieth centuries. Many of these churches had been forcibly converted into Orthodox churches, and the Roman Catholic section of the Liquidation Commission considered that they now ought to be restored to the Catholics. A move of this kind was bound to be opposed by the Orthodox hierarchy and to encounter difficulties arising from the fact that the Orthodox had been in possession of the churches for many years. For example, some former Catholics would almost certainly prefer to remain in the Orthodox communion, which in the course of time they had come to adopt as their own. But in spite of the difficulties the Provisional Government showed its good will by at least beginning the restoration of Catholic property and allowing Catholic churches to extend their holdings. On July 27, 1917, it approved the restoration of a Capuchin monastery at Winnica in Podole to which its church and all its property were to be returned.[33] On August 28, 1917, it also voted to restore to

[31] Ministerstvo vnutrennikh . . . , July 29, 1917, No. 3879, pp. 1–2. ZZVP, II, No. 128, p. 18; No. 150, p. 11.
[32] Wasilewski, *op. cit.*, p. 171.   [33] ZZVP, II, No. 71, p. 7.

the Catholic church in Berdichev the Carmelite monastery suppressed in 1866.[34] It further agreed that the Samara Catholic church could accept the legacy of an engineer named Chiliński, who had willed his home to the church for the establishment of a school and orphanage for Roman Catholic children.[35] St. Catherine's church in St. Petersburg similarly received the government's permission to acquire property for the establishment of a Roman Catholic shrine and school.[36]

Though these efforts at restitution were small in comparison with the enormous losses of the Church in the nineteenth century, they nonetheless illustrate the goodwill of the government, overwhelmed as it was by problems arising out of the war, the disruptive efforts of the formerly oppressed nationalities, and the revolutionary temper of the population—especially the peasantry. But the government's various measures remained disconnected and unorganized; and what was really needed was the systematic organization of relations between the government and the sovereign Catholic authorities in Rome. These relations could be based only on the freedom of religion. On July 14, 1917, the government had issued a decree which guaranteed freedom of conscience to every citizen of the Russian state. This meant that the use of political and civil rights was in no way dependent on religious affiliation, and that no one could be persecuted or restricted in his rights on account of his religious affiliation. The decree also provided that the religious affiliation of children under nine years of age was to be determined by their parents. If the parents disagreed, their children were to belong to the father's faith. If parents separated, the children were to take the faith of the parent with whom they stayed. If the parents were dead or unknown, or if it proved impossible to establish the actual religious affiliation of a child, its guardians or those who adopted it were to decide which faith it was to take. In this way the decree safeguarded the religious freedom of all citizens, including children.

The thorny question of passing from one religious confession to another had also to be tackled. The decree on freedom of conscience declared that those who had reached the age of fourteen needed no

[34] *Ibid.*, No. 127, pp. 2–3.
[35] *Ibid.*, No. 127, pp. 2–3.   [36] *Ibid.*, No. 110, p. 17.

permission or declaration from any authority to join another religion or to have no religion at all. Any legal obligations and relations, such as taxes, for example, flowing from membership of a religious group would be terminated by an oral or written statement to the local court. The law also provided for those who did not join any religious group at all. They had merely to inform the local administration which, in turn, was to communicate with the appropriate parish or religious body. Children under the age of nine were to be allowed to transfer their religious allegiance when both their parents did the same. But if only one parent joined another religion and no agreement could be reached between the parents on their children's faith, the children were to remain in the confession of which they were members. On the other hand, children over nine years of age could not be enrolled in another faith without their consent. The decree also declared that the civil acts of persons with no religious affiliation fell within the competence of the organs of local administration in accordance with a decree of October 17, 1906, which prescribed the procedures and rules for Old Believers and sects.[37]

This decree on freedom of conscience laid the basis of religious freedom not only for Catholics but for all the peoples of Russia. The Roman Catholics in Russia were, however, in a peculiar position in that the great majority of them were Poles and that they all owed religious allegiance to authorities outside Russia. This meant that their relations with the Russian government called for special attention. On June 17, 1917, at the instance of Alexander Lednicki, chairman of the Liquidation Commission, the government ordered the minister of the interior to elaborate a draft law incorporating the changes already recommended in the existing laws governing relations between Church and State in the Russian empire.[38] The ministry wasted no time and was able to give the government a draft for discussion on July 26, 1917. As approved, the new law on freedom of association was comprehensive and dealt with the whole range of Catholic problems from church building to the appointment of bishops. For example, it laid down that the restoration of old churches, the collection of voluntary offerings for

[37] *Ibid.*, No. 131, pp. 8–10.   [38] *Ibid.*, No. 111, pp. 36–37.

the building or repair of churches or for other religious needs, and the creation of parishes were to be left to the appropriate Roman Catholic authorities, and that the civil authorities were merely to be informed of what was taking place.[39] On the appointment of bishops it said that the archbishop of Mohylew, diocesan bishops, bishops with the right of succession, and apostolic administrators were to be named by the Apostolic See in agreement with the Russian government, but that candidates were to be presented to the Apostolic See by the local clergy. The appointment of other categories of prelates, however, was not to need the agreement of the Russian government.[40]

The new law also dealt with the establishment of new dioceses and related problems. The immense area of the archdiocese of Mohylew made it very difficult to exercise the ministry; hence the supreme authority of the Holy See in the matter of new dioceses was at last recognized, and it could now be invoked to establish a new diocese wherever needed. But negotiations with the government would still be necessary over the expenses involved in setting up such a diocese.[41] The law further provided that the archbishop and the diocesan bishops were to appoint an official to preside over their consistories and a secretary to run their chanceries. These officers, together with the members of the consistory and the chancery clerks, could be laity or clerics of the Roman Catholic faith. But the local civilian authorities had to be informed of their appointment.[42]

When founding schools, the Roman Catholic authorities were to be subject to the general laws for establishing private educational institutions.[43] But seminaries, with their courses of theological and general instruction, their discipline, and their choice of students, now came within the exclusive competence of the diocesan authorities. Appointments to rectorships, inspectorships and professorships, on the other hand, had to be reported to the local civilian authorities. In order to enter a seminary, students must have completed the four classes of the middle school. During their course, or after its completion, they also had to pass an examination in Russian lan-

[39] *Ibid.*, No. 140, pp. 8 and 48–49.
[40] *Ibid.*, No. 140, p. 49.
[41] *Ibid.*, No. 140, p. 50.
[42] *Ibid.*, No. 140, p. 50.
[43] *Ibid.*, No. 140, p. 50.

guage, Russian history, and geography, corresponding to the fifth and sixth classes of the middle school.[44] The new law recognized the Roman Catholic ecclesiastical academy as the higher institution of learning for the Catholic clergy. The administration of the academy was entrusted to the diocesan bishops; but its immediate supervision devolved on the archbishop-metropolitan, who appointed the rector after consultation with the diocesan bishops and with the consent of the government. Appointments to professorships, however, and to other posts in the academy had merely to be reported to the government. Only those who had completed the regular course of training were to be admitted to the academy; and the stipend which they were to receive was to be fixed by the archbishop after consultation with the diocesan bishops. It was also to be the archbishop who conferred scholastic degrees.[45] The law also gave the diocesan bishops the right to supervise religious instruction in the schools of their diocese. The language used for religious instruction was to be the native language of the pupil, and it was to be determined by the pupil's parents or guardians. Schools which gave no religious instruction in the Roman Catholic faith were to introduce it if parents or guardians asked for it.[46]

Under the tsars one serious injustice to the Catholics in Russia had been the forcible suppression of monastic institutions. The law on freedom of association now remedied this by permitting the formation of Roman Catholic organizations of every kind—societies, brotherhoods, clerical congregations, and monastic orders. This gave the Catholics reason to hope that the future would see a renaissance of the Catholic religious orders, which had once been such a common feature of Catholicism in the lands of the former Commonwealth of Poland-Lithuania.[47]

While the legal position of the Church was being defined, the Social Council of the clergy also faced the problem of getting information to the widely scattered priests and Catholics of Russia. This was, in fact, a constant subject of discussion among the organizers of Christian Democracy. One suggestion was that informed

---

[44] *Ibid.*, No. 140, pp. 51–52.   [45] *Ibid.*, No. 140, pp. 52–53.
[46] *Ibid.*, No. 140, pp. 53–54; Antoni Około-Kułak, *Kościół w Rosji, dawniej, obecnie, i w przyszłości* (Cracow, 1928), pp. 24–25.
[47] ZZVP, II, No. 140, p. 50.

and qualified priests travel about the immense territories of the archdiocese to present to the faithful the Church's view on social and political programs and parties.[48] An effort was also made to get literature to the provinces.[49] A pastoral letter on political and social matters was another measure advocated.[50] A printing press and the publication of pamphlets were also proposed.[51] Finally, a firm decision was taken to acquire a printing press, if possible; at any rate, it was definitely decided to publish a diocesan chronicle or newsletter. The Social Council then, on November 29, 1917, discussed this plan fully.

The new Archbishop Ropp, the onetime organizer of Christian Democracy in Wilno, agreed on the need for an archdiocesan organ of information, but also cited two fundamental obstacles—the lack of funds and the lack of personnel. The Council proposed that the pastors should bear the expense. Two copies of the chronicle were to be sent to each parish; one copy was to be kept in the parochial archives, and the other was to be available for consultation. As to the editor of such a newsletter, undoubtedly, a qualified person could be found in the archdiocese; the editor would be given a post that would leave him sufficient time to edit the archdiocesan chronicle. The Council agreed to approach Father Wasilewski to inquire whether he would accept the editorship if it were offered to him.[52] Actually, he had accepted the editorship; for his work in this task he was to receive 50 rubles monthly.[53] The title was to be *The Chronicle of the Archdiocese of Mohylew and of the Mińsk Diocese* (hereafter cited as *The Chronicle*), and this publication was to be a monthly. Further investigation showed that 1,000 copies would cost 70,000 rubles annually—if it were issued monthly.

Besides the use of *The Chronicle*, the clergy generally agreed that they would use sermons and conferences to inform the people on crucial issues. To this end it was suggested that a political and

[48] General Meeting of the St. Petersburg Clergy, March 3, 1917; First Meeting of the Organizing Committee, March 10, 1917.
[49] General Meeting of the St. Petersburg Clergy, March 3, 1917; also meeting of November 23, 1917.
[50] First Meeting of the Organizing Committee, March 10, 1917.
[51] *Ibid.*, March 10, 1917.
[52] Meeting of the Social Council, November 29, 1917.
[53] *Ibid.*, December 6, 1917.

social catechism be drawn up, which would provide the clergy with material.[54] This concern about the acquaintance of the clergy with the social question originated in the fear that some of the older clergy might be adverse to a progressive social and political program.[55]

At this distance much of this activity seems to have been conducted in a secluded world. Although the Socialists are mentioned once in the minutes, they are mentioned only at a meeting on January 23, 1918, when the attitude to be taken toward the Bolshevik decrees of separation of Church and State are discussed.[56] But the minutes of the meetings come to an abrupt end. However, the attitude taken toward that decree is known from *The Chronicle*, which in an isolated issue of January 1920 gives a survey of events from the suppression of the original *Chronicle* in June 1918. Originally, the Catholic clergy thought that the decree affected only the Russian Orthodox Church. They reasoned that only what had been united with the State could be separated from it, namely, the Orthodox Church. Far from ever having been united with the Russian state, the Roman Catholic Church had been considered an alien confession and had been persecuted by the tsarist government.[57] Events showed that this view of the matter had been naive in the extreme.

Such was the history of the relations of the Roman Catholic Church in Russia under the Provisional Government. But it still does not give a complete picture of the development of Catholicism. In the western provinces, for example, the opening of schools among the Poles, who formed a majority of the population, went on apace; and although these schools were essentially Polish rather than Catholic, they included the Roman Catholic faith as an integral part of their educational program. The widespread opening of such

[54] First Meeting of the Organizing Committee, March 10, 1917.
[55] General Meeting of the St. Petersburg Clergy, March 3, 1917.
[56] For the decree, see P. V. Gidulianov (ed.), *Otdelenie tserkvi ot gosudarstva*, 3rd ed. (Moscow, 1926), pp. 368–369; for the English translation see Curtiss, *op. cit.*, pp. 332–333; for the danger that eventually confronted the Church because of this decree, see James J. Zatko, "A Contemporary Report on the Condition of the Catholic Church in Russia, 1922," *The Harvard Theological Review*, LIII (1960), 277–295. The "maximalists" are mentioned in the minutes of the Meeting of the Social Council, January 23, 1918.
[57] *Kronika . . .* , January 1920, a copy of which is in this writer's possession.

schools in 1917–1918 points to the strength of Catholicism in the border areas. In Kiev, Podole, and Wołyń, for instance, the Poles established 36 *gymnasiums,* a university in Kiev, and nine professional secondary schools. The number of primary schools established was 500 in Wołyń, 546 in Podole, and 194 in the Ukraine, with a total of 73,688 pupils and 1,663 teachers. In December 1917, Wilno also had 60 primary schools with 7,000 pupils. By contrast, only 500 Polish primary schools existed in the whole of the territory occupied by the Germans. In the Mińsk province seven secondary schools existed in Mińsk itself and one each in Borysów, Łożańsk, Ihumen, Bobrujsk, Słuck, Nieśwież, Mozyr, and Dokszyce. In the Mohylew province the Poles opened 200 primary schools, as well as two secondary schools at Mohylew and Orsza. The primary schools were supported by voluntary contributions from the Polish peasants.[58]

Catholic public opinion acclaimed the new relationship between Church and State, for the Catholics interpreted it as meaning the liberation of the Roman Catholic Church and the elimination of the inequalities.[59] The restoration and restitution were undoubtedly small and bore no comparison to the losses inflicted on the Church in the nineteenth century. But the efforts of the government clearly indicated its good will and presaged a better future for the Catholics in Russia. Though the Provisional Government has often been criticized for its failure in nationality and peasant affairs, the settlement which it made with the Roman Catholic Church illustrates statesmanship at its best and suggests the kind of solution which the government intended to provide if Russia had not been overwhelmed by the Bolshevik revolution.

But the destruction in the previous century could perhaps not have been undone even with the best of efforts. It was impossible by law to restore Catholicism to those who had been assimilated into the Orthodox Church, or to reinstate the hundreds of monks in their monasteries even if the monasteries themselves could have been made available. Nor could legislation resurrect overnight the

---

[58] W. Konopczyński, "Polish Institutions in Lithuania and Ruthenia," *The Eastern Provinces of Poland* (Paris, 1918), pp. 47–51.

[59] *KP,* October 12, 1917. The Vatican also expressed itself optimistically about future relations, *KW,* April 2, 1917.

churches, priests and laity, now lost to the Catholic Church. The very organization of the section of the Liquidation Commission dealing with Catholic problems suggests in itself the vast damage inflicted on the Church: freedom of clerical appointment and activity, matrimonial laws, stolen church property, religious instruction for Catholics, and the building of churches and monasteries. All these problems centered around the restoration of the Church to a position of freedom from a position of inferiority. Yet how their complexities could have been resolved in practice must remain in the realm of the hypothetical.

III

The Church Organizes

Fortunately for the Catholics, the Bolshevik seizure of power found them organized in greater strength than they had been for many decades.[1] Just as the Orthodox Church had strengthened its position by restoring the patriarchate in the person of Tikhon on November 18, 1917, so the position of the Catholic Church had been strengthened by the elevation of Bishop Ropp of Wilno to the archdiocesan see of Mohylew, a worthy choice for the turbulent

[1] Interpretations of the Bolshevik Revolution abound. E. H. Carr's distinguished, *The Bolshevik Revolution, 1917–1923*, 3 vols. (New York, 1951-1953), is favorable to the Socialist ideal. W. H. Chamberlain, *The Russian Revolution, 1917–1921*, 2 vols. (New York, 1935), was comprehensive, perhaps even yet unsurpassed by Carr. Sidney and Beatrice Webb, *Soviet Communism: A New Civilization*, 2 vols. (London, 1936), and Sir John Maynard, *Russia in Flux* (London, 1946), are optimistic toward the revolution as a real step to communism, particularly economic democracy. For Jan Kucharzewski, *The Origins of Modern Russia* (New York, 1948), the Soviet system is a new Russian despotism and Soviet imperialism is tsarist in reality. N. A. Berdiaev, *The Russian Idea* (New York, 1948), feels that the Soviet system has deep roots in Russian culture and in the Russian soul's yearning for collectivism. N. S. Timasheff, *The Great Retreat: The Growth and Decline of Communism* (New York, 1946), interprets the events as an attempt to remake society, an attempt that is defeated by the environment; the communist regime thus is forced to return to traditional and national values.

As to the dynamics of the system, Trotsky in his *History of the Russian Revolution* (New York, 1936), considers that the Socialist ideal was tarnished by the failure of the world revolution, the emergence of a new bureaucracy, and the Thermidorean Reaction. W. W. Rostow, *The Dynamics of Soviet Society* (New York, 1953), stresses power and its priority in decision-making. On the other hand, Waldemar Gurian, *Bolshevism: An Introduction to Soviet Communism* (Notre Dame, 1952), makes ideology the central hypothesis in his

rcvolutionary times that were sweeping Russia.[2] This towering figure from the gentry—educated in law at the University of St. Petersburg, and in theology at Fribourg and Innsbruck—dominated the scene of Catholicism in Russia, even after his exile in Warsaw. Adding strength was the new bishop of Mińsk, Zygmunt Łoziński. Later Edward O'Rourke became the first bishop of Riga on September 29, 1918. The diocese of Riga numbered about 600,000 Catholics.[3] In 1919 Bishop Peter Mańkowski took possession of the restored see of Kamieniec-Podolski. The gradual filling of vacant sees fortified Catholicism.[4]

The Church was organized into six dioceses: the archdiocese of Mohylew under Archbishop Ropp, and the dioceses of Kowno, Łuck-Żytomierz, Kamieniec-Podolski, Mińsk, and Saratov or Tiras-

interpretation and considers Bolshevism a secular religion with a demonic priesthood enforcing total claims. Nathan Leites, *The Operational Code of the Politburo* (New York, 1951), finds that ideological commitments play a decisive role: for the sake of an envisioned good society, the citizen must be controlled.

Others, like Barrington Moore, Jr., *Soviet Politics: The Dilemma of Power* (Cambridge, 1951), emphasize the role of industrialization as leading to a more rational political and social order.

An important work which tries to present a total picture of the Soviet Union, its institutions, political, social, and economic, is W. W. Kulski, *The Soviet Regime* (Syracuse, 1954). As to particular aspects of the Soviet development, its political developments are traced in that most excellent work, Merle Fainsod, *How Russia is Ruled* (Cambridge, 1954), which sees the governing formulas of the Soviet dictatorship in alternating repression and relaxation. The social developments of the Revolution are well treated by Timasheff, *op. cit.*, with a good presentation of the development of social classes. The economic problems are dealt with in a quite technical manner by Alexander Baykov, *The Development of the Soviet Economic System* (New York, 1948), in manner overly trustful by Maurice Dobb, *Soviet Economic Development since 1917* (London, 1948), and in a readable style by Henry Schwartz, *Russia's Soviet Economy* (New York, 1950). The classical work on Soviet agriculture is Naum Jasny, *The Socialized Agriculture of the USSR* (Stanford, 1949).

[2] Jan Wasilewski, *Arcybiskupi i administratorowie archidyecezji mohylowskiej* (Pińsk, 1930), pp. 177–186. For a sympathetic Catholic account of the restoration of the patriarchate, see Albert M. Ammann, *Abriss der Ostslawischen Kirchengeschichte* (Vienna, 1950), pp. 592–594; John S. Curtiss, *The Russian Church and the Soviet State, 1917–1950* (Boston, 1953), pp. 26–39, a work that is marked by a definite naiveté when dealing with Soviet policy toward the Church. For Archbishop Ropp's elevation, see Jan Wasilewski, *op. cit.*, p. 180; ZZVP, I, No. 84, p. 3; papal documents were published in *Kronika archidyecezji mohylowskiej*, January 1918; see also James J. Zatko, "The Roman Catholic Church and its Legal Position under the Provisional Government in Russia in 1917," *The Slavonic and East European Review*, XXXVIII (1960), 486.

[3] OR, January 21, 1920, and June 18, 1920.

[4] Jan Wasilewski, *op. cit.*, p. 185.

pol.[5] These dioceses constituted one ecclesiastical province, the province of Mohylew. The archdiocese of Mohylew, embracing Russia proper and Siberia, extended from the shores of the White Sea to Kharkov and from Belorussia to the frontiers of China and Japan. On the other hand, the diocese of Tiraspol included in its domain southern Russia, the Caucasus, Crimea, Georgia, and the Tartar regions.[6] These vast dioceses were reorganized when in 1921 the deaneries of Irkutsk, Omsk, Tomsk and Tashkent were constituted as the Apostolic Vicariate of Siberia. A papal bull of the date February 2, 1923, established the diocese of Vladivostok under Bishop Charles Śliwowski with residence at Harbin.[7] The diocese of Vladivostok included the *Primorskaia* and *Amurskaia oblast,* and part of Sakhalin. The Polish churches in Manchuria were administered by Bishop Śliwowski.

The Vatican itself took a hand in the vigorous reorganization of the Church in Siberia. In February 1921, Monsignor Jean B. M. de Guebriant, vicar apostolic of Canton since 1916, was appointed apostolic visitator for Siberia, and he planned to leave for the visitation in the spring.[8] Monsignor de Guebriant was accompanied on his journey by Father P. Kluge, O.F.M., whom he appointed as the head of the new seminary in Vladivostok.[9]

Besides Siberia, Georgia also came within the purview of the Vatican. The Holy See sent the Dominican Bishop M. Gabriele Moriondo as vicar apostolic of the new republic of Georgia and as apostolic administrator of the Caucasus and Crimea.[10]

Although the parishes of the western provinces were of normal size, the parishes in the interior and in the east were proportionately as vast as the two sees of Mohylew and Tiraspol; at times the parish would surpass the boundaries of the *guberniia.* Besides, as difficult

[5] In exile, Bishop Kessler wrote *Geschichte der Diozöse von Tiraspol* (Dickenson, 1931).

[6] Antoni Około-Kułak, *Kościół w Rosji dawniej, obecnie, i w przyszłości* (Cracow, 1928), p. 6, a brief work of great value, for the author was frequently an eyewitness of the events he describes.

[7] Jan Wasilewski, *op. cit.,* p. 185; *Elenchus cleri et ecclesiarum archdioeceseos Mohiloviensis in Russia in diem 1 Januarii 1926* (Warsaw, 1926), p. 4; Około-Kułak, *op. cit.,* pp. 6–7; *Polska,* February 17, 1918; *Annuario Pontificio per l'anno 1924* (Rome, 1924), p. 242; *AAS,* XV (Rome, 1923), 255.

[8] *OR,* February 7, 8, 1921; *Elenchus cleri . . .* (1926), p. 4.

[9] *OR,* December 26, 27, 1922.   [10] *OR,* May 2, 3, 1921.

as the spiritual care of the Catholics was in these endless spaces, efficient administration was also hampered by the fact that the parishes were not organized in deaneries, and hence were immediately subject to the bishop. Archbishop Ropp, therefore, proceeded to organize the parishes of Russia proper and Siberia into deaneries, thus actually providing a stronger organizational structure to face the stormy future. For instance, the archbishop established the deanery of Smoleńsk with Father Około-Kułak as dean. Within the deanery he included the parishes in Wiazma, Mazalce, Roslavl, and Smoleńsk with twenty-six priests and some tens of thousands of Catholics. This organization of the deanery used the frontiers of the old Polish state, which had had a bishop in Smoleńsk.[11]

Along with the efforts at reorganization, the structure of the Russian Catholic Church—that Eastern rite Slavonic Catholic Church distinct from the old Byzantine-Slavonic Church—also came under consideration. Here Metropolitan Szeptycki, archbishop of Lwów, played a significant role;[12] according to him, the Catholic Church of the Byzantine-Slavonic rite provided an important base for a mass movement toward reunion of the Orthodox Church with the Roman See. In order to accomplish this truly heroic work, the metropolitan strongly emphasized the difference between the Orthodox, who accept episcopal authority, and the Protestants, who reject ecclesiastical authority, a distinction neither quite complete nor exact. According to Archbishop Szeptycki, to the Orthodox the Latins must give assurance that to unite churches is not to become Latin and to lose Orthodox traditions and nationality. The Russian Catholic Church of Slavonic rite, therefore, by preserving Russian usages, was doing a work of charity for the Russian church. The

[11] Jan Wasilewski, *op. cit.*, p. 180; Około-Kułak, *op. cit.*, pp. 6–7; *Polska,* February 17, 1918.

[12] Roman Maria Alexander Count Szeptycki was born on July 29, 1865, into a Polish family of Latin rite. After completing the *gymnasium* in Cracow in 1883, he served in the Austrian army from 1883 to 1884. At this time he fell ill with scarlet fever, a disease that left its mark on him for life. After his army service, he studied law at Cracow, where he obtained his doctorate. Having entered a monastery of the Basilian fathers in Dobromil in 1888, he studied theology with the Jesuits in Cracow. From 1899 to 1901 he was the bishop of Stanisławów, and in 1901 he rose to the rank of metropolitan of Halicz and archbishop of Lwów, a position he held until 1944. See G. Luzhnitskii, *Ukrainska Tserkva mizh skhodom i zakhodom* (Philadelphia, 1954), p. 687.

metropolitan condemned as contrary to the decrees of the popes the opinion that each convert should choose his own rite. The remedy proposed by the metropolitan demanded a sharp change in the public opinion of the Western church, which must learn to regard Catholics and priests of Eastern rite as equals. On the other hand, a correct notion of the Church, of infallibility and primacy, must be instilled into the minds of the Orientals. Westerners must understand the different mentality of the Eastern Christians and adapt themselves; religious congregations and secular clergy could render their work fruitful and acceptable by joining the Eastern rite themselves. These workers were not to act as though they were missionaries to a pagan country.[13]

After having been interned six months in the monastery prison of Suzdal and exiled to Jaroslav,[14] metropolitan Szeptycki arrived in St. Petersburg in 1917, where he presided over the first synod of the Russian Catholic Church of Eastern Rite (May 18–31, 1917). Archbishop Ropp, Bishop Cieplak, and Bishop Łoziński showed a most friendly attitude to the synod. Indeed, Bishop Łoziński, even before he had become bishop, had helped place at the disposal of the Eastern rite Catholics the church of St. John, the so-called Maltese church, established by Tsar Paul I.[15] The synod, sitting in St. Catherine's church in St. Petersburg, effected the basic organization of the rite. Metropolitan Szeptycki appointed Father Leonid Fedorov as the exarch of the Russian Catholic Church.[16] This act must be considered the beginning of the independent existence of

---

[13] *OR*, February 19, 20, 1923.

[14] *OR*, February 19, 1921; Luzhnitskii, *op. cit.*, p. 538.

[15] D. Kolpinskij, "Początki katolicyzmu wschodniego obrządku w Rosji," *Kościół katolicki w Rosji: Materiały do jego historji i organizacji* (Warsaw, 1932), p. 29, a valuable account of the origin and growth of the Byzantine rite for Russian Catholics, by one of the clergy that belonged to that rite.

[16] See Paul Mailleux, S. J., *Exarch Leonid Fedorov* (New York, 1964), for a biography of the exarch. Fedorov, ordained in 1911, had returned to Russia and been arrested, and then exiled to Siberia, because of his effective work among the Russian Orthodox. After his return he became the exarch for the approximately 3,000 Russian Catholics of the Byzantine rite. He died a prisoner in Viatka, March 7, 1935. See also Paul Mailleux, "The Catholic Church in Russia and Exarch Fedorov," *Religion in Russia: A Collection of Essays Read at the Cambridge Summer School of Russian Studies*, edited by George Bennigsen (London, 1940), pp. 31–48; Luzhnitskii, *op. cit.*, pp. 684–685.

the Russian Catholic Church, which until then had been under the direction of the Latin bishops.[17]

Archbishop Szeptycki's activities ranged much wider than St. Petersburg. He envisioned a Catholic patriarchate in Kiev.[18] Nor was his influence insignificant among the Orthodox Ukrainians, for when he went to Kiev to attend the Ukrainian *sobor* (synod) he was received with great joy, but his plans for a union of churches failed totally and dismally.[19] The confused religious situation in Ukraine, the debate between the Moscow-oriented Orthodox and the Ukrainian Orthodox Autocephalous Church,[20] the struggle over "Ukrainization" of the Orthodox rite,[21] and the hopelessly turbulent political atmosphere made any systematic effort at union of churches a doomed project from the beginning. The metropolitan's influence was not limited to Ukraine but made itself strongly felt in Belorussia, where the Union had been a means toward Westernization and Latinization. It may be that the influence of the vigorous metropolitan and the Ukrainian nationalists had inspired the Belorussian nationalists to seek to establish the Byzantine-Slavonic Catholic Church as a national church.[22]

Undoubtedly, amid the confusion of war and revolution, the figure of Szeptycki appeared like a colossus; but his efforts disappeared amid the smoke. Indeed, the wisdom of establishing a church, small and weak in numbers, and freeing it from the support of the better organized and stronger Latin church (which for all its strength could not survive) may at least be questioned, for the Russian Catholic Church could be destroyed by eliminating its

---

[17] Martha E. Almedingen, *The Church in Russia Today* (New York, 1923), pp. 30–31; Luzhnitskii, *op. cit.*, pp. 540–541.

[18] Luzhnitskii, *op. cit.*, p. 678.

[19] E. Edlinskii, "Uniia s Rimon i metropolit graf Sheptitskii," *Revolutsiia i tserkov* (1924), Nos. 1–3, p. 109; *OR*, August 25, 1922.

[20] S. K., "Ukraińska Prawosławna Cerkiew," *Sprawy narodowościowe*, I (1927), 63–64, summarizes the events in the Ukrainian Orthodox Church during the revolutionary period; *OR*, August 26, 1922, illustrated how closely Rome watched the events in the Ukraine; for secondary accounts, Luzhnitskii, *op. cit.*, pp. 545–547, and Ammann, *op. cit.*, pp. 623–624.

[21] *OR*, June 22, 1921, and December 4, 5, 1922.

[22] Leon Wasilewski, "Sprawa wznowienia Unji Wyznaniowej," *KP*, May 31, 1917.

only exarch. Moreover, Archbishop Szeptycki's approach to the problem of union seems tinged with political plans, a cultural romanticism and ecclesiastical nationalism, which would exclude from work among Eastern Christians all but Slavonic rite clergy and congregations. Admittedly, the whole program of the Russian Catholic Church based its appeal on satisfying the requisites of Russian nationality.[23] Actually, the Russian Catholics themselves disagreed: one party preferred the Latin, while another preferred the Oriental.[24]

Another element of strength for the church was the national organization of the Poles throughout the Russian Empire. As early as March 1917, the Poles in Kiev organized a congress of fifty Polish organizations with 150 persons present.[25] In Siberia, in practically every Polish colony there was a Polish House (*Dom Polski*), where the Polish societies of the area met. When any critical question of general import arose, the organizations met in the *Dom Polski* and chose delegates for a common assembly.[26] The Poles in Belorussia, too, made themselves heard by demanding incorporation into Poland. The Polish culture, incidentally, allied itself with the Catholicism of the area; among these Poles, however, were adherents of other religions. This petition for incorporation

[23] Kolpinskij, "Początki katolicyzmu . . .," *op. cit.*, pp. 25, 28. See Jan Ostrowski, *Z za Kulis Kurji biskupiej w Leningradzie* (Moscow, 1929), p. 370, for a letter of Archbishop Ropp's, without date but in the year 1921, where he writes: "I have nothing against Szeptycki, but his activity, supported by Ukrainians and Germans, is political and anti-Polish; it is not Catholic and does not lead to agreement and unity. . . ."

[24] Almedingen, *op. cit.*, pp. 64–65. On this problem, see James J. Zatko, "A Contemporary Report on the Condition of the Catholic Church in Russia, 1922," *The Harvard Theological Review*, LIII (October 1960), 284, where Monsignor Constantine Budkiewicz reports that Russian converts frequently wanted to disassociate themselves as far as possible from the Orthodox Church and its usages; see also p. 284 for the difficulties between the Latin clergy and the Russian rite Catholic clergy. See again Ostrowski, *op. cit.*, pp. 228–229, for a letter of John Troigo to Archbishop Ropp, July 21, 1921: "Generally the activity of Father Fedorov and of Father Abrikosov, who has the same ideas, is provoking criticism from our clergy . . . . The tactics of Father Fedorov somewhat provoke the Latin clergy"; also p. 236, for a letter of Troigo to Archbishop Ropp, December 2, 1921: "The matter of the Eastern rite concerns us greatly; as I have already written, generally the attitude of the Latin clergy is negative."

[25] *KP*, May 7, 1917.

[26] *KP*, July 7, 1919; "Polonja na dalekim wschodzie," *Przegląd powszechny* (1923), pp. 281–284.

was placed before the Central Powers Council of Regency on December 19, 1917.[27]

With the German withdrawal in 1918 came the first attacks on the Polish and Catholic population—which indicated that protection was needed in Belorussia. The Regency Council addressed a petition to the chancellor, George Count von Hertling, for protection of the Polish people in the areas from which the Germans were withdrawing in accordance with the Treaty of Brest.[28]

However, these efforts to co-operate with Germany were doomed to failure as Germany went down to defeat in 1918. Hence, the Polish-Catholic element could look for support only to a resurrected Poland, a position that involved dangers as well as protection.

[27] "Deklaracja Polaków z polskiej i polsko-białoruskiej części Litwy," *Naród i Państwo,* January 12, 1918.
[28] "Rzecz na Białej Rusi," *Naród i Państwo,* October 10, 1918; *OR,* March 18, 1920.

IV

The Bolshevik Government Attacks

The Bolshevik overthrow of the Provisional Government found the Catholics, therefore, not unprepared for the storm that threatened to overwhelm them in the very near future. Some elements in the Catholic Church welcomed the October Revolution, in spite of the generally favorable policy of the Provisional Government toward the Catholics.[1] Nevertheless, the Bolshevik attitude generated hostility, and no amount of good will could hide the fact that war would be waged on religion on two fronts. An ideological campaign for materialistic atheism to replace religious "prejudices" was an imperative; and the Bolshevik demand for a unitary, monolithic state structure would result in political action against the church that would have as its objective the prevention of "a state within a state."[2] The Bolshevik demands were great: all church and monastic funds in banks and co-operatives were to go to local Soviets; libraries and printing presses were to be placed under commissars; all "enemies of the people" were to be registered. Only then could the State leave religion alone.[3] The Bolshevik declara-

---

[1] Francis McCullagh, *The Bolshevik Persecution of Christianity* (New York, 1924), pp. 201, 240. This is an eyewitness account of the persecution, marked however by occasional errors.

[2] "Sovetskaia politika v religioznom voprose," *Revolutsiia i tserkov*, No. 1 (1919), pp. 2–3.

[3] *Pravda*, January 31, 1918.

tions indicate the confusion resulting from theory and action. Theory dictated that, for the State, religion was a private affair and at the same time that it was the duty of the Communist Party to combat religious prejudice. Still the governmental power remained the only instrument for combat in any real sense.[4] The Communist Party resorted to governmental action.

Before the coup of October 25, 1917, the Bolsheviks had responded to the peasants' hunger for land by proclaiming a program of all land to the peasants. Therefore, on the very morrow of the Bolshevik victory, October 26, 1917, the Bolsheviks published a decree on the liquidation of landed estates. This decree (1) abolished private ownership of land by estate owners without payment of any kind of compensation; (2) transferred to the provisional control and administration of regional rural communities or to district Soviets of peasant representatives all the land belonging to estate owners, Crown appanage estates, convents, monasteries, etc., with all their livestock, machinery, buildings, and productive equipment; (3) ordered punishment for any damage to confiscated property as a severe crime, because henceforth the confiscated property must be considered as belonging to the whole people; (4) but did not confiscate land belonging as private property to peasant farmers.[5] In 32 provinces of European Russia, 22,800,000 *desiatins* of land (each *desiatin* being one and three-fourths acres) were made available in this way, according to the data for 1919. Of this newly available land 4.6 per cent was retained for state operation, mainly as state farms; 1.7 per cent went into *kolkhozy*, and 93.7 per cent was subdivided. Thus the roughly 20,000,000 *desiatins* which became available to the peasants increased their prerevolutionary holding of 95,000,000 *desiatins* by more than 20 per cent.[6]

Of all this land, the church lands formed but a small percentage. Official data for the 42 provinces of European Russia, except the North Caucasus, show 119,400,000 *desiatins* of allotment land and 89,500,000 *desiatins* of private land in 1905. The church lands in

[4] *Pravda*, May 15, 1921.

[5] Alexander Baykov, *The Development of the Soviet Economic System* (New York, 1948), pp. 16–17.

[6] Naum Jasny, *The Socialized Agriculture of the Soviet USSR* (Stanford, 1950), pp. 152–154.

1905 comprised but 335,000 *desiatins,* and in 1911 they had dropped to 319,000, a pittance in comparison with the total holdings in Russia.[7]

While the central authorities fulfilled their pledges to the peasants by confiscating the landed estates, in the borderlands where the chief strength of Catholicism lay, there were similar developments in process. A manifesto of the first Provisional Government of Peasant and Worker Soviets of Belorussia in 1917 proclaimed the nationalization of the land: all land of estates and of great land-owners, monasteries, Orthodox churches, Catholic churches, and of the clergy with all movables and immovables, woods, waters, and mineral rights became the property of the working people of Belo-russia.[8] A similar decree of the Provisional Government of Workers and Peasants in Ukraine in 1917 nationalized the estates, transfer-ring them from landowners to peasants.[9]

Small as the total holdings of the churches and monasteries were, the share of the Catholic Church in these lands was even smaller. During the course of the nineteenth century, the monasteries and their lands had disappeared. Nevertheless, some churches had con-siderable property. Outside Russia proper, parish churches norm-ally possessed about 33 *desiatins* of land; but there were also churches, like St. Catherine's in St. Petersburg, with property in buildings. St. Catherine's endowment ran to 30,000,000 rubles.[10] Hence, although the lands of the church were not vast, their con-fiscation meant the total loss of its whole store; yet the disaster was not something new in the Catholic Church's experience in Russia, for its property had often been seized before.

More important to the Church's influence was the series of decrees that in rapid succession nationalized all the schools, ele-mentary and secondary, as well as theological seminaries and

[7] *Ibid.,* p. 143. For the political conflict of the Bolsheviks and the Social Revolutionaries over land policy, see E. H. Carr, *The Bolshevik Revolution, 1917-1923,* II (New York, 1952), 32–41.

[8] *Politika sovetskoi vlasti po natsionalnom voprosu za tri goda 1917-XI-1920* (Moscow, 1920), p. 24, the official statement of what had been done in nation-ality policy.

[9] *Ibid.,* p. 110.

[10] Antoni Około-Kułak, *Kościół w Rosji dawniej, obecnie, i w przyszłości* (Cracow, 1928), p. 11.

academies; granted legal recognition to civil marriages and divorces only; and finally ordered the record books on births, marriages, and deaths turned over to a governmental bureau.

Only on January 23, 1918, was the fundamental decree on separation of Church and State issued.[11] The decree declared the Church separated from the State, and forbade local laws or regulations interfering with the freedom of conscience or granting special privileges by reason of religious belief. These articles of the decree were a fundamental blow at the privileged position of the Orthodox Church. When the decree abolished every legal restriction connected with the profession of certain faiths or with the nonprofession of any faith, it undoubtedly provided for the freedom of Roman Catholics, Russian Catholics, Old Believers, and all the sects that had suffered discrimination in times past. Small wonder then that Catholics greeted this aspect of the decree with relief. Exarch Fedorov said at his trial: "We were subjected to persecution in the time of the tsar, and we had to contend with great difficulties under the Kerensky *regime*. That was the reason why Archbishop Ropp and all the Latin Catholics breathed a sigh of relief when the October Revolution took place. But the Russian Catholics also felt very happy, as it was only when the Soviet *regime* came that the Greco-Catholic Church was placed on a footing of equality with all other denominations. For this reason I myself welcomed with enthusiasm the decree for the separation of Church and State. I welcomed it with all the joy of a man who hated the unnatural alliance that had existed between the two in Russia. . . ."[12] The prospect of deliverance from a position of inferiority, endured for

[11] John S. Curtiss, *The Russian Church and the Soviet State, 1917–1950* (Boston, 1953), p. 46. For the decree, see P. V. Gidulianov (ed.), *Otdelenie tserkvi ot gosudarstva,* 3rd ed. (Moscow, 1926), pp. 368–369; *Certain Legislation Respecting Religion in Force in the Union of Soviet Socialist Republics* (London, 1930), a publication which points up the repressive aspects of the Soviet laws; *The First Code of Laws of the Russian Socialistic Federal Soviet Republic* (Petrograd, 1919), especially on civil marriage, p. 25, and divorce, pp. 28–29; *Pravda,* January 21, 1918; *OR,* June 3, 1921.

[12] McCullagh, *op. cit.,* pp. 204, 239. *Kronika archidyecezji mohylowskiej* (January 1920), p. 1, indicates that the Catholic authorities felt the decree was aimed at the Orthodox church, since what was not united to the government could not be separated; the Catholic Church was reckoned among the "foreign confessions." This invaluable document was made available to this writer by Monsignor Bronislas Ussas, Warsaw.

over a century, evoked from the Catholics a loyal attitude to the new political authority in Russia; only the future was to show how misplaced that loyalty was and how unmerited.

In contrast to the Catholic authorities, the leadership of the Orthodox Church, gathered in a *sobor,* denounced the separation of Church and State as "a malicious attack upon all the structure of the life of the Orthodox Church and an act of open oppression against it." This synod threatened all participants in the legislation and execution with ecclesiastical penalties, even excommunication. Appealing in a more popular vein to the Orthodox people, the synod called the decree an act of violence against the conscience that would be worse than the Mongol yoke, forgetting that the attitude of the Mongols had actually made the Church's position very favorable in Russia. Later, on March 5, 1918, Patriarch Tikhon condemned in no uncertain terms the peace of Brest Litowsk. Thus from the very beginning there was open warfare between the Orthodox Church and the Bolsheviks over the decree on separation, while the Catholics hoped to find relief from oppression in that very decree.[13]

Other provisions of the decree were not as welcome as the simple separation of Church and State. Religious oaths were abolished, and all civil acts were to be registered only by a government department. More fundamental, churches were not to be juridical personalities nor were they to own property. Thus the economic and legal basis of the churches' strength was being undermined. If the church could not act as a juridical person in law, then it and its representatives were deprived of the strength and protection of concerted action and were thus isolated and exposed as individuals to the power of law. Moreover, to deny churches the right to possess property was to deny them the opportunity to exist in security and to expand their activity.

As a logical consequence of the churches' inability to own property, the decree nationalized all existing church property by transferring ownership to the people. Thus at a stroke there vanished the Catholics' accumulation of church properties that had not been the gift of Russian governments, but had been salvaged largely

[13] Curtiss, *op. cit.,* pp. 52–53. See also *New York Times,* March 13, 21, 1918.

from the confiscations and closures of the nineteenth century. The properties of the Catholic Church in Russia had been until 1917 under the administrative direction and control of the Ecclesiastical College. The funds administered by it went back to the efforts of Archbishop Siestrzencewicz, that controversial first archbishop of Mohylew; subsequently, Tsar Alexander I (1801–1825) decided on January 18, 1820, to establish a capital fund, whose income was to be used for ecclesiastical necessities. The Ecclesiastical College resolved to begin collecting the sums on January 1, 1823, from the secular clergy to establish the fund. The diocese of Mohylew was to pay 300 rubles a year, while the diocese of Wilno was to contribute 1,000 rubles, the diocese of Kowno 600 rubles, the diocese of Łuck-Żytomierz 450 rubles, the Kamieniec-Podolski and Mińsk dioceses 100 rubles and 50 kopecks. Thus the sum contributed annually amounted to 2,575 rubles. Over and above this, the Wilno chapter was to contribute 5,575 rubles from its properties annually. These contributions lasted until 1843. After the confiscation of several monasteries in 1832, the capital of these monasteries was added to the fund. Again when church properties had been confiscated in the years 1842 and 1843, Nicholas I by an imperial decree consented to assigning the pensions connected with the properties to the capital fund. This fund, which in 1826 amounted to 18,080 rubles, had by 1908 risen to 6,423,865 rubles. This sum included the value of immovables in St. Petersburg to the amount of 1,640,400 rubles and borrowed money to 2,387 rubles. The income for the year 1907 was 209,274 rubles. The minister of internal affairs was empowered to permit expenses up to 900 rubles; sums beyond that could be expended only by the consent of the Emperor.

The Ecclesiastical College also had control of the capital deriving from foundations, left by individuals for religious services or for religious institutions. The interest from these funds was forwarded semiannually to the churches specified in the foundations. In 1908 this capital had reached 1,119,730 rubles.

In the year 1846 Nicholas I at the request of the bishops established a building fund by withdrawing 300,000 rubles from the original capital; the interest from this amount was to provide funds for the repair of churches in the Empire. After 1906, the interest accruing was divided among the dioceses in the following manner: 5,857 rubles 50 kopecks went to the archbishop of Mohylew; the bishops of Wilno, Łuck-Żytomierz, and Kowno received 3,100 rubles. By 1908 the capital of the building fund had reached 374,320 rubles.

Finally, there were the sums collected for the support of the clergy in the Samara and Saratov *guberniias*. The local authorities collected the requisite sums and paid their clergy, but the remainder after 1879 they had to send to the Ecclesiastical College. Thence by 1908 arose a capital fund of 34,953 rubles. The interest was used for the support of retired clergy.

Thus, in the year 1917 the Ecclesiastical College administered property in Russia of this value:

1. Sustaining Fund of the Empire	4,984,673	rubles
Interest	202,349	"
2. Sustaining Fund of the Kingdom	353,087	"
Interest	13,720	"
3. Foundations:		
a. Permanent Investments	1,522,672	"
Interest	60,107	"
b. Temporary Investments	202,125	"
Interest	7,994	"
4. Building Capital	375,300	"
Interest	14,380	"
5. Saratov Funds	38,615 24	kopecks
Interest	1,497 35	"
6. Houses' Value	3,640,400	rubles
Total	11,381,009 rubles 59 kopecks (sic)	

These then were the funds of the Catholic Church when the Ecclesiastical College ceased to exist on August 25, 1917. When therefore church property was confiscated and proclaimed the property of the people, the Catholic Church in Russia suffered a major economic disaster. Its economic strength had been built up actually over centuries in the Polish-Lithuanian Commonwealth and the century and a half of the Empire of the tsars.[14]

[14] A. Petrani, *Kolegium Duchowne w Petersburgu* (Lublin, 1950), pp. 119–124. See also the *Kronika . . .*, January 1920, p. 8, for the attempt to nationalize the funds of the Ecclesiastical College.

As crippling as was the nationalization of church property, it did not prove to be as catastrophic for the moral authority and influence of the Catholic Church as did the separation of the school from the church and the prohibition of religious instruction in state and public schools as well as in private schools where general subjects were taught. To the Catholic clergy this appeared as the vital blow, for it struck at what they considered one of their essential functions as priests.[15] Moreover, in the light of an instruction published in December 1917, over the signature of Lenin and Lunacharskii—the people's commissar of education—the decree was to be interpreted in the most sweeping sense. The instruction pointed out that education was completely removed from the hands of the clergy and subjected to the People's Commissariat of Education. Comprehended within this transfer were all parochial schools, teachers' seminaries, theological schools and seminaries, diocesan schools, missionary schools, academies, lower, middle, and higher schools and institutes under clerical control with all articles, movable and immovable properties, buildings and their lands, lands required for the schools, libraries, valuables, capital, and all that belonged to the schools. A more sweeping statement could hardly be formulated.[16] When therefore the decree on the separation of Church and State appeared and also separated the church from the schools, the scope of its effectiveness had already been defined.

The decree, therefore, touched the Catholic schools from the very top to the bottom. The diocesan seminaries, the Theological Academy at St. Petersburg with its valuable library, dating back to the time of Peter Skarga in the sixteenth century, the parochial schools, and the right of teaching religion in public schools were all torn from the Catholic Church and transferred to the Commissariat of Education. For instance, the church of St. Catherine in St. Petersburg had for decades supported a boys' *gymnasium* and a girls' *gymnasium*, a vocational school, and 11 elementary schools. In St. Catherine's elementary schools 20,000 Catholic children were being educated, while the *gymnasium* provided an education for 1,500 young men and women.[17]

[15] McCullagh, *op. cit.*, pp. 184, 189, 202, 241.
[16] *Pravda*, December 22, 1917.
[17] Jan Wasilewski, *Arcybiskupi i administratorowie archidyecezji mohylowskiej* (Pińsk, 1930), p. 188.

How vast the network of schools is suggested by the figures given for the year 1919 in the *Zhizn Natsionalstei*. In the Mińsk *guberniia* alone in 1919 there were 261 schools with 12,079 students and 304 teachers. In 19 other provinces there were 100 schools and 16 workers' clubs and 16 libraries with 48,000 volumes. Until 1919 the *Tsentralni grazhdanskii komitet Tsartva Polskogo* directed 1,021 schools with 48,000 students. Priests did much of the work in these schools, educating the children in a Catholic and national spirit; hence, the Bolsheviks considered the schools centers of "chauvinism" and Catholicism. All these schools were closed, and only a very small part of them reopened under the supervision of the Soviet government.[18]

Not merely the actual control of the school was objected to by the government, but in July 1918 the Polish schools in St. Petersburg received a circular from the commissar of education for the St. Petersburg district and the commissar of the middle schools that renewed the prohibition against teaching Latin and religion in the schools and using priests as instructors. Religious pictures and religious books were also excluded from the schools.[19]

In Moscow, because of a lack of teachers that would present the subjects in a communist spirit, the government decided to close the Polish schools and to reorganize them with communist teachers and sympathizers.[20]

These changes the Bolshevik Government determined to formalize in the constitution. Between the initiation of the project on January 28, 1918, and the final approval on July 10, 1918, under the influence of Jakov M. Sverdlov and Joseph Stalin a committee of fifteen appointed for the task by the Central Executive Committee wrote the Constitution of the Russian Socialist Federated Soviet Republic. A bill of rights, expressed in class terms, formed the first part of the constitution. Freedom of speech, of press, of association, of assembly, and of access to education was reserved expressly for the working class. Liberty of conscience was guaranteed for the "workers"

---

[18] Komorovskii, "Kulturnye dostizheniia Poliakov RSFSR," *Zhizn natsionalnostei* (January 1923), p. 232, a favorable report on Soviet policy toward the Polish minority in the Soviet state.

[19] *Polska*, September 15, 1918.

[20] *Zhizn natsionalnostei* (February 1919), p. 4.

by separating Church from State and from the school. Freedom of religious and antireligious propaganda was the prerogative of every citizen.

The second part of the constitution defined the governmental structure, or rather formalized the existing structure. The primary objective was to establish a dictatorship of the proletariat, a strong central government. Members of the onetime "exploiting" classes, that is, businessmen, police agents of the *ancien regime,* monks and priests of all denominations, were disfranchised and denied the right to hold public office.[21] Thus clergy were relegated to the status of second-class citizens, deprived of any rights at all.

Moreover, the Bolshevik government, in order to control the activities of the Polish citizens and organizations in Russia, as early as November 28, 1917, organized the Commissariat for Polish National Affairs, thus controlling the Commission for the Liquidation of the Affairs of the Polish Kingdom. This commissariat was to aid in the preservation, listing and description of objects of antiquity and art belonging to the Polish people. These objects were understood to include antiques, art objects, libraries, museum articles, collections, historical documents, archives, church bells, and church equipment.[22] This was but a temporary pause in the traditional Russian anti-Polish attitude.

[21] Merle Fainsod, *How Russia is Ruled* (Cambridge, 1954), pp. 295–296, a detailed and well-balanced account of the Party and State structure's development. For a study of the constitutional efforts of this period, see G. V. Kulakov, *Konstitutsiia SSSR i obrazovanie sezdov sovetov v skhemakh,* 4th ed. (Moscow, 1925), devoted to the Constitution of 1924. G. S. Gurvich, *Osnovy sovetskoi konstitutsii,* 8th ed. (Moscow, 1930), is the most detailed to that date; the constitution of the RSFSR is given, pp. 310–325, and the declaration of the laboring and exploited classes, pp. 308–309; freedom of conscience is discussed in its constitutional meaning, pp. 160–161. *Osnovy sovetskogo gosudarstva i prava* (Moscow, 1917), published by the Ministry of Justice, gives a brief discussion of the constitution of the RSFSR, pp. 101–102; a Stalinist interpretation of the freedom of conscience, pp. 200–201; and very little space to the separation of Church and State in 1918, p. 201. E. B. Genkina, *Obrazovanie SSSR,* 2nd ed. (Moscow, 1947), and G. P. Barinov, *Osnovye voprosy konstitutsii SSSR* (Moscow, 1948), are both propagandistic works. V. N. Ivanov, *Osnovye prava i obiazanosti grazhdan SSSR* (Moscow, 1952), pp. 76–79, discusses freedom of conscience, but still under the Stalinist "personality-cult."

[22] *Politika sovetskoi vlasti . . .,* pp. 86–88.

V

The Catholic Opposition

The anti-Catholic program of the Bolshevik government developed more fully only with time. Indeed, the decree on the separation of Church and State was received with relief by the Catholics—however objectionable some features of that decree may have appeared, for instance, the regulations on education. Moreover, the decree left many details doubtful: What were to be the relations with the new government? How were property regulations to be carried out? Still the clergy debated the decree not in order to resist it, but in order to discover some way of conforming with the decree without doing violence to the Catholic conscience and canon law.[1]

Catholic hopes of reaching a working agreement with the government rose sharply when the department of religious affairs of the Commissariat of Justice requested Archbishop Ropp to take part in consultations on the separation of Church and State.[2] After the archbishop had agreed and asked only to be informed of the date, several months passed without further notice; in order to discover the reason for the delay, he sent Monsignor Constantine Budkiewicz, a man of great business ability and consummate address, as his dele-

[1] *KW,* March 19, 1923; Francis McCullagh, *The Bolshevik Persecution of Christianity* (New York, 1924), pp. 174, 239; M. Milich, "Protsess rimsko-katolicheskogo dukhovenstva," *Revolutsiia i tserkov,* Nos. 1–3 (1923), pp. 109–110, a very valuable article which surveys the activity of the Catholic clergy from 1917 and interprets it from the Soviet viewpoint.
[2] *Kronika archidyecezji mohylowskiej,* January 1920, p. 1.

gate to Moscow. There the monsignor learned, to his dismay, that there had not been and would not be consultations with religious leaders, but that the chancery of P. A. Krasikov, head of the department of religious affairs, would draw up its own instruction on the decree of separation.[3]

The worst fears of the clergy were aroused and their most optimistic hopes were dashed with the promulgation of the Instruction on Separation of Church and State on August 24 or 30, 1918. This instruction deprived all religious and all religious organizations of their character as legal persons and declared their property the property of the people. It contained a formula to be signed by committees of parishioners, consisting of at least twenty persons, in order to obtain the use of a church building and its ecclesiastical equipment. These committees were in no sense the "owners" of the churches, which remained the property of the people, represented by the government. Under the guise of the instruction, the government really intensified its control, for it regulated the use of the church and supervised the inventory of church property.[4]

Soon after the issuance of the instruction, apparently still in August of the same year, the clergy of St. Petersburg met and decided that it was not possible or lawful to sign the agreements demanded by the government. A few days later at another meeting, it was resolved not to give way to the signing of documents but to send a protest to Moscow, and, if possible, to do so in co-operation with the Orthodox bodies.

Without delay the archbishop, together with the Russian Catholic exarch Fedorov and the Orthodox bishops, lodged a sharp protest with the Commissariat of Justice, but without avail.[5] Soon afterwards the commissariat demanded that a delegate be sent in order to discuss details involved in carrying out the instruction. Monsignor Budkiewicz, already engaged as intermediary between the government and the archbishop, was delegated; and the government in-

[3] Jan Wasilewski, *Arcybiskupi i administratorowie archidyecezji mohylowskiej* (Pińsk, 1930), p. 182; *Kronika . . .,* January 1920, p. 1.

[4] Jan Wasilewski, *Arcybiskupi i administratorowie . . .,* pp. 182–183; Antoni Około-Kułak, *Kościół w Rosji, dawniej, obecnie i w przyszłości* (Cracow, 1928), pp. 26–27. The *Kronika* dates the instruction September 30, 1918.

[5] *Kronika . . .,* January 1920, p. 1.

formed him that the separation of Church and State involved three areas in particular: (1) the churches and church property; (2) the parochial registers of births, marriages and deaths, which were now to be transferred to the control of the government; (3) control of the administration and income of cemeteries. Monsignor Budkiewicz, speaking in the name of the archbishop, agreed that an arrangement, amicable and complete, could be reached with the archbishop about the registers, but any renunciation of property must be done in negotiations between the government and the Apostolic See itself.[6]

When it became clear that the government intended to enforce the decree in the sense of the instruction—by force if need be—the Catholic clergy, mostly of St. Petersburg, began to hold a series of consultations. These conferences, originally held under the leadership of Archbishop Ropp, continued from December 18, 1918, until April 7, 1920. There were at least thirteen such consultations, whose purpose was not to oppose the law but to seek ways of reconciling the church law with the civil law, so as to enable the Church to survive the revolutionary times. The problems facing the Church in Russia formed the substance of the discussions and reports, and the attitudes to be taken to these problems were also studied: the decree of separation, the instruction, the seizure of church property, the nature of communism, the possibility of a Catholic belonging to the Communist Party.[7]

At an important meeting in the first half of December 1918, Monsignor Budkiewicz read to the assembled clergy a document in which, with the consent of Archbishop Ropp, he proposed that the clergy ignore, as being contrary to canon law, the form of the agreement published in the instruction and ordered to be signed by parishioners who were to receive from the government the use of the fabric of the church and the articles of worship. The representatives of the parishes must point out to the government that the Church cannot be deprived of its independence, and the government must be satisfied with accepting a form which would transfer church

---

[6] *Ibid.*, p. 2; Jan Wasilewski, *Arcybiskupi i administratorowie . . .*, p. 183; McCullagh, *op. cit.*, p. 161.
[7] N. V. Krylenko, *Sudebnye rechi, 1922–1930* (Moscow, 1931), p. 17; McCullagh, *op cit.*, pp. 156–517; Milich, *op. cit.*, p. 106.

property only to the custody of parishioners. Should the government refuse to accede to this demand, the parishioners representing the parish must insist that they be allowed to introduce into the government's form of agreement such corrections and modifications as would make the document acceptable to Catholics. If this were refused by the government, then the parishioners may sign—but only under the protest that they sign under compulsion. Moreover, the representatives of the parishes must not rush to renounce church property, but should wait and procrastinate as much as possible. Finally, priests ought to keep one copy of the parish registers outside the church, and deposit another copy with the diocesan consistory. If the authorities demand the registers, they must be told that the registers have been sent to the diocesan consistory.[8]

It was only at a conference on March 27, 1919, that definite plans were laid for organization of Catholic committees to protect ecclesiastical property. As a result of this meeting, Archbishop Ropp published in the Mohylew diocesan *Chronicle* a circular letter dated April 2, 1919, which outlined the plan of conduct for the Catholic parishes of Russia. Perhaps it was felt that the uncompromising attitude of Monsignor Budkiewicz was somewhat unrealistic for revolutionary times. Moreover, Archbishop Ropp was convinced that the Bolshevik government would not last very long, that it was but a phase in a revolutionary era. Hence, he looked upon the arrangements of committees as temporary expedients to save the property of the Church and to save the Church itself in Russia.[9] In this circular letter, therefore, the archbishop permitted the parochial clergy to organize committees of parishioners to take over church property and thus protect it. These committees, furthermore, were to protect the churches and their valuables against irreligious forces. If the government insisted upon the signing of agreements, then they were to be signed but every effort must be made to avoid obnoxious conditions. The committees, in close dependence on the pastors, would take over the church property, so far as the government was concerned, protect it within the bounds of canonical prescription, sign the agreements with the government, and under-

[8] *OZ* (Moscow, 1923), pp. 2–3; see also McCullagh, *op. cit.*, pp. 160–161.
[9] *Kronika . . .*, January 1920, p. 2; *OZ*, p. 2; Krylenko, *op. cit.*, p. 20; McCullagh, *op. cit.*, pp. 159, 210, 233; Milich, "Protsess . . .," *op. cit.*, p. 110.

take to find means to help support the clergy and the church fabric. Since the total effectiveness of the committees depended on their close co-operation and co-ordination, the archbishop proposed establishment of a central committee—to be formed by each of the parochial committees selecting two members to participate in the central committee. The tasks of this central committee were to conduct relations with the central government within the parochial committees' competence, to supervise the united action of all the parochial committees, to assist the local committees in achieving their ends, and to organize in St. Petersburg the necessary means for the support of ecclesiastical government, including the support of the archdiocesan *curia*, the archbishop, the auxiliary, the chapter, and the seminary.[10]

Organization, therefore, began. Some agreements had already been signed when there was imminent danger of having the church closed unless an agreement were signed. A critical instance was the church and chapel of the Theological Academy with its library of 70,000 volumes and an especially good section of *Polonica*. This library, founded by Peter Skarga (1536–1612) in Wilno, was a precious national and historic monument. As to the Academy chapel, about fifty persons arrived to sign the agreement, among them some Orthodox who had come to sign on behalf of Catholics. The chapel was entrusted to Father Michael Dmochowski, and the agreement signed and sent to the local Soviet in St. Petersburg.[11]

The organization of Catholics had hardly begun, when Archbishop Ropp was arrested on April 19, 1919. Rumors of his arrest had drifted out to the Western world as early as February, when on February 2, 1919, the papal secretary of state, Cardinal Peter Gasparri, lodged a vigorous protest with Lenin himself, demanding the instant release of the archbishop. Lenin replied immediately to Cardinal Gasparri that the archbishop had not been arrested, but that his nephew had been arrested for speculation.[12] In April, however, there was no error. Bolshevik extremists wished to shoot the archbishop out of hand, but cooler heads prevailed and planned to use him in an

---

[10] *Kronika* . . ., January 1920, p. 2; *OZ*, pp. 3–6; Krylenko, *op. cit.*, p. 17; McCullagh, *op. cit.*, p. 158; Jan Wasilewski, *Arcybiskupi i administratorowie* . . ., pp. 183–184.

[11] *KW*, March 19, 1920.   [12] *OR*, April 2, 1919.

exchange of prisoners to liberate Karl Radek, the communist leader, who was in a German prison.

The archbishop's place of confinement was in Grochov Prison, St. Petersburg, but it was continually changed, undoubtedly for security reasons; his arrest, however, failed to halt Catholic activity. The eventuality of his arrest had been foreseen, so immediately Archbishop Cieplak took over the government and leadership of the Church in Russia, in accordance with the declaration left at the *curia* by Archbishop Ropp himself.[13]

Archbishop Cieplak's very first act in assuming authority was to address a circular to the Catholics of Russia, requesting prayers for their imprisoned metropolitan. Nor did he rest with that for, after futile efforts in St. Petersburg to obtain the release of the archbishop, he sent a telegram to Moscow to the Council of People's Commissars (*Sovnarkom*) and at the same time sent a delegation of Catholics from St. Petersburg to Moscow.[14] The affair seemed likely to issue successfully, when on May 16, 1919, the vice-chairman of *Narkomnats*, S. S. Pestkowski, informed Archbishop Cieplak that the metropolitan's arrest would be changed to house arrest. Indeed, on May 24, 1919, the archbishop and Monsignor Anthony Malecki visited the metropolitan.

In order to strengthen the impression of Catholic solidarity, on May 25, 1919, after services in St. Catherine's church conducted by Archbishop Cieplak, there was a huge procession of Catholics— reported as being 13,000—to the building which housed the headquarters of the *Cheka* (the Chrezvichaina Kommissiia, the Extraordinary Commission in Charge of Security, i.e., the secret police) in hopes of thus winning the release of the metropolitan, but to no avail. During the night following the demonstration there were

---

[13] *Kronika . . .,* January 1920, pp. 3, 4–6. The next place of confinement was Shlaperna Prison. On May 16 the archbishop was placed in the house of the police inspector; at the end of June he was transferred to a prison at Viborg. For an eyewitness account of the harsh conditions in Grochov prison, see Jan Wasilewski, *W szponach Antychrysta: Wspomnienia księdza z Rosji Bolszewickiej* (Cracow, 1932), pp. 31–34, where Wasilewski, a fellow prisoner of the archbishop, describes the conditions of 170 people jammed into two small rooms. See also *ibid.,* pp. 34–45, for a description of the archbishop's imprisonment in Shlaperna prison, formerly used only for political prisoners; its inmates during the archbishop's confinement were aristocracy and intelligentsia.

[14] *Kronika . . .,* January 1920, p. 5.

attempts by the police to seize a number of clergymen, but the attempt failed for the clergy managed to hide.[15]

Archbishop Cieplak personally visited the headquarters of the *Cheka* in order to negotiate the release of the metropolitan and of the clergy arrested after him: Fathers Ladislas Issajewicz (who was about 80 years of age), John Wasilewski, Anthony Racewicz, and Aleksei Zerchaninov, a Russian rite Catholic priest. Another delegation was sent to Moscow with Father Stanislas Ejsmont at the head of it. In co-operation with the archdiocesan central committee Archbishop Cieplak sent a telegram to the president of the Council of Ministers in Warsaw through the Commissariat of Foreign Affairs; for the metropolitan and the other priests seemed to have been imprisoned as Polish hostages. Undoubtedly, the arrest of Archbishop Ropp and the other priests was timed with the Polish offensive, which by Eastertide, April 19, 1919, had driven the Bolshevik forces out of Wilno. Still another delegation went to Moscow, but failed as completely as did the other two. On June 20, 1919, Archbishop Cieplak again telegraphed Pestkowski, reminding him that his former assurances had so far been without effect; the archdiocesan central committee sent a similar telegram. The reaction to all this was that on July 5, 1919, the metropolitan was transferred to Moscow and lodged successively in the notorious Lubianka prison and then in the Butyrka prison. After a few days he was permitted to reside at the parish of the Immaculate Conception, on the condition that he would not undertake any parochial duties or the government of his archdiocese. Still he remained in contact with Archbishop Cieplak, Monsignor Budkiewicz, and even with the papal nuncio in Warsaw, Achille Ratti.[16]

Thus the news of Archbishop Ropp's imprisonment reached Benedict XV (1914–1922) in Rome. The pope, first of all, made use of the good offices of King Christian (1906–1947) of Denmark to send a telegram from the papal secretary of state, Cardinal Gasparri, to Lenin himself. After July 10, when the metropolitan had been allowed to reside at the parish of the Immaculate Conception, the Apostolic See availed itself of the good offices of the Polish govern-

---

[15] *KP*, September 5, 1919; *Kronika* . . ., January 1920, p. 5.
[16] *Kronika* . . ., January 1920, p. 6; *KP*, September 5, 1919; Jan Wasilewski, *Arcybiskupi i administratorowie* . . ., pp. 172–173, 184–185.

ment, proposing that Archbishop Ropp be exchanged for Bolshevik prisoners being held in Poland. It proved impossible to exchange the archbishop under these conditions. Finally, Monsignor Achille Ratti, the nuncio in Poland, presented a memorandum to the Bolshevik plenipotentiaries by means of the Polish Red Cross. The Bolsheviks then recognized Archbishop Ropp as a subject of the pope, with whom the Soviet government was not at war. Therefore, because of the regard shown to George Chicherin, the commissar of foreign affairs, and because of the age and sufferings already undergone by the archbishop, the government agreed to the immediate release of the archbishop as a subject of the pope and in exchange for Radek.[17] The archbishop started for Poland on November 17, 1919, and arrived in Warsaw, November 27, 1919, in the evening.[18]

The imprisonment and exile of Archbishop Ropp did not leave the Church leaderless in Russia; into the position of authority stepped Archbishop Cieplak, a man of heroic mould, as is suggested by his willingness to replace the metropolitan in prison. However, the new administrator did not find universal support among his clergy; some indeed thought him too weak for the difficult times that faced the Church.[19] Nonetheless, with the removal of the metropolitan, new problems faced the Catholic authorities in St. Petersburg. The effort to find a workable relationship with the Soviet authorities had failed, and even the signing of agreements had not improved relations with the government. Inspection of churches was frequently combined with sacrilege, as, for instance, at Gatchina, when the species of the Eucharist were cast upon the floor.[20] Archbishop Ropp's arrest had been followed by other arrests; news from the distant parts of the Empire was alarming.[21] Bolsheviks were report-

---

[17] *OR*, December 28, 1919, and March 22, 23, 1920.

[18] *OR*, December 28, 1919; Franciszek Rutkowski, *Arcybiskup Jan Cieplak* (Warsaw, 1934), p. 166, a valuable biography, for Father Rutkowski was active in Russia and was also one of the priests tried in 1923. For a popular biography in English see Joseph Ledit, *Archbishop John Cieplak* (Montreal, 1964).

[19] *OR*, March 22, 23, 1920; see Jan Ostrowski, *Z za Kulis Kurji biskupiej w Leningradzie* (Moscow, 1929), p. 221, for a letter of Troigo to Archbishop Ropp, July 1, 1921: "At the head of the government of the archdiocese, as Your Excellency knows, there stands a man . . . without principle and will, without any talent for rule in normal times, to say nothing of the present times . . . . In critical times, when the good of the Church demanded it, we forcibly pushed the archbishop into action. . . ."

[20] *Kronika* . . ., January 1920, p. 4.   [21] *Ibid.*, p. 6.

edly arresting or killing priests, seizing church property, and nation-
alizing churches—and Catholics were abandoning Russia in a flood.
To add to the confusion, postal and railroad communications broke
down. The number of priests available to minister to the needs of
Catholics decreased daily, and there was no seminary and no Theological Academy to brighten the future. Finally the Bolsheviks
removed children and adolescents as far as possible from the influence of religion in order to demoralize them, as the Catholics saw
the situation.[22]

From the beginning there had been among the clergy opponents
to Archbishop Ropp's policy of signing the agreements with the
Bolshevik government; the chief exponent of this viewpoint was
Monsignor Budkiewicz. The monsignor did not consider Ropp's
opinions quite canonical, especially his opinion about concluding
agreements with the Soviets before obtaining the permission of the
pope to do so. He considered the unauthorized signatures fictitious.[23]
Monsignor Budkiewicz demanded a strictly legal course; he felt,
too, that events had refuted the archbishop's basic contention that
the Soviet government would not last very long. The monsignor
thought that instead of the fictitious, temporary agreements, a
permanent settlement could be made in time by energetic representations to the Soviet government and by negotiations with the
Vatican; and, in fact, he tried to find a *modus vivendi* but met governmental obstruction at every turn.[24]

[22] *OR*, April 2, 1920; Jan Wasilewski, *Arcybiskupi i administratorowie . . .*,
p. 174. While it is sometimes said that the role of the government toward the
Church was rather passive during the Civil War, e.g., John S. Curtiss, *The
Russian Church and the Soviet State* (Boston, 1953), pp. 106, 196, reports
that diplomatic agents of the allied government indicate how the agents of
the Bolshevik government were actively persecuting church and clergy. See,
for instance, *A Collection of Reports on Bolshevism in Russia* (London, 1919),
where reports from Vladivostok tell of twenty-five priests shot at Perm (p. 26),
churches being closed, and a bishop being buried alive (p. 28); a report from
the consular officer at Ekaterinenburg transmitted via Vladivostok told that
the Bolsheviks in 1919 were particularly oppressing the Orthodox clergy and
religion (p. 42), and that thirty Orthodox priests had been massacred at Osa
(p. 43)—actions that hardly represent a passive policy. See also the *New York
Times*, February 15, 1919, for the letter of Archbishop Sylvester of Omsk to
the archbishop of Canterbury, Randall Thomas Davidson.

[23] *Pravda*, March 24, 1923; Krylenko, *op. cit.*, pp. 20, 32; McCullagh, *op.
cit.*, p. 208.

[24] Krylenko, *op. cit.*, pp. 18–20; McCullagh, *op. cit.*, p. 259; OZ, pp. 10–11.

Archbishop Cieplak also felt the problem of the arrangements made under the old policy. He especially objected to the "twenties" which were so destructive of unity and made possible infiltration by communists. In other areas, too, he felt it necessary to disagree with Archbishop Ropp, for Cieplak was convinced that the government of the Soviets would last a long time, an unvarying personal opinion of his.[25]

As early as September 12, 1919, Archbishop Cieplak issued a circular in which he very cleary and forcibly declared his views of the canonical problems and the canonical principles involved. Church property, he declared, and especially the articles of worship, are the inviolable and sacred property of the church, because they had been dedicated by the donors for the service of the church exclusively and because they had been consecrated, and thus set apart from worldly uses. Therefore, to take possession of them, to hand them over to unauthorized persons, and "to execute agreements or other civil documents about them without the permission of the ecclesiastical authorities," is not only a violation of the rights of the church but also a profanation and a sacrilege, in which consequently no Catholic can co-operate. On the other hand, church property, that is, the temporal goods of the church, is also inviolate, because it has been given to the church by benefactors for the church's own use. On this account, wrote the archbishop, an energetic protest must be made against nationalization of such property. Should nationalization be carried out, the archbishop called upon all parishioners to do their part in defense of the church, by renewing their protests to obtain justice and respect for their rights.[26]

The clerical conferences, too, held on January 8, 1920, and January 23, 1920, reviewed the relations of the Church to communism in general. At the meeting of January 8, 1920, the question was raised about the possibility of a Catholic belonging to the Communist Party, and a resolution was passed denying that a Catholic could do so. The meeting also voted to buy communist publications and works on communism, so that the clergy might be better in-

[25] *Kronika . . .,* January 1920, p. 3; *Pravda,* March 24, 1923; McCullagh, *op. cit.,* pp. 202–203.

[26] *Kronika . . .,* January 1920, p. 3; Krylenko, *op. cit.,* p. 18; McCullagh, *op. cit.,* pp. 161–162.

formed and thus better equipped to instruct their listeners. The archbishop requested Father Witold Iwicki to prepare a report on the subject for the next meeting. At the next meeting, January 23, 1920, the report after being read and discussed had emphasized the incompatibility of a Catholic joining the Communist Party.[27]

However, the meeting of February 18, 1920, was more decisive in establishing a line of conduct to be followed. Here the problem of the central committee was discussed, and the clergy agreed that one of the functions of the committee should be to protect the Church against persecution. Archbishop Cieplak proposed that the work of the parochial committee should be to make the parishioners acquainted with the actual state of affairs in order to pass from the defensive to the offensive, to obtain freedom for religious instruction in the school buildings, and to remove obstacles to the performance of religious duties.[28]

Monsignor Budkiewicz supported this line of policy by a document on the question of signing the agreements under existing conditions. He declared that the signing of the agreements in 1918 had been dictated by expediency and the expectation that the Bolshevik regime would soon fall; but inasmuch as this expectation had proved erroneous, there now existed no legal basis for signing these agreements without the previous consent of the Holy See. Therefore to sign the documents would be to deprive one's self of Holy Communion and to break away from the Church. The monsignor, enumerating some of the reasons against signing, declared it would suffice to explain to the Bolsheviks that it was against the law of the Church. He was convinced, too, that though the Bolsheviks would put pressure on Catholics to sign the agreements, they would not really close and sequestrate the churches for they were sensitive to European public opinion. Finally, he felt that refusal to sign would give Catholics a tactical advantage, as the Bolsheviks would then have to deal with a population that had not committed itself by agreements and would have to reckon more carefully with a population in protest than with one in retreat.[29]

Prudent as the monsignor's plan might have been in less turbulent

---

[27] *OZ*, pp. 6–9; McCullagh, *op. cit.*, pp. 157, 205.
[28] *OZ*, pp. 9–10; McCullagh, p. 158.
[29] Milich "Protsess . . .," *op. cit.*, p. 106; McCullagh, *op. cit.*, p. 159.

times or with an enemy less consistent, it showed a misunderstanding of the ultimate objective of Bolshevik action against religion. It supposed that the Bolshevik government would be satisfied with the attainment of limited objectives, e.g., the separation of Church and State, the nationalization of churches and schools, the elimination of ecclesiastical privilege; certainly, it failed to take into consideration that the total objective of the Bolshevik government included the complete destruction and disappearance of religion from the new social order being built by communists. Hence, the strategy of Monsignor Budkiewicz avoided disaster as little as did the strategy of Archbishop Ropp, because no strategy could avoid it.

The clergy, therefore, in line with the new policy began to refuse to sign new agreements and to reject the agreements that had been made. Over and above this overt rejection of the agreements, Archbishop Cieplak organized secret schools of religious instruction for the children and youth in St. Petersburg and established in Moscow regular theological courses. Under the guidance of Monsignor Malecki, the archbishop established a secret seminary to help supply the dwindling number of clergy. The Theological Academy had already been transferred from St. Petersburg to Lublin for the school year of 1918–1919.[30]

In 1920 St. Catherine's church in St. Petersburg, known as "the converts' church," organized a popular lecture series for Catholics and non-Catholics; these lectures were given every Monday evening, and were carried on until 1923. They touched all the pertinent religious topics of the day; nor were they the exclusive monopoly of the clergy. Indeed, the clergy gave but one lecture of the four a month. These lectures were given in a strictly nonnational spirit; Monsignor Budkiewicz presented this view strongly when a national clash arose: "On our part we can honestly say that we have done our utmost to get rid of purely national bitternesses which have caused so many misunderstandings in the past. We are neither Poles nor Lithuanians nor Letts, when we deal with you. We are simply Catholics. Why can you not be simply Orthodox, and then we could meet on the ground of purely religious divergences? This would ease the position. Do you not see that we have fully mastered your

[30] *Polska*, August 18, 1918; Jan Wasilewski, *Arcybiskupi i administratorowie . . .*, pp. 175, 181; Rutkowski, *op. cit.*, pp. 93–111, 172–187.

language and your ways and your customs, hitherto strange to us, and we have done all this in order to be better equipped to help you, when you may have need of us? We will not come unasked. All we claim in return is sympathy and understanding and peace."[31] The parish clergy in St. Petersburg can in no sense be accused of following a line of narrow nationalism.[32]

Inasmuch as the Bolshevik attack was directed against all religions, the Catholic Church in Russia began to look for a kind of "collective security" by co-operating with the other religious groups in Russia. Excellent relations had been maintained between the Russian Catholic Church of Oriental Rite and the Old Believers. As far back as 1916 and 1917 conversations were held with the Old Believers, initiated by Bishop Innocent of Nizhni-Novgorod and Bishop Gerontii of Petrograd. Bishop Innocent went so far as to express hope of coming to an agreement with the Catholics.[33]

As the revolutionary ferment grew and the Bolsheviks seized power, the need was felt for closer co-operation with the Orthodox, especially against the atheistic propaganda that was being broadcast throughout the vast land. This idea originated with Exarch Fedorov, upon whom the Latin bishops relied to make contacts with the Orthodox with a view to resisting also the nationalization of church property. Meetings often took place in the apartments of Monsignor Budkiewicz, who was, indeed, interested in a more uncompromising policy toward the Soviet government in the matter of the church agreements. Among the clergy who attended these meetings aimed at co-operation was the Orthodox metropolitan of St. Petersburg himself, i.e., Metropolitan Benjamin, who was later executed by the Bolsheviks for his stand against the seizure of church valuables.[34]

In the effort to win the sympathy and co-operation of the Orthodox Church, the papacy played a striking and important role, even

[31] Martha E. Almedingen, *The Catholic Church in Russia Today* (New York, 1923), pp. 57–58.

[32] See Almedingen, *op. cit.*, pp. 54–63, where the author vindicates the Polish Catholic clergy from the charge of a narrow Polish nationalism in Russia, a charge all too frequently repeated by Bolshevik propagandists.

[33] D. Kolpinskij, "Początki katolicyzmu wschodniego obrządku w Rosji," *Kościół katolicki W Rosji: Materiały do jego historji i organizacji* (Warsaw, 1932), p. 30.

[34] Kolpinskij, *ibid*, pp. 29–30; Milich, "Protsess . . . ," *op. cit.*, p. 107.

if it was not always effective in obtaining the desired results. When the first rumors of the execution of the tsar and the heir reached Western Europe in July 1918, there was no news as yet of the massacre of the entire imperial family. Benedict XV interested himself in the fate of the empress and her daughters. He asked the Bolshevik government to transfer the imperial widow and the grand duchesses to some neutral country, where the papacy undertook to provide for them. However, news came through the Austrian consul in Munich in Bavaria, that the Bolsheviks did not know the whereabouts of the tasarina and the grand duchesses.[35]

More calculated to win the friendship of the Orthodox were the papal moves to relieve the persecution of the Orthodox as such. In 1919 the president of the Supreme Administration of the Orthodox Church in areas not taken by the Bolsheviks, Sylvester, the archbishop of Omsk, addressed a letter to Benedict XV. The letter was dated February 7, 1919. Addressing the pope as "Venerable Father," Archbishop Sylvester described the horrors of Bolshevik conduct toward the Orthodox Church: the churches of the Moscow Kremlin, of Yaroslav, and Simferopol sacked, other churches desecrated, the Metropolitan Vladimir of Kiev, five bishops, and hundreds of priests murdered. He begged the Holy Father by reason of human sympathy and brotherly Christian feeling to intervene as representative of the Christian church.[36] After the pope's reply of reassurance to Archbishop Sylvester, Cardinal Gasparri, the papal secretary of state, telegraphed Lenin, declaring that a reliable source had informed the Vatican that the ministers of the Russian Orthodox Church were being persecuted. The Holy Father, wrote Cardinal Gasparri, demanded that ministers of every religion whatsoever be respectfully treated.[37]

George Chicherin, the commissar of foreign affairs, replied in a lengthy note that the source mentioned by Cardinal Gasparri was undoubtedly in error. The separation of Church and State had been effected, and religion was treated as a strictly private affair. He guaranteed that no minister of the Orthodox Church was persecuted

[35] *OR,* June 28, 1918, July 22, 23, 24, 26, 1918, August 3, 1918, and October 14, 1918.

[36] *OR,* July 2, 1919.

[37] *OR,* April 2, 1919; "Sluzhiteli kulta v sovetskoi vlasti," *Revolutsiia i tserkov,* Nos. 3–5 (1919), pp. 52–53.

for his religious beliefs; on the other hand, any one of the clergy who would engage in conspiratorial and counterrevolutionary activity would be subjected to the laws and punishments as other citizens of the State. The commissar noted, too, that the Vatican had failed to denounce the amassing of wealth by the clerical orders; nor had the Vatican noticed the frauds, such as relics, by which the clergy of the Orthodox Church had maintained their domination. In view of the papal protest against persecution of the Orthodox Church, the commissar felt it unfortunate that the Vatican had not protested against the atrocities committed against the Russian people by the Czechoslovaks, by the governments of Kolchak, Denikin, and Petliura, and the present leaders of Poland.[38] The ironic denial of persecution just at the moment when the arrest of Archbishop Ropp impended suggests the reliability of the Bolshevik diplomatic correspondence of this period.

Another occasion offered itself to increase sympathetic contact with the Orthodox Church when an attempt had been made on the life of Patriarch Tikhon in the summer of 1919. Imprisoned though he was, Archbishop Ropp had managed to write a letter of sympathy to the patriarch. The patriarch, after excusing his delay in replying because of his wound, congratulated the archbishop on his situation having improved, an obvious reference to the archbishop's taking up residence at the parish of the Immaculate Conception. The patriarch expressed his gratitude for the papal intervention, for in the perilous times fraternal charity was especially dear. He would be especially grateful if the archbishop would find a means of expressing to His Holiness the patriarch's sincere gratitude for this most Christian action.[39]

In spite of this very friendly attitude expressed here freely, Tikhon, under pressure from the Bolsheviks, repudiated any rapprochement with the Vatican. Whether this was the real sentiment of the patriarch is doubtful, in light of the statement he made when free of the Bolsheviks.[40] Thus, ultimately the prospects of co-operation were destroyed at a time when that co-operation was

---

[38] *OR*, April 2, 1919; *Pravda*, March 15, 1919.

[39] *OR*, August 1, 1923; S. Tyszkiewicz, *Sovetskoe bezbozhie i papstvo* (Rome, 1950), p. 3, written from the Roman Catholic viewpoint.

[40] *OR*, August 1, 1923; Tyszkiewicz, *op. cit.*, p. 4.

most necessary to the survival in freedom. The long ecclesiastical conflict, as bitter as it was long, bore evil fruit even in modern times.

Foreseeably, these new tactics of the Catholics in Russia were such as to provoke a vigorous reaction by the Soviet government to this challenge to its authority. Arrests followed, and the years 1919 and 1920 were the worst for the Catholic Church during the period of War Communism. Ignatius Dubowski, the bishop of Łuck-Żytomierz, on October 28, 1919, in an appeal to the Polish bishops and Polish government in Warsaw described the full horrors of Bolshevik occupation after the German withdrawal: massacres of both Poles and Ruthenians of every class, and burial alive—these horrors exposed by a commission on which Bishop Dubowski had a representative. The Bolsheviks tried to seize the seminary and the church in order to convert it into a theater. After an attempt to assassinate the bishop had failed, news of the intention to arrest him caused the bishop and his chaplain to flee and hide five days and nights in tombs; only the relief of Żytomierz by the Poles and Petliura restored order temporarily. But liberation did not come soon enough to save Fathers Boleslas Lisiecki, Theophilus Szeptycki, and Adolph Kowalski.[41]

Aloysius Kessler, the bishop of Tiraspol, resided at Saratov. The original national base was formed of the Germans who had settled in the Volga region at the request of Catherine II, in which region in 1914 there were 192 German colonies in the provinces of Saratov and Samara; of these, 38 were Catholic. In 1914, the Black Sea region had 1,077 colonies, and the Catholics there numbered 195,-641 according to the census of 1897. The nationalities included in the diocese of Tiraspol were Russians, Poles, Armenians, Kirghiz, Circassians, Ossetins, Daghestanis, Germans, French and Italians.[42]

On August 14, 1918, the Bolsheviks had entered Saratov, according to the letter sent by Bishop Kessler to a friend on December 7, 1919. They occupied his house, the seminary, the *curia*, the property

[41] *OR*, December 13, 1919; Około-Kułak, *op cit.*, p. 28; M. Tokarzewski, *Przyczynek do historji męczeństwa rzymsko-katolickiego w dyecezjach kamie-nieckiej i łucko-żytomierskiej, 1863–1930* (Łuck, 1931), p. 28.

[42] Richard J. Bollig, "The German Catholic Schools in Southern Russia, *The Catholic University of America Educational Research Monographs* (Washington, 1931), pp. vi, 609, 622.

of the seminary and the cathedral church. The bishop walked ten days to Odessa, where he arrived ill. There the Bolsheviks tried to arrest him, after they found a letter of his in which he had threatened Catholics with excommunication if they favored the Bolsheviks. Following the withdrawal of the French and Germans, the Bolsheviks inflicted unspeakable horrors about them. The rector of the seminary was arrested and spent days before the revolutionary tribunal. The bishop would undoubtedly have been arrested, had he not been hidden by friends. Three priests had been slain. Bishop Kessler had no contact with Saratov, but before escaping he had appointed vicars general for various parts of the diocese.[43]

Even Archbishop Cieplak failed to escape the intensified anti-Catholic drive. On March 31, 1920, he preached a sermon in St. Catherine's church, which the government construed as filled with an anti-Soviet spirit; the police interpreted this as sanctioning the anti-Soviet spirit and activities of the lower clergy, for whom they held him morally and actually responsible. In order to cut off the open "antirevolutionary" activity carried on under a "religious" guise, the Petrograd *Cheka* arrested the Catholic archbishop on Holy Thursday, 1920. At the investigation the archbishop stated that he considered himself a Soviet citizen, that he held loyalty to the Soviet government to be his duty, and that co-operation with its enemies was not permissible for Catholics. The Catholics of St. Petersburg organized protests and public manifestations against the arrest of the archbishop; in fact, they were able to win to their side some 800 marines. The *Cheka* found, therefore, that no connection could be established between the archbishop and Polish agents; it demanded a written statement that neither he nor his clergy would engage in political activity. It also tried to extort from him an approval of all the decrees issued by the government, but this the archbishop consistently refused to give.[44] In order to emphasize

[43] *OR*, February 15, 1920.

[44] Około-Kułak, *op. cit.*, p. 28; Jan Wasilewski, *Arcybiskupi i administratorowie* . . . , p. 175, where the author erroneously puts the arrest in the year 1921; *OR*, April 24, 1920. See also Jan Wasilewski, *W szponach Antychrysta* . . ., pp. 72–78, for a description of the archbishop's arrest and cross-examination; Dzierżyński himself conducted the examination; according to Wasilewski, *W szponach* . . ., p. 75, Catholic officers from the Red Navy and Catholic sailors played a decisive role.

its position, the *Cheka* on April 17, 1920, informed the representatives of the Polish clergy that the smallest attempt at anti-Soviet activity would be mercilessly punished. It felt that the arrest of Archbishop Cieplak had had its effect, namely, halting what the *Cheka* considered anti-Soviet activity.[45]

Another form of harassment applied by the Bolshevik government was the exposure of "fradulent" relics. By force of circumstances, the Orthodox Church was more subject to this particular pressure; and exposure of relics of traditional heroes like St. Tikhon Zadonskii, St. Cyril of Belozersk, and many others went on at a rapid and blasphemously merry pace.[46] On August 26, 1919, the Bolsheviks resolved to expose the remains of St. Andrew Bobola in Połock and ordered the Catholic clergy to send representatives for the opening of the grave. Strong protests by Archbishop Cieplak, the central committee, and a demonstration by Catholic workers from the Putilov works caused the Bolsheviks to give up their plan, and the remains of St. Andrew Bobola remained undisturbed until 1922.[47]

Among the more serious losses of the Church in Russia at this time was the loss of the chapel of the Theological Academy. On June 5, 1920, the Catholic Committee, whose chairman was Alexander Pawłowski, a prominent Catholic layman in St. Petersburg, was ordered by the local commissar for the separation of Church and State to surrender the chapel of the Theological Academy. Before leaving the Academy chapel, they were to prepare an inventory, but they were not told where to send the inventory. The committee protested to the chief authorities in St. Petersburg, on the grounds that the chapel was but a wing of the Academy, that the valuable historical frescoes were under the protection of the Polish Liquidation Commission; and they petitioned for protection against the unwarranted demands of local officials. The Commis-

---

[45] "Rabota petrogradzkikh ksendzov," *Revolutsiia i tserkov*, Nos. 6–8 (1920), pp. 102–103; Rutkowski, *op. cit.*, p. 214.

[46] For reports on the exposure of Orthodox saints' relics, see *Pravda*, April 4, 23, 1919; M Gorev, "Vskrytie moshchei Tikhona Zadonskogo i Mitrofana Voronezhskogo," *Revolutsiia i tserkov*, No. 2 (1919), pp. 9–23. For a table of relics exposed during 1918, 1919, and 1920 see *Revolutsiia i tserkov* Nos. 9–12 (1920), pp. 74–81.

[47] Jan Wasilewski, *Arcybiskupi i administratorowie* . . ., p. 174; *Kronika* . . ., January 1920, pp. 6–7.

sariat of Justice on June 16, 1920, investigated the charges and confirmed the complaints but, nevertheless, sealed the chapel; and it was no longer under the control of the committee.

Once again on November 5, 1920, the neighboring parish committee received from the new chairman of the commission for the separation of Church and State an order for a new inventory of the chapel with a view of closing it. Pawłowski, Father Troigo, and Archbishop Cieplak lodged a new protest with the Commissariat of Justice. Without injecting propaganda into the affair they based their protest on the religious needs of the populace; the essence of the problem was religious, even though the affair involved Polish people. Here again the Orthodox tried to help protect the chapel; and the Protestants helped in the search for property stolen from the chapel and Academy.

The moving force behind these activities was Archbishop Cieplak, who always turned to the representative of the Commissariat of Foreign Affairs in St. Petersburg, I. E. Zolkind, or to the central authorities themselves.

When Zolkind stated that nothing further could be done about the stolen property until more information was obtained on the whereabouts of the stolen goods, Archbishop Cieplak sent this information, but there was no help forthcoming from the government.

The committee, therefore, determined to question Zolkind personally; so with Father Troigo and the layman Pawłowski as leaders, the committee went to do their task, but Zolkind's secretary informed them that they should put the matter into the hands of the Red Cross. However, a chance visitor, W. P. Hartmann, reported that Zolkind had informed him that the Red Cross had no authority to receive complaints. So, the matter ended with the committee sending Zolkind a protocol on the subject. The archbishop's appeals to Moscow also remained without effect, and the chapel was lost as far as the Catholics of St. Petersburg were concerned.[48]

[48] *KP*, March 28, 1923.

VI

The Catholic Church in Russia and International Problems

As difficult as the internal situation in Russia made the position of the Catholic Church, greater difficulties arose from complications in the world of international conflict. There was a twofold aspect to this problem, namely, insofar as Poland was in conflict with the Soviet government and insofar as papal diplomacy was construed by the Soviet government as pursuing objectives hostile to the Soviet government.

The background included the disastrous experience of Catholics and Poles with the Bolshevik governments when the Bolsheviks in the Mińsk and Mohylew provinces in November 1917, and that of Wilno in December 1917, had perpetrated crimes against the population and against the churches. When the Bolsheviks retreated before the German armies in February 1918, they reportedly plundered everything.[1]

It is no small wonder, then, that when in the spring of 1919 the Polish army began its advance to liberate the western provinces, the Catholic population, including the Catholic clergy, welcomed them with open arms. The Soviet government criticized severely what they considered the "polonophile" activity of the Catholic priests in Belorussia, who had declared that the Soviet government was but a temporary phenomenon, that the Polish legions would

---

[1] "Z ziem wschodnich od Rosji przez okupację odciętych," *Naród i Państwo* (April 13, 1918), pp. 59–66.

soon come and hang every Bolshevik. The government muttered threats that this anti-Soviet activity of priests, or "ksendzov," and teachers in Polish schools would not go unpunished.[2] Because of the indiscriminate rapine of the Bolsheviks when in occupation, both the Catholics and Orthodox were anti-Bolshevik in disposition; moreover, the young people were reportedly joining the Poles against the Russian Bolsheviks and the old people were trying to associate themselves with those "of the Polish faith."[3]

As the Polish army approached Mińsk in August 1919, Bishop Zygmunt Łoziński issued two proclamations, one to the advancing Polish troops and the other to the people in Mińsk. The address to the Polish troops welcomed them as liberators and crusaders against the enemies of God and society. Wishing to protect the local population from any harm, he called upon the soldiers to deal justly with the native population. The bishop also appealed to the population of Mińsk to preserve peace and order and to beware of *provocateurs*. He assured the large Jewish population that there was no danger to them as Jews, and finally he appealed to the militia to do its work conscientiously.[4]

On August 8, 1919, the Bolsheviks had withdrawn from Mińsk, and the Polish troops entered the city. There was no street fighting. Then, on August 10, 1919, the Polish troops gathered at the cathedral for a thanksgiving service, but Bishop Łoziński failed to get there in time to say mass, for he was still on his way from his hiding place in the forests. General Szeptycki proclaimed the return of Mińsk to Poland after 146 years of separation, and in order to emphasize the fact that the entry of Polish troops symbolized not a conquest but a reunion of old provinces of the Commonwealth, proclaimed a civilian administration for the area.[5]

The diplomatic and military developments centering around the aspirations of the Ukrainians also involved the Catholic Church in Russia in most serious problems at the same time that the Polish armies entered Belorussia. Upon the collapse of the Austro-Hungarian Empire, an armed force of Ukrainians took possession of the city of Lwów on November 1, 1918; however, by November 22,

---

[2] *Zhizn natsionalnostei* (March 23, 1919; April 27, 1923).
[3] *KP*, June 1, 1919.
[4] *KP*, August 5, 1919.   [5] *KP*, August 10, 1919.

1918, the Polish element in the city had dislodged the Ukrainian force and the city was in Polish hands, though in the countryside the Ukrainian armed bands remained.

The Peace Conference at Paris attempted to bring about a truce by means of a special commission and brought considerable pressure to bear upon Poland in the latter part of April 1919. When at this point the Ukrainian forces launched an offensive, the Poles managed in May 1919 to mount a counteroffensive that forced the Ukrainian troops to withdraw beyond the eastern boundary of Galicia, the river Zbrucz. By this time the Red Army, supporting the pro-Soviet Ukrainian government of Khristian Rakovskii, a Bulgarian-born communist, had expelled the Ukrainian Directory under V. Vinnichenko and defeated the Ukrainian forces under Simon Petliura, the supreme commander *(Holovnyi Ataman)* of the Ukrainian troops. On February 6, 1919, the Red Army had entered Kiev. The Soviet government lasted seven months, until the end of August 1919, when the White forces of General Denikin took Kiev and the surrounding territories. However, by the end of 1919 the forces of Denikin were being expelled too by Soviet armies, and late in December a new Soviet government had entered Kharkov. In the meantime, in December 1919 Piłsudski had made an agreement with Petliura by virtue of which, in return for Galicia and western Wołyń, he promised to aid Petliura in dislodging the communists from Ukrainian territory on the right bank of the Dnepr. Piłsudski's policy was to establish an independent Ukraine that might serve as a buffer against the Soviet state[6] and maintain naturally friendly relations with Poland, her western neighbor.

Into this welter of confusion a new factor had intruded itself, the diplomacy of the Vatican. On April 25, 1919, Benedict XV received the Ukrainian ambassador, Count Michael Tyszkiewicz, in an official

[6] For the internal developments in Ukraine, see Richard Pipes, *The Formation of the Soviet Union* (Cambridge, Mass., 1954), as well as Adam Żółtowski, *Border of Europe: A Study of the Polish Eastern Provinces* (London, 1950), pp. 171–173, 181–190, who balances the treatment of Pipes by considering the problem of Ukraine not merely as a Ukrainian-Russian problem but rather as a Polish-Russian-Ukrainian problem. For the religious composition of Galicia, see S. Pawłowski, *Ludność rzymsko-katolicka w Polsko-Ruskiej części Galicji*, Prace geograficzne, No. 3 (Lwów, 1919), which emphasizes the assimilative process in Galicia. See also M. K. Dziewanowski, "Piłsudski's Federalist Policy, 1919-1921," *Journal of Central European Affairs*, X (1950), 113–128, 271–287.

audience; the count also handed his credentials to the papal secretary of state, Cardinal Gasparri. The reaction in pro-Soviet and some anti-Soviet circles was violent. The Paris Ukrainian National Committee accused the Vatican of following a policy of dismemberment toward Russia, in hopes of surrounding Poland protectively with Catholicized states, Ukraine and Belorussia, and of using Polish imperialism to subject these countries to Poland.[7]

Pro-Soviet sources saw in Jesuit Father Xavier Bonn the intermediary who convinced Petliura that the only way for a rapprochement with Poland was through the Vatican; and it was to gain the pope's support that Petliura sent Tyszkiewicz to the Vatican.[8]

The Bolsheviks quoted Petliura as saying that the Italian government had paid the Vatican for the Vatican's share in the allied victory with materiel, and that Petliura now requested the use of this materiel.[9]

Count Tyszkiewicz's position in the Vatican was difficult because he was a Catholic representing a nation whose majority was Orthodox; and it certainly did not ease his situation at all to have to represent Orthodox Ukraine against Catholic Poland. When he presented his credentials to Cardinal Gasparri, he also lodged a protest against the attack of General Joseph Haller on southeast Galician territory and the use of force against a Catholic nation. One might have expected formidable difficulties from the Vatican, but Benedict XV pursued a policy of supporting the nations which were arising on the ruins of the Hapsburg Monarchy and the former Russian Empire. Papal recognition enabled Count Tyszkiewicz to use to the best advantage the Catholic press in Italy and Switzerland, thus presenting the case of the Ukrainian nation to the Catholic world. In the diplomatic sphere, the Vatican indicated to the apostolic nuncio in Paris and papal representative at the peace conference, Bonaventure Cerretti, titular archbishop of Corinth, that he was to support the efforts of Count Tyszkiewicz to gain for the Ukrainian state recognition in Paris.[10]

[7] "Petlura and the Vatican," *Soviet Russia*, III (1920), 214, but to be used with care as being strongly pro-Bolshevik and anti-Catholic.

[8] *Ibid.*, p. 214. [9] *OR*, October 30, 1920.

[10] G. Luzhnitskii, *Ukrainska tserkva mizh skhodom i zakhodom* (Philadelphia, 1954), pp. 563–565; *Annuario Pontificio per l'anno 1922* (Rome, 1922), p. 270.

When Count Tyszkiewicz left Rome for Paris, he left Father Bonn as *chargé d'affaires* at the Vatican and P. Kasmanskii as the secretary of the Ukrainian mission. Thanks to the efforts of this mission, on February 16, 1920, Benedict XV appointed Father John Genocchi (1860–1926) the apostolic visitor for Ukraine. At the beginning of April 1920 Genocchi arrived in Vienna, but had to proceed to Warsaw, for the Polish government would not allow him to enter Lwów. In Warsaw he waited in vain for permission, but in the meantime the Bolsheviks had opened the offensive that brought them to the gates of Warsaw. Genocchi then returned to Vienna, where he entered into close relations with the Ukrainian political emigration; but even so, he was unable to enter Ukraine, and eventually returned to Rome in the first half of January 1922.[11]

Count Tyszkiewicz's mission in Paris seemed to include two objectives: to obtain international recognition of Ukraine and to obtain this by a wide propaganda on behalf of the Ukrainian cause. As a Catholic, the count was anxious for the establishment of a church union in Ukraine; but pro-Soviet sources viewed this from a political standpoint: the counterpart to the church union between the Vatican and Ukraine was to be a political union with Poland. How unrealistic this interpretation was is suggested by Tyszkiewicz's protest against Polish action in Galicia.[12]

As all this developed, the Bolshevik government on January 29, 1920, approached the Polish government with feelers for peace; but the Poles doubted Bolshevik sincerity. After hesitating as to what course to follow, for opinion in Poland was divided about the expedition against the Bolsheviks and its extent,[13] the Polish government decided to open negotiations; but on April 20, 1920, the Bolsheviks refused to negotiate at the place indicated by Poland, namely, Borysów. Thereupon, the Bolsheviks opened in the spring

[11] Luzhnitskii, *op. cit.*, pp. 565–568; F. von Lama, *Papst und Kurie in ihrer Politik nach dem Weltkrieg* (Illertissen, 1925), pp. 398–401, strongly pro-papal; D-r Kremer, "Vatikan i sovietskoe pravitelstvo," *Revolutsiia i tserkov*, Nos. 1–2 (1924), p. 10.

[12] "Petlura and the Vatican," *op. cit.*, p. 214; for the Soviet construction of the diplomatic contracts between the Vatican, Kolchak, and Denikin, see N. M. Sheinmann, *Vatikan mezhdu dvumia mirovymi voinami* (Moscow, 1946), p. 34.

[13] *KP*, September 2, 1919, the disagreement in the Polish governmental circles over Piłsudski's policy is clearly stated in Stanislas Grabski, *The Polish-Soviet Frontier* (New York, n. d.), pp. 17–22.

an unsuccessful offensive against the Poles from the Dźwina river; Poland replied with a drive, beginning April 1920, against Kiev, which General Edward Rydz-Śmigły took on May 8, 1920. North of Kiev the front followed the Dnepr, and then the Berezyna and the Dźwina to the city of Riga.

The political program of Piłsudski included an independent Ukraine; hence, the proclamation of April 26, 1920, to the people of Ukraine announced his determination that the Ukrainians should solve their national and religious problems freely, without pressure from any country, including Poland. For this reason Piłsudski's occupation was purely military and temporary, and the civil administration remained entirely in the hands of the Petliura government in Kamieniec-Podolski.[14]

In the light of the ferocity which the Bolsheviks used against religion, the diplomatic involvement of the Vatican with the Ukrainian cause and the Vatican's hopes of church union, and finally the idealism of Piłsudski's program formulated in the proclamation of April 26, 1920, it is small wonder that the Catholics of the southeast welcomed the Polish armies as they advanced through Podole, Wołyń, and Kiev. Bishop Peter Mańkowski, ordinary of the restored see of Kamieniec-Podolski, and Bishop Ignatius Dubowski of Łuck-Żytomierz, together with all their clergy, could hardly restrain their joy at the striking Polish victory. Most solemn services of thanksgiving were joyfully conducted everywhere; speeches and agitation on behalf of the Polish cause swept Catholic circles, where, indeed, it had its greatest support. The leaders of this movement were, understandably, the Polish Catholic clergy. The word everywhere was that the Bolsheviks had gone forever, so complete and smashing did the victory of gallant Polish arms appear.[15]

The consternation that struck the hearts of the Catholics, more especially of the Catholic clergy, when news came of a Bolshevik offensive in the north from Smoleńsk on May 14, 1920, may well be imagined. That the Catholic clergy had mortally offended the

[14] For clear statement of Piłsudski's policy for an independent Ukraine and Belorussia, see Grabski, *op. cit.*, pp. 17–18.

[15] M. Tokarzewski, *Przyczynek do historji męczeństwa rzymsko-katolickiego w dyecezjach kamienieckiej i łucko-żytomierskiej, 1863–1930* (Łuck, 1931), p. 30.

Bolsheviks is clear from the Soviet press, where the activity of bishops and priests in stimulating or organizing the effort against the Bolsheviks or in celebrating days in honor of Piłsudski were denounced.[16] The breakthrough by Budenny on June 8 in the southern sector forced the Polish forces to begin the evacuation of Kiev on June 11, 1920. The clergy who had compromised them- selves were advised to leave; the Jewish population warned the clergy, remembering that the clergy had protected them during the pogroms, that the Bolsheviks knew all and that the clergy must flee to save themselves. Thus not only Bishops Mańkowski and Dubowski, but also many parish priests were forced to leave and to seek safety in Poland; others among the clergy who were mem- bers of "bourgeois" families had to flee for that very reason. Still, there were heroes who stayed behind; some returned from the safety of Poland, among them the aged Canon John Lewiński and Father Anthony Liniewicz.[17] Undoubtedly, among the giants of those days must be reckoned the bishop of Kielce, Augustine Łoziński, who had been interned for a year at Mohylew after having been carried off by the Red armies from Poland. He was scheduled to be freed in January 1921, but escaped from the train that was taking him to freedom and returned to the prison camp to minister to the Catholics there. Having finally been caught, he was sent to Poland and arrived at Wilno on July 12, 1921.[18]

In the north the Bolsheviks launched a drive on July 7, 1920, that broke the left wing of the Polish line on the Wilja river and enabled the Bolshevik armies to advance with phenomenal speed— Wilno fell to them on July 14, and Grodno on July 20. The rapid advance endangered the very capital, Warsaw.

The Vatican once again demonstrated its interest in Polish inde- pendence. In a letter of August 5, 1920, to Cardinal Pompili, the bishop of Velletri and vicar general of Rome, Benedict XV ordered prayers to be offered for Poland on the following Sunday in the historic church of the Gesù. The pope emphasized the papacy's traditional interest in Poland, even at a time when European nations

[16] *Revolutsiia i tserkov,* Nos. 6–8 (1920), p. 102; Nos. 9–12, pp. 54–55.
[17] Tokarzewski, *op. cit.,* p. 31.
[18] *OR,* July 21, 1921; *Annuario Pontificio per l'anno 1922* (Rome, 1922), p. 152.

remained silent. He hoped, too, that the example of the Church in Rome would be followed by Catholic bishops all over the world. Indeed, the independence of Poland had been included in the papal proposal of August 10, 1917, as well as in relations with President Wilson and the heads of states.[19]

Meanwhile, on the field of battle, Polish forces had had to withdraw to the very gates of Warsaw, but the retreat, skillfully executed, was orderly and the Polish forces remained intact. Supplies and equipment from France had been halted at the border by German and Austrian "neutrality" and by the definite hostility of Czech leaders, Masaryk and Benes.[20] In mid-August 1920, according to a plan devised by Piłsudski, and not, as is frequently averred, by Weygand,[21] the Polish army struck the divided Bolshevik forces of Tukhachevskii and Budenny,[22] and very soon cleared central

[19] *OR*, November 9, 1918, January 30, 1920, February 2, 3, 1920, July 24, 25, 26, 27, 1920, and August 8, 14, 1920. For a statement of the United States policy toward Poland and Russia, see *Notes Exchanged on the Russian-Polish Situation by the United States, France and Poland*, No. 155 (New York, 1920), where the United States policy aimed at a united, free, and autonomous Poland (p. 461); the United States also recognized the independence of Armenia (p. 464).

[20] As to the hostility of the Czechs, the book of Viscount D'Abernon, *The Eighteenth Decisive Battle of the World: Warsaw, 1920* (London, 1921), suffices to document it: President Thomas Masaryk's advice not to give aid to the Poles because it would be militarily ineffective and liable to destroy the authority of the Western allies in the peace negotiations (pp. 20–21); the halting of supplies at the border (p. 48). See an excellent survey of Polish-Czech relations, Zygmunt J. Gąsiorowski, "Polish-Czechoslovak Relations, 1918–1922," *The Slavonic and East European Review*, XXXV (1956), 172–193, with pp. 183–187 devoted to the Czech attitude during the Polish-Soviet War.

[21] According to the documentary evidence, General Maxim Weygand did not take command in the matter of defense. This is the evidence of D'Abernon, *op. cit.*, pp. 56, 81–82, 87–88, 92. Piłsudski himself describes his offer to Weygand to share the supreme command, as well as Weygand's refusal, based upon Weygand's lack of knowledge of the army's strength and resources; see Józef Piłsudski, *Rok 1920*, Pisma Zbiorowe, VII (Warsaw, 1937), 152–153. General Weygand himself acknowledged that the victory of the Vistula was a Polish victory, as stated in Harold D. Fisher, *America and the New Poland* (New York, 1928), p. 260; for the American military aid, see pp. 260–261. *Polsha na sovetiskuiu Rossiiu* (Moscow, 1954), blames the defeat at Warsaw on the "traitors" Trotsky and Tukhachevskii (p. 197), declares that the Polish delegation opposed the principle of self-determination supported by the Soviets (p. 212), and finally asserts that the border proposed at Mińsk was based on the Curzon line (p. 218); the negotiations between the two states are described, pp. 212–218.

[22] For Trotsky's disapproval of the invasion of Poland, see Isaac Deutscher, *The Prophet Armed* (New York, 1954), pp. 463–464.

Poland of the enemy, who was also forced to abandon Galicia. The Poles crossed the Zbrucz river in the south, while in the north they fought a hard victorious battle on the Niemen river.

The protracted negotiations for a truce were to begin at Mińsk on August 14, 1920, when the military advantage, which the Bolshevik diplomats were hoping to exploit, had changed and rested now with the Poles. The interrupted negotiations were resumed in Riga, where on October 12, 1920, the preliminaries of peace and an armistice were signed.[23]

The frontier ran from the river Dźwina—from the Russian-Latvian border, practically due south with Mińsk remaining on the Russian side of the border—down to the Zbrucz river, which it followed to where it empties into the Dniestr. Claims to war damages were resigned by both sides, and both undertook not to interfere in one another's internal affairs nor to support armed bands aimed against the peace and welfare of the other party. Minority rights were to be respected, and Poland was assured the return of libraries, archives, art and historical monuments, stolen by the Russians during the nineteenth century.

The treaty was signed on March 18, 1921, and of particular significance for Catholics in Russia was Article Seven, which guaranteed the religious liberty and rights of the Polish population in Russia. This article caused a veritable flood of demands by Catholics in Russia for a return of their property, seized under the pretext of nationalization. The local departments of justice, for instance, from Saratov, Astrakhan, and others, turned to the central authorities for the proper interpretation of Article Seven. The central authorities in Moscow construed the treaty in the following sense: (1) that even after the Treaty of Riga, the Roman Catholics of Russia remain subject to the laws of the Russian Socialist Federated

[23] For the preliminary peace and the Treaty of Riga, see Leonard Shapiro (ed.), *Soviet Treaty Series*, I (Washington, 1940), 67–69, 105–116. The details of the negotiations are contained in a book by one of the participants, Grabski, *op. cit.*, pp. 23–26, 34–35; Jan Dąbski, *Pokój Ryski* (Warsaw, 1931). See also *Livre Rouge: Recueil des documents diplomatiques relatifs aux relations entre la Russie et la Pologne 1918-1920* (Moscow, 1920); *Sovetskaia Rossiia i Polsha* (Moscow, 1921), also contains the exchanges between the two governments. Typical of works on the subject is James Shotwell and Max Laserson, *Poland and Russia, 1919-1945* (New York, 1945), where the authors still repeat (p. 7) the old error: "The Curzon Line was an effort to establish a frontier on ethnographical rather than political lines."

Soviet Republic; (2) that, consequently, the churches are put at the disposal of believers in the same manner and under the same conditions as other churches; (3) that the Treaty of Riga does not have the effect of a restitution edict, nor do the organs of the Catholic Church, parochial or central, acquire the status of legal persons; (4) that Article Seven deals with goods that had their origin in Poland.[24]

Thus by 1921, when the Treaty of Riga was finally in effect, the policies initiated by the Bolsheviks in 1917 had had very considerable effect. The Roman Catholic Church had lost its property as well as its funds, built up over centuries due to the efforts of the Catholics themselves. The leadership had been decimated by exile; the clergy had suffered murder and deportations as well. Isolated from Rome as well as from Poland, the Catholic Church had now to face the future alone, ruined in wealth and numbers.

The peoples and lands of Belorussia, Lithuania, Livonia, Curland, Ukraine—with their varied history of the Rurikevich dynasty and princes; the Livonian Knights; the Teutonic Knights; the Grand Duchy of Lithuania; the Polish-Lithuanian Commonwealth; the Partitions and Russia, with their religious conflicts and reconciliations; the Roman Catholic Church; the Orthodox Church; the Greek Catholic Church; and the Jesuits—had lived and survived within the very shadow of death. And the miracle of the Vistula, which had seemed to change the course of history but had only delayed it for some twenty years, seemed indeed a real miracle, guaranteeing life and freedom. But the end was not yet in sight.

[24] *Revolutsiia i tserkov,* Nos. 1–3 (1922), pp. 36–37. See Jan Ostrowski, *Z za Kulis Kurji biskupiej w Leningradzie* (Moscow, 1929), p. 307, for Archbishop Ropp's view of the Peace Treaty of Riga: "The Treaty of Riga is so infinitely stupid, that I think we can expect little from it." The letter was addressed to Archbishop Cieplak, without date, but in 1921.

VII

The Catholic Church and the Famine

The years 1917 to 1921 had seen the Catholic Church in Russia move through a whole cycle of hope and fear: the March Revolution had held out promise of liberation from tsarist oppression, but the Bolshevik revolution had destroyed that promise. The Bolshevik decree on the separation of Church and State had really meant the complete subjugation of the church by the civil authorities and the church's exclusion from the life of society, except for strictly religious activities, understood in the narrowest possible sense. Nevertheless, harassment was not destruction, and the Catholic Church, its organization, and its efforts for an independent life continued, even under the most difficult circumstances of the Civil War, the Polish-Soviet War, and persecution systematically applied. During those years, exile, flight, murder, and death had seriously decreased the number of clergy available for work among the Catholics in Russia, and little did these Catholics realize that those events were but a prelude to the final destruction of the organized life of the Church.

With the year 1921 the period of War Communism came to an end; but the heritage of that turbulent period produced conditions in Russia that led to the proclamation of the New Economic Policy. The economic life of the country had been completely paralyzed. First of all, the output of the large scale industries in Russia had declined catastrophically from the year 1913. If the index of output for 1913 is 100, then by 1920 the production of large-scale industry had fallen to a low of 12.8. This disastrous condition in industry was matched in agriculture, where in 1921–1922 agricultural production was little more than half of the prewar level. In 1922 grain acreage was 32 per cent below the prewar level. Added to the agricultural disaster were two successive droughts in 1920 and 1921. Millions were threatened by starvation; demoralization and suffering allegedly produced even cannibalism.[1]

It was perfectly clear to the Soviet government that it had on its hands a major disaster, one that could not be alleviated from the government's own resources. Besides its political and diplomatic problems with the "capitalist" countries, the government saw its foreign trade collapse almost entirely. The allies had lifted the naval blockade on January 16, 1920; but the financial blockade, that is, the refusal of the leading English, French, American, Scandinavian, and Estonian banks to have any financial dealings with the Soviet government, continued in force until the middle of 1921. This almost total cessation of economic intercourse with the outside world helped to produce economic stagnation.[2] Consequently, the Russian government had to depend on the charitable services of governments and social organizations throughout the world in order to obtain the food and medical supplies which the suffering people of Russia so badly needed.[3]

Within Russia itself, Patriarch Tikhon appealed to the Eastern patriarchs, the pope, the archbishop of Canterbury, and the Protestant episcopal bishop of New York for charitable aid in August 1921, as soon as the scope of the disaster became clear.[4] This action, of course, enhanced Tikhon's position in Russia. Tikhon's personality had been of great value in maintaining support for the Russian

[1] For data on the economic policies and the industrial decline, see Alexander Baykov, *The Development of the Soviet Economic System* (New York, 1948), pp. 3–8. For the agricultural decline, see Naum Jasny, *The Socialized Agriculture of the USSR: Plans and Performance* (Stanford, 1949), pp. 200–202.

[2] See Baykov, *op. cit.*, pp. 28–29, for the details of the decline in trade.

[3] A detailed history of the American effort in the relief work is H. H. Fisher, *The Famine in Soviet Russia: The Operations of the American Relief Administration* (Stanford, 1935).

[4] Patriarch Tikhon's appeal is contained in a confidential report to the Department of State. See the *NAD, RS*, File No. 861.404/18, December 9, 1921.

Orthodox Church. The Bolshevik acts of sacrilege and their crude and dogmatic materialism had alienated many people, particularly the peasants who looked upon the disaster as God's visitation of Russia because of the Bolsheviks. Attendance at church grew, and interest in religious questions increased. The Orthodox Church seemed in a fair way to win back some of her old position.[5] Indeed, there seemed to be a feeling among the Russian people that religion was the only common bond among them. Bolshevik authorities were alarmed by this seeming revival of religious interest and ecclesiastical life.[6]

In spite of their disapproval of the increased prestige of Tikhon, the Soviet authorities hoped to exploit Tikhon in their relations with the Western world, even though at first they suppressed the patriarch's appeal to the leaders of the Christian world. When the situation had grown more desperate, Lenin sent Maxim Gorky, the distinguished writer, to persuade the patriarch to make his appeal not only to Christian leaders but also to heads of states. Evidently, Bolshevik leaders hoped not only to obtain famine relief but they regarded Tikhon's appeal as a subsidiary means of entering into diplomatic relations with Western states. Probably suspecting this, Tikhon refused to enter into any negotiations with the heads of states but agreed to approach the leaders of the Christian churches. As a condition for taking action, he demanded that the relief funds be distributed through the church; perhaps he felt that if the government had exclusive control of the money and material, the army, government officials, and their relatives would have priority—a conviction that undoubtedly motivated his attitude on the later question of church valuables.[7]

The Orthodox leaders also formed an All-Russian Church Committee for famine relief; but the government insisted on centralized

[5] This information on the Orthodox Church is contained in a confidential report of *NAD, RS*, File No. 861.404/17, August 30, 1921; File No. 861.404/18, December 9, 1921. However, much of the information in these reports must be used with great caution, as subsequent references will illustrate.

[6] *NAD, RS*, File No. 861.404/18, December 9, 1921; see also File No. 861.404/19, November 21, 1921, for a report on the religious situation in Russia at that time.

[7] *NAD, RS*, File No. 861.404/18, December 9, 1921, which describes fully the negotiations between Patriarch Tikhon and Gorky.

government control of the relief administration.[8] When, as a result, contributions fell off, the government reversed itself in December 1921, declaring that church societies might conduct collections for famine relief and that the central ecclesiastical authorities ought to make arrangements with local church groups for the disbursement of relief.[9] In spite of this apparent concession, on January 26, 1922, the Soviet press raised the fateful question of church valuables and their use for famine relief.[10]

This suggestion, so casually dropped in the Soviet press, was not an isolated incident. As the prestige of the Orthodox Church revived, Soviet authorities had already sounded the alarm. A circular, signed by Emelyan Jaroslavskii, deplored the fact that many party members still remained in the zone of Orthodoxy and demanded the participation of all party members in antireligious propaganda.[11] Moreover, the conduct of the Soviet government in the matter of church valuables indicated that its objective was to destroy the prestige of the church and religion in general by depicting them as opponents of famine relief.

After two preliminary reports in the Soviet newspapers on church valuables,[12] *Izvestiia* announced on February 24, 1922, a government decree that ordered the local Soviets to remove all church valuables from churches and use them for famine relief. The decree gave the local Soviets a month's time to seize the treasures from the churches of all religions, unless the removal essentially impaired the cult itself. Periodic accountings of confiscations were to be made and reports were to be published on the valuables thus confiscated.[13]

Patriarch Tikhon immediately condemned the government's action as sacrilegious, because it also involved the seizure of vessels and utensils used in the divine service. He pointed out that the church

[8] John S. Curtiss, *The Russian Church and the Soviet State, 1917-1950* (Boston, 1953), p. 107, naively accepts the idea that the Soviet government in its relations with the churches during the famine was sincerely interested in famine relief rather than in discrediting the churches by any means whatever. The evidence against this view will be pointed out in the course of the chapter.

[9] P. V. Gidulianov and P. Krasikov, *Tserkov i gosudarstvo po zakonodatelstvu RSFSR* (Moscow, 1926), p. 52.

[10] *Izvestiia*, January 26, 1922; Curtiss, *op. cit.*, p. 107.

[11] *New York Herald Tribune*, January 19, 1921.

[12] *Pravda*, February 11, 1922; Izvestiia, February 12, 1922.

[13] *Izvestiia*, February 24, 26, 1922.

had agreed to use for famine relief the valuables not immediately involved in divine service and that he wished to preserve for church use consecrated articles only.[14] While much could be made of the fact that some churchmen declared the sale of consecrated articles for famine relief was not unknown to church history or canon law,[15] neverthless Tikhon felt that the church valuables seized by the government would not go to famine relief, as already stated by him in his conversation with Gorky. Indeed, if the government were really interested in using the seized valuables for relief, Tikhon had already taken steps to provide funds for relief equal in value to the church treasures. When he was informed of the government decree, Tikhon notified the Soviet authorities that the church as an institution was willing and able to raise a sum of money equal to the worth of the valuables to be seized under the decree. The funds were to be raised by a subscription and by a sale of a portion of the church valuables. Moreover, this money was to be spent by the church or under its direction. Tikhon had also approached Colonel William Haskell, director of the American Relief Administration in Russia, to inquire whether this organization would assist the church in selling the valuables in America and whether it would take over the funds so realized and apply them for relief purposes. Thinking that such an action would be construed by the Soviet authorities as interference in Russia's internal affairs, Colonel Haskell felt constrained to refuse help. Significantly the colonel informed the patriarch that the funds realized from the sale of church valuables would not be applied by the Soviet government to relief work. The American Relief Administration already had more food and supplies at all ports and on all lines leading into Russia than the Soviet transportation system could handle.[16]

The government, on its side, proceeded to the seizures and to a

---

[14] A. A. Valentinov, *Chernaia Kniga* (Paris, 1925), pp. 253–254. The statement was issued on February 15, 1922.

[15] For instance, Curtiss, *op. cit.*, pp. 112–113.

[16] *NAD, RS*, File No. 861.404/30, April 20, 1922, a memorandum of conversation with Mr. Colton of the American YMCA, April 18, 1922. Curtiss, *op. cit.*, p. 116, seemingly is convinced that the church valuables were used for famine relief; but see his doubts on p. 124. McCullagh, an eyewitness, was certain that the money realized would not go for famine relief; see Francis McCullagh, *The Bolshevik Persecution of Christianity* (New York, 1924), pp. 8, 14–15. See also *NAD, RS*, File No. 861.404/51, June 15, 1922.

campaign of arrests, involving eventually the patriarch himself and so prominent a man as Metropolitan Benjamin of Leningrad, who was tried in August 1922, and condemned to be shot.[17] Moreover, a dissident group, called the Living Church, obtained control of the central administration of the church. The Soviet government supported this group against the church headed by the patriarch.[18] Emigré Orthodox bishops and leaders did not make the situation of the patriarch any safer or easier. They had gathered at Karlovtsi in Serbia in December 1921 and called for the destruction of the Bolshevik government, claiming that the Karlovtsi synod spoke for the silenced patriarch.[19]

Needless to say, the government's policy on church valuables was directed not only against the Orthodox Church but fell with a fine impartiality on all religious groups. Inventories of valuables were made in all churches—but especially in the synagogues, to silence the charge that the Jews supported the seizure of church valuables.[20] The blow, therefore, fell upon the Catholic Church in Russia as well.

That the Catholic Church in Russia could not long escape the attentions of the Soviet government is suggested by the growth of

[17] Curtiss, *op. cit.*, p. 122, says of Metropolitan Benjamin's trial that the government "probably after long and detailed investigation," held a great trial. However, the proceedings clearly show a hasty and foregone conclusion. See *Pravda*, July 27, 1922, and August 6, 1922; *OR*, July 10, 11, 12, 1922, and August 6, 1922; Valentinov, *op. cit.*, pp. 198–238, for an eyewitness account of the trial; McCullagh, *op. cit.*, pp. 50–51.

[18] See Curtiss, *op. cit.*, pp. 129–153, where he follows the events in considerable detail but is a victim of the fiction that the revolutionary is always the progressive, liberal, and democratic. The Living Church, as a matter of historical fact, was the tool of an undemocratic government and used undemocratic methods against its opponent, e.g., the patriarchal church. See *NAD, RS*, File No. 861.404/48, May 31, 1922, which also includes a report from *Izvestiia*, May 17, 1922. See also *OR*, November 26, 1922, for a report on the Living Church; *OR*, April 2, 1922, and February 17, 1923, describes the splintering of the Living Church; *OR*, January 31, 1923, describes the birth of a new schism; *OR*, May 7, 8, 1923, describes the deposition of Patriarch Tikhon by the Living Church. See *Pravda*, May 25, 1921, for an article by E. Jaroslavskii about the road to socialism and the role of the Living Church.

[19] *OR*, December 19, 20, 1921, points out the action of the synod declaring that atheism is the enemy on one side and Catholicism on the other. *OR*, September 14, 1921, June 9, 1922, and August 2, 1922, illustrates how closely Rome watched events in the Orthodox Church. *OR*, October 14, 1922, gives Tikhon's statement repudiating the synod.

[20] *NAD, RS*, File No. 861.404/51, June 15, 1922, on the situation of the Russian Church and the confiscation of church property, May 26, 1922.

Russian religious interest in the Catholic Church. Indeed, the Eastern rite Russian Catholic Church and the activities of Metropolitan Szeptycki were certain to draw attention to that church.[21] Moreover, the Catholics and clergy of Russia had been in touch with the Orthodox Church. Exarch Fedorov together with a member of the All-Russian Synod, Kuznetsov, had lodged one of the first protests against Soviet antireligious policy. Because of the efforts of Exarch Fedorov, the clergy of the Orthodox Church and the Catholic Church held several meetings in the apartments of Monsignor Budkiewicz and sent a protest to Moscow as early as February 26, 1919. This protest had been signed by Archbishop Ropp, Exarch Fedorov, and the Orthodox metropolitan of Petrograd, Benjamin. Exarch Fedorov also was engaged in promoting a union between the Orthodox Church and the Catholic Church in Russia, a matter on which he reported to the clergy at their meetings.[22] Moreover, two government decrees, one on the preventive censorship of sermons and the other a prohibition of teaching religion to children under eighteen years of age, certainly presaged difficulties for the Catholics.[23] Obedience to these decrees would undermine the basic teaching function of the clergy, a fact to which they testified at their trial. An article in *Bezbozhnik* emphasized the law that no schools with religious instruction for children under eighteen years of age were to be permitted to exist.[24]

Although the decree on church valuables helped to create the final crisis between the Soviet government and the Catholics, it cannot be said that the Catholics were slow in the work of famine relief. As early as August 1921 Archbishop Cieplak had appealed

[21] *NAD, RS*, File No. 861.404/18, December 9, 1921, on the revival of religion in Russia, Part II.

[22] *BA*, paper on the separation of Church and State in Bolshevik Russia, prepared by Monsignor Budkiewicz and read by him at a meeting of the Roman Catholic clergy, January 9, 1920. (The Budkiewicz Archive is in the possession of Monsignor Bronislas Ussas, Warsaw, Poland.) See *OZ* (Moscow, 1923) p. 15, where the meeting of the Orthodox and Catholic clergy is reported, and *OZ*, p. 49, where Fedorov states that he reported to the Latin clergy on the progress of negotiations for a union of churches. See also James J. Zatko, "A Contemporary Report on the Condition of the Catholic Church in Russia, 1922," *The Harvard Theological Review*, LIII (October 1960), 290–291.

[23] McCullagh, *op. cit.*, p. 110.

[24] *NAD, RS*, File No. 861.404/31, April 21, 1922, contains a summary of the whole article.

to Catholics to assist the famine-stricken. At about the same time, August 5, 1921, Benedict XV in a letter to the papal secretary of state, Cardinal Gasparri, indicated the calamity that had over-taken Russia. The pope requested Cardinal Gasparri to approach the heads of state about immediate effective aid for the Russian people. He also appealed to the charity of all in Russia's hour of need.[25] Nor was this an uninvited gesture. Previously George Chicherin, the commissar of foreign affairs, had confirmed the crying need as well as the offer of Fridtjof Nansen to organize relief, although Chicherin denied that he had sought help from any government.[26] The Red Cross, too, on August 9, 1921, asked by telegram for papal support in the relief program for Russia, a request that the papal secretary of state answered affirmatively on August 11.[27] Nor did the pope delay. He appointed Archbishop Luigi Maglione the papal representative to the International Relief Commission and to the organizational meeting to be held in Geneva. Pope Benedict also sent 1,000,000 lire for relief, which were to be distributed by the exiled Archbishop Ropp and Archbishop Cieplak, recognized by the Soviet government as subjects of the pope because of their episcopal character.[28] In order to mobilize the authority and support of the League of Nations, the pope directed to its assembly an eloquent appeal for famine-stricken Russia, recom-mending Russia to the solicitude of the governments represented there.[29]

Nor did the pope's efforts stop at words or attempts to organize relief to be sponsored by others. By December 1921 the news agency Stefani reported that fifty train cars of papal relief had entered Russia; moreover, efforts were being made to obtain permis-

[25] *AAS*, XIII (1921), 428–429; see *OR*, August 8, 9, 1921, for the letter of Benedict XV; *OR*, August 10, 1921, an editorial on the problem. Previous notices of the famine and epidemic of cholera had already appeared in *OR*, July 11, 22, 1921, and August 1, 2, 1921.

[26] *OR*, July 22, 1921.

[27] *OR*, August 18, 1921. See *OR*, August 25, 1921, for Nansen's telegram to the pope asking his moral support and suggesting an appeal to the whole Christian world. For the Nansen-Gasparri correspondence on Italian prisoners in Russia, see *OR*, December 21, 1921.

[28] *OR*, August 18, 1921, and October 2, 1922.

[29] Alban du Hamel, *Le pape et la Société des Nations* (Paris, 1932), p. 103. See *OR*, September 25, 1921.

sion for Archbishop Ropp to enter Russia and together with Archbishop Cieplak assume charge of the distribution of papal relief.[30]

Pope Benedict's magnanimous efforts to help the Russian people in spite of the government's antireligious policy were halted by his death on January 22, 1922; but his successor, Pius XI (1922–1939), proved just as interested in the relief work. As early as March 12, 1922, the Vatican and the Soviet government were concluding an agreement for a papal relief mission to Russia.[31]

On the eve of the conference at Genoa, which met April 10 to May 19, 1922, Pope Pius sent a letter to the archbishop of Genoa, Josue Signori, commending his appeal for prayers for the success of the conference. The pope declared that the archbishop had exactly interpreted the papal desires; furthermore, the pope extended the appeal to the faithful of all the world. He expressed the hope that the conference would provide the conditions for effective aid to suffering people and would also help to dispel international hatreds, the sad heritage of war.[32]

Pius XI also addressed a letter, dated April 29, 1922, to his secretary of state to stress the need of reconciliation and to express his sympathy for the Russian people, with whom he desired communion in the "same mysteries." Papal representatives throughout the world were instructed to present these views zealously to the governments and people to whom they were accredited. Emphasizing the need of reconciliation rather than the mere cessation of hostilities, he called upon the representatives of nations at the conference to work for the common good in a spirit of Christian charity and mutual confidence.[33]

Even prior to the publication of the pope's letter of April 29, news

[30] *OR*, December 19, 20, 1921.

[31] *Mezhdunarodnaia politika RSFSR v 1922 g.* (Moscow, 1923), p. 27; *OR*, April 7, 1922, and May 5, 1922.

[32] *OR*, April 8, 1922; *AAS*, XIV (1922), 217–220, gives the Italian and French versions of the papal letter, dated April 7, 1922. See *OR*, April 15, 1922, for an editorial on the public reaction to this letter.

[33] *OR*, April 30, 1922; see *AAS*, XIV (1922), 265–270 for the letter of Pius XI to Cardinal Gasparri, April 29, 1922. It is ironic that exactly on April 29, 1922, the Polish plenipotentiary in Mińsk, W. Z. Białopiotrowicz, was protesting to the commissar of foreign affairs the plundering of the Roman Catholic cathedral in Mińsk, and was himself placed under arrest for a while. This letter is in the possession of Monsignor Bronislas Ussas, Warsaw.

of the ecclesiastical situation in Russia had reached the Vatican. Without delay the Vatican sent Monsignor Giusseppe Pizzardo, the papal undersecretary of state, to Genoa, where he arrived on May 6, 1922, carrying an important memorandum to the conference. The memorandum pointed out that the rapidity of events did not permit the Holy See to approach the governments through its accredited representatives; consequently, the Holy See took advantage of the presence of government representatives at Genoa to send them the text of the memorandum directly. Inasmuch as the conference was engaged in the historic task of admitting Russia to the family of nations, the Vatican wished to safeguard in Russia those religious interests which are the basis of all civilization. The Holy See, therefore, demanded that, in any accord which the representatives of the powers would establish, three clauses should be expressly included: (1) full liberty of conscience for all Russian citizens or foreigners is guaranteed in Russia; (2) the public and private exercise of religion is guaranteed; (3) the immovables that belonged or belong to any religious confession, whatever it be, will be returned to it and respected.[34]

To this papal effort to safeguard the interests of all religions in Russia by international guarantee, the reaction of the leading statesmen at Genoa was not encouraging. Louis Barthou, representing France, felt that the first and second articles of the papal program could be discussed, but not the third; Lloyd George observed that he did not see how it was possible to act without interfering in Russia's internal affairs, but agreed that the note must be read and some action taken. This was the total result of the pope's efforts.[35] Ironically, on April 16, 1922, Easter Sunday, while Joseph Wirth, a Catholic of the Center Party, went to the Genoa cathedral for mass,

---

[34] *OR*, May 15, 16, 1922; du Hamel, *op. cit.*, p. 104. Once again it is ironic that just while efforts were being made to obtain international guarantees for the freedom of religion in Russia, the international guarantees in the Treaty of Riga were being flouted; on April 27, 1922, the Polish *chargé d' affaires* was protesting these violations in a memorandum to the commissar of foreign affairs.

[35] *OR*, May 12, 1922. For the Soviet documents see *Genuezskaia konferentsiia: materialy i dokumenty* (Moscow, 1922). Karel Radek, *Vneshnaia politika sovetskoi vlasti Rossii* (Moscow, 1923), is silent on the Vatican and on Genoa. See also the survey of diplomatic history, Bor Vaks, *Ot Oktiabra do Genui Mezhdunarodnye otnosheniia RSFSR* (Moscow, 1922).

George Chicherin and Emil Rathenau slipped away quietly to Rapallo, where the famous treaty was signed.[36]

Although these efforts to work with the conference failed, the possibility of a direct agreement between the Vatican and the Bolsheviks seemed to grow stronger. When asked what impression the papal letter to Gasparri had made on Chicherin and the Russian delegation, Maxim Litvinov replied in the most flattering terms, indicating that the impression was the best possible, especially since the letter had come while Russia was in such difficult circumstances. The pope's words, he asserted, were a great comfort at a time when efforts were being made to restore peace to Russia. He even expressed the hope that Chicherin might conclude an agreement with the Vatican on purely religious matters.[37] An atmosphere of apparent good feeling having been established, Monsignor Pizzardo met Vladimir Vorovskii to define points of an accord between the Holy See and Russia for a papal mission in Russia. As chance would have it, Chicherin arrived on the scene, and the monsignor took the occasion to express papal views on the questions of liberty of conscience and a guarantee for the free exercise of religion in Russia. Still this informal meeting did not have any effect on the conference, and the only result was the accord for the papal relief mission.[38] This accord provided for the work of three Catholic "orders" in Russia, the Congregation of the Most Holy Redeemer (popularly known as the Redemptorists) to work in northern Russia, the Society of Jesus to work in central Russia, and the Society of the Divine Word to work in southern Russia.[39]

These negotiations evoked the most fantastic interpretations. The Orthodox Archbishop John of Latvia felt that the Soviet government, having failed to destroy the influence of the Orthodox Church, would now strike a new blow against that church by an agreement with the Vatican. The introduction of Roman Catholicism into Russia, he declared, would uproot the last mainstay of the old regime.

---

[36] Lionel Kochan, *Russia and the Weimar Republic* (New York, 1954), p. 52.
[37] *OR*, May 3, 1922.
[38] *OR*, May 16, 17, 1922, where the meeting with Chicherin is described.
[39] *NAD, RS*, File No. 861.404/59, July 17, 1922, where the report speaks of the members of the Society of the Divine Word as "Brothers of the Word of God."

In the communist strategy Catholic propaganda was to cause the whole Orthodox structure to crumble. The majority of peasants would anyhow be unable to make a distinction between the two religious confessions, a fact that the archbishop described as the most insidious element in the new plan.[40] The instruments of this new alliance between the Soviets and the Vatican were to be the Jesuits, described as the hereditary enemies of the Orthodox Church. Reportedly, there were, and had been for a considerable time, large numbers of representatives of the Jesuit order in Moscow, including Bishop Ropp. The pope, who is said to have left the Jesuit order before being elected pope, acted entirely on the instructions of Count Ledóchowski, the superior general of the Jesuit order! According to the same report, the Vatican felt it could bring the Russian church under papal domination only if Tikhon were eliminated, a condition which the Bolsheviks thought had now been fulfilled. The Jesuits and the Vatican, on their part, promised that after a conclusion of a concordat, they would do all in their power to put pressure on the governments of Italy, France, and Belgium to hasten their recognition of the Soviet government.[41]

There were other reports that negotiations had begun between the Vatican and the Soviets for an agreement that would recognize the rights of Roman Catholics and permit all the missionaries of the Catholic religion to work in Russia—a report that was denied by the Vatican at least twice.[42] Another rumor that negotiations were in progress between the Vatican and Russia allegedly produced tensions in French and Vatican relations.[43]

The most violent reaction came from the Russian emigrés, who apparently felt that the Vatican was planning to exploit the difficulties of the Orthodox Church in order to benefit the Catholic Church. The Russian National Committee in Paris published an offensive open letter even before they had read the papal memorandum to

[40] *NAD, RS,* File No. 861.404/49, June 5, 1922, includes a report whose source is said to be the Orthodox archbishop, John of Latvia, a source described as reliable and in direct contact with Tikhon: the amazing statements and speculations suggest the extent of reliability.

[41] *NAD, RS,* File No. 861.404/49, June 5, 1922, contains a supplement to the information provided by Archbishop John. For a fantastic report on Catholic activity among the Russian emigrés, see *NAD, RS,* File No. 861.404/86, February 16, 1923.

[42] *OR,* April 17, 1922, and May 5, 1922.   [43] *OR,* May 7, 1922.

the Genoa conference: detailed descriptions were published of the meeting between Chicherin and Archbishop Signori, of Chicherin's audience with the pope. While the outcry was almost universal among the emigrés, there were others among them who retained their sense as well as their dignity, e.g., Father Peter Izvolsky of Brussels, a friend of Cardinal Mercier, that great churchman and philosopher.[44] Of course, the documents do not show that the Vatican ever attempted to take advantage of the Orthodox Church, but rather had used its high position in the world, both of religion and diplomacy, to intervene on behalf of the Orthodox Church.

Moving to implement the papal policy toward Russia, Pius XI, in an apostolic letter of July 10, 1922, approached all the patriarchs, primates, archbishops, and bishops of the Catholic world with a request for aid. While he recalled the work of Benedict XV and his own efforts at Genoa, the pope praised the generosity of all, especially the efforts of the more prosperous regions of America, nor did he fail to mention the Congress of the United States, which had voted a large sum of relief money. All these efforts, he noted, had necessarily proved insufficient because of the daily worsening situation; therefore, he called upon all possessed of Christian and human feeling to expand their charitable efforts. Since it was of primary importance that the funds made available were spent properly, he had decided to send a special mission to distribute this relief without distinction of religion or nationality. As an example of generosity, the pope set aside 10,000,000 lire for Russian relief.[45]

No time was lost in organizing the mission. Father Edmund Walsh, a Jesuit and scholar, was placed at the head of the mission. To make clear the purely charitable character of the mission, Father Walsh declared that the members of the mission eschewed all political and religious propaganda.[46] There were thirteen priests

---

[44] McCullagh, *op. cit.*, pp. 101–106, gives considerable detail; Pierre Hanski, "La Tragédie de l' église Russe," *Etudes*, CLXXII (1922), 295–312; M. J. Rimsky, "L' aide pontificale aux affamés de Russie," *Etudes*, CLXXII (1922), 651–661.

[45] *AAS*, XIV (1922), 417–419; *OR*, July 28, 1922.

[46] *OR*, August 5, 1922. For a description of Father Walsh's Papal Relief Mission as an effort to establish the Catholic Church in Russia, see *NAD, RS,* File No. 861.404/65, August 14, 1922. In spite of papal statements and Father Walsh's declarations, outsiders persistently described the Vatican policy as aimed toward a self-interested exploitation of the Russian religious situation.

on the commission. It established five centers of operation and fed about 160,000 persons a day. The papacy expended about $1,500,000 in this charity.[47]

The papal relief mission, after pausing at Constantinople, disembarked in Crimea on August 19, 1922, and proceeded to set up two centers in Crimea for relief work. The work began officially on August 29, when Father Edward Gehrmann, a member of the Society of the Divine Word, gave an address. By the middle of September the Eupatoria center was caring for 21,000 children, while in Dianko 14,000 children were being administered to. The population of the two districts, according to a report from the mission, consisted mostly of Germans, Poles, Czechs, and Estonians, among whom were many Catholics. According to the same report, the number of children in danger of starvation in both districts reached 40,000. Nor was the work of the mission limited to the relatively simple process of feeding so many thousands; the section of the mission working from Krasnodar requested medical supplies to combat typhus and malaria, supplies which were sent by the pope to the extent of 1,000,000 lire.[48]

This work was carried on with the knowledge of the Soviet government, which openly acknowledged the extent of the papal relief work, at the same time pointing out that the differences between the Roman and Russian churches were minor—perhaps a remark calculated to encourage the impression that the government stood behind an agreement between the two churches.[49] Furthermore, when medical supplies for the papal mission arrived in Moscow, the commissar of public health and the head of the Russian Red Cross were on hand to receive them. Both these officials sent a telegram to the Holy See, thanking the pope for the generous gift

---

Indeed, the difficulties of the Roman Catholic Church provided sufficient matter and scope for Father Walsh's talents and energy. For a survey of Father Walsh's career, see the *New York Times*, November 1, 1956, which summarized his life and activities when giving notice of his death October 31, 1956.

[47] *OR*, September 16, 1922.

[48] *OR*, December 7, 1922, and March 18, 1923. For a report of a new outbreak of typhus, see *OR*, June 4, 5, 1923.

[49] *OR*, January 18, 1923.

and expressing the hope that he would continue to aid the Russian people.[50]

A testimony to the splendid work of the papal relief mission came from the letter of a religious living in the south of Russia to a fellow religious living in Constantinople. In a letter of September 27, 1922, he wrote that he had learned the previous week that the mission was in Rostov. He hurried to Rostov, where he found two Spaniards, Don Pedro Voltas and Don Angelo Vergara, struggling to learn Russian. He noted that the mission distributed its goods without fanfare to all who were in need, whatever their religious affiliation. With their weak Russian, the two Spaniards even went to visit the suffering in their homes. The writer paid great tribute to the work of the Italian Red Cross, directed by Prince Pignatelli, the nephew of Cardinal Granito Pignatelli di Belmonte. The supplies the religious brought back to his home and the contact with the members of the mission did much to restore his courage and his spirits.[51]

While the papal relief mission energetically carried through the papal program, Pius XI continued to appeal to the world, Catholic and non-Catholic, for further aid. Still he did not fail to notice in an address to a secret consistory on December 11, 1922, that in Russia, in addition to the disasters visited upon an innocent population, religious and civil liberty was restricted.[52] Mild words, indeed, for persecution was rife.

---

[50] *OR*, March 18, 1923. However, see, James J. Zatko, "A Contemporary Report on the Condition of the Catholic Church in Russia, 1922," *op. cit.*, p. 288, where Monsignor Budkiewicz writes to the nuncio in Warsaw: "We had thought that the Russian government would be grateful for the Apostolic See's assistance in the famine, but this hope has deceived us. Russian officials endeavor to discount that aid both in their newspapers and in their conversations. This ungrateful attitude toward the Holy See appeared most strongly in the matter of the purchase of the sacred vessels. As we know now, the Roman Curia, after the decree on the so-called expropriation of valuables, by telegraph offered the Russian government to pay an equivalent price for the sacred objects. But the government not only did not give an answer, but also designedly exposed the sacred objects to profanation, and at the same time imprisoned and put on trial even priests who had maintained a passive attitude in the matter."

[51] *OR*, December 16, 1922.

[52] *AAS*, XIV (1922), 611; *OR*, December 11, 16, 1922.

VIII

The Attrition of the Church

During the period of the Civil War and the Polish-Soviet War, the government had been unable to bring all its force to bear upon the Roman Catholic Church. However, the imposition of a preconceived social order without religious content was only delayed, not dropped. While the government had to concede a certain amount of liberalization in the economic sphere, it used the interval to settle permanently the problem of religion in a society formally atheistic and militantly antireligious. The choice which confronted the Catholics of Russia was either immediate destruction or ultimate submission. The total power of the State was now issuing a challenge to the Catholics.

The totalitarian grasp of the Bolshevik government soon made itself felt. A government decree of December 26, 1921, ordered the preventive censorship of sermons, a measure that exceeded anything the tsars had done; almost immediately afterwards on January 3, 1922, another decree forbade the teaching of religion to anyone under fourteen years of age.[1] However extreme these decrees might seem, they did not strike at fundamental principles held by the Catholics in Russia.

The antireligious policy of this period had already been deter-

[1] BA, letter of the Polish *chargé d' affaires* to the commissar of foreign affairs, April 27, 1922, pointed out that even the tsars did not go so far as to subject sermons to a preventive censorship. See also Francis McCullagh, *The Bolshevik Persecution of Christianity* (New York, 1924), p. 110.

mined by the Tenth Party Congress in March 1921. Antireligious activity was proclaimed one of the fundamental tasks of the party that demanded the organization of antireligious propaganda and agitation in the form of publications, lectures, and films.[2] Moreover, party members who engaged in religious services and who refused to participate in antireligious propaganda because of material or family reasons were to be dealt with sternly.[3] Then, the Eleventh Party Congress, which met in March and April of 1922, resolved to create a special agency to publish antireligious literature.[4]

On the philosophical level, this antireligious policy coincided with a popular materialism, quite crude in its conception of matter and life. In fact, these cruder forms of materialism demanded not only the destruction of religion but also of anything like philosophy.[5]

The policy outlined at the party congresses was implemented in the following months. The Atheist Publishing House was founded. Soon antireligious publications poured from its presses; school books of the old regime were suppressed, and new texts with the religious element entirely excluded were printed. The vast cost of these publications at a time of economic crisis suggests how important the party and government considered their antireligious program.[6]

The Communist Organization of Youth (known as the Komsomol), organized in 1918, undertook a truly violent and aggressive program of antireligious activity. Perhaps alarmed at the decline of revolutionary fervor in the first days of the New Economic Policy, the Komsomol officials determined to use their members for antireligious demonstrations during the Christmas holidays. These demonstrations were to consist of parodies of religious services and religious events, e.g., the birth of Christ; they were calculated to dissuade religiously-minded persons from celebrating Christmas. The vulgarity of the demonstrations reached abysmal depths. In Petrograd a carnival parade, with a Protestant "pastor," an "Orthodox priest"

[2] Vsesoiuznaia kommunisticheskaia Partia, *VKP (b) v rezolutsiiakh i resheniiakh sezdov, konferenstii i plenumov* TSK, part I, pp. 449–450.

[3] *New York Herald*, June 19, 1921; *NAD, RS,* File No. 861.404/16.

[4] *VKP (b) v rezolutsiiakh*, part I, p. 530.

[5] John S. Curtiss. *The Russian Church and the Soviet State, 1917-1950* (Boston, 1953), p. 202, speaks of this policy of eradicating religion as not making the textbooks "overly antireligious."

[6] See Gustav Wetter, *Dialectical Materialism* (New York, 1958), pp. 128–129.

and his wife, a Jewish "rabbi," and a Moslem "mullah" marched to a church and there proceeded to stage parodies. In Rostov the carnival included a "burning of the gods." The Komsomols burned Jehovah, Allah, Christ, and the Mother of God—"They burned as though they were alive, they shriveled, their heads drooped, and their hands shook."[7] From the provinces came claims of thousands attending the Komsomol "Christmases"; however, for all the glowing reports, not long afterwards complaints appeared in the press about the failure of the Komsomol carnivals. As early as January 27, 1923, the carnivals were being described as failures with only small numbers attending in Moscow itself. An analysis of the causes of failure suggested that there was lack of popular support for such carnivals. For instance, an article in *Pravda* on February 25, 1923, declared that only where the majority supported an antireligious policy could such carnivals be staged successfully.[8] However, the lessons of failure are hard to learn, so even more elaborate plans were made for the Easter of 1923, but with similiar disappointing results.[9] Indeed, the Easter of 1923 was to be memorable for more than the Komsomol blasphemies.

To stimulate antireligious fervor, reports in the press described peasants closing churches and synagogues and turning them into study or recreation centers. Icons were being removed from public places, religious holidays were voted abolished, and God was voted out of existence.[10]

The barrage of propaganda was supplemented late in 1922 with a periodical, *Bezbozhnik*, that was meant to serve as the organizational journal for the antireligious movement. For the benefit of the "godless" agitators, it published the material needed for a "scientific" atheistic propaganda to liberate the masses from the bondage of religious prejudice. The articles, however, were hardly scientific, though they made a pretense of using a learned jargon, e.g., in the discussion of evolution. The cartoons were of a kind to offend sensibilities of fair-minded people rather than to dispel prejudice in the

[7] *Pravda*, November 15, 1922, and January 6, 17, 18, 1923. See also the description of a "godless" Christmas in the *New York Times*, January 9, 1923.
[8] *Pravda*, January 27, 1923, and February 25, 1923.
[9] E.g., *Pravda*, April 1, 12, 1923, and May 1, 1923; *New York Times*, June 11, 1923.
[10] *Pravda*, January 27, 30, 1923, and February 16, 17, 20, 21, 22, 28, 1923.

dawn of "scientific knowledge."[11] In the autumn of 1924 the contributors and supporters of the periodical met in Moscow to organize a society, The Friends of the Newspaper *Bezbozhnik*. This soon developed into the League of the Militant Atheists.[12]

Great claims were made for the advance of atheism and the creation of a nonreligious society.[13] However, confidential reports suggest that this was propaganda rather than actual fact. For instance, in the Smoleńsk area a voluntary association of the opponents of religion had strongly propagandized against the Orthodox Church in the Jartsevo region. Directives had been passed to all antireligious agencies of the Communist Party on how atheists are to penetrate among their follow citizens in order to liberate them from the oppressive influence of the Orthodox clergy. Antireligious cells were formed among the factory and farm workers. There were, in fact, only two groups of 35 atheists among 173,000 inhabitants. The officials of the voluntary antireligious association complained about the lack of antireligious activity; they demanded that copies of *Bezbozhnik* be distributed among factory and farm workers in large quantities.[14] However, war, emigration and new oppression breed success; for the Smoleńsk Archive also mentions that the Catholic church in Smoleńsk, that of the Immaculate Conception of Mary, now included only about 100 members; in 1904 it had numbered 6,736 members.[15]

This vast expenditure of money and energy illustrates the importance the Bolshevik government attached to the antireligious campaign. In fact, it indicates that the concern was not merely with the enemies of the revolution; the effort to spread atheism is something quite different from the elimination of enemies of the regime. Ultimately, the antireligious policy was dictated by the metaphysics of

[11] This writer has examined the following numbers: *Bezbozhnik* (1925), Nos. 1, 2, 3, 4, 5, 6; (1926), Nos. 1, 2, 3, 4, 5, 6, 7, 8, 9, 10; (1928–1929); all these are available at the Hoover Library, Stanford University, Stanford, California. See also *Pravda*, January 11, 1923, which illustrates the efforts to spread *Bezbozhnik* among the workers, as well as the conflicts that these efforts produced in "backward" areas. For a general view of Soviet antireligious policy, see Edmund Walsh, *The Last Stand* (Boston, 1931), pp. 167–219.

[12] For the organizational procedure, see the Smoleńsk Archive, WKP 458, pp. 31–34.

[13] Cited in Curtiss, *op. cit.*, p. 206.   [14] Smoleńsk Archive, WKP 459, 19252.

[15] Smoleńsk Archive, WKP 499, 295.

the regime: its determination to create an irreligious society. In
this effort to create a certain form of society without respect for the
desires of the members of that society the Bolshevik regime betrayed
its fundamental character.

In pursuing its goals, the Bolshevik government was not satisfied
with popular agitation and propaganda. The fearful famine then
devastating Russia was made the occasion of a double onslaught
against the Roman Catholic Church in Russia. The government
began once again to demand the signature of contracts for the use
of the nationalized churches, which were declared to be the property of the Russian people; in addition, the confiscation of church
valuables for alleged famine relief proved a two-edged sword
against the churches: to discredit them if they refused to give up
church valuables and to hamstring them if they did.

Archbishop Cieplak had already anticipated the problem of the
use of church valuables for famine relief. In a circular letter of
January 3, 1922, he insisted that the Catholic Church's position on
church property and the church valuables was defined by canon
law, which forbade the sale or surrender of church property to any
group, including the State. Appealing to the Bolshevik decree on
the separation of the Church and State, he denied that the State had
any right to interfere in the internal life of the Church. Finally,
according to the archbishop, the Treaty of Riga provided international guarantees for the Roman Catholic Church in Russia.[16] Hoping to solve at least the problem of signing contracts for the use
of nationalized churches, the archbishop had inquired of the
apostolic nuncio in Warsaw, Archbishop Lorenzo Lauri, whether
an agreement between the Vatican and the Bolshevik regime on
the matter was possible; but the nuncio replied that the pope had
refused to make any such agreements with the Soviets. However,
if there were any danger that the churches might be closed, the
pope wished to be informed at once.[17]

[16] M. Milich, "Protsess rimsko-katolicheskogo dukhovenstva," *Revolutsiia i
tserkov* (1923), p. 104, which gives a hostile Soviet construction to the conduct of the Roman Catholic clergy; *Izvestiia*, March 24, 1923.

[17] Milich, "Protsess . . .," *op. cit.*, p. 104; *Izvestiia*, March 24, 1923; see
Franciszek Rutkowski, *Arcybiskup Jan Cieplak* (Warsaw, 1934), pp. 220–222,
for Archbishop Cieplak's letter of November 22, 1922, to Bishop Adolph

In accordance with defined policy, when the decree on church valuables appeared, the archbishop refused to sanction their surrender. Father Michael Rutkowski, the pastor of Yaroslav, had telegraphed the archbishop for instructions; the archbishop replied by telegraph that the demand for church valuables was illegal and that, consequently, the demand even for an inventory of these valuables must be rejected. Hence, many Catholic priests refused to submit their churches even to an inventory.[18]

The reaction of the government was all that could be expected. Churches were plundered throughout the archdiocese of Mohylew. The relics of St. Andrew Bobola, once successfully defended against desecration, were now desecrated and brought to Moscow. In the Ukraine fifty-two of sixty-eight churches were robbed. In fact, the rapidity and extent of the raids suggest that the government had been prepared for such an operation, which was but one aspect of its program.[19]

With the present evidence it is difficult to estimate the exact worth in church valuables which the Catholic churches lost. The data published in the Soviet press show the wide extent of the seizures; however, these reports are probably not to be taken at face value, since the government had much to gain from exaggerated reports of ecclesiastical wealth. On September 3, 1922, *Izvestiia* published a statement of the valuables collected from the beginning of the campaign until August 10, 1922. Although this report did not include the valuables seized in the churches of Siberia and Petrograd, the results until August 10 are indicative of the extent of the confiscation:[20]

Szelążek, Polish Ministry of Religious and Public Education, where the archbishop describes his appeal to the Holy See through Archbishop Lorenzo Lauri, the nuncio in Warsaw, and through the People's Commissariat of Foreign Affairs, and the reply that came through Lauri. Archbishop Lauri's reply is published in Rutkowski, *op. cit.*, p. 247.

[18] Milich, "Protsess . . .," *op. cit.*, p. 102; *Izvestiia*, March 24, 1923; Rutkowski, *op. cit.*, p. 243.

[19] Curtiss, *op. cit.*, p. 202, speaks of the antireligious movement of 1921 and 1922 as "marked by caution," a statement in conflict with the conduct of the confiscations during 1922.

[20] *Izvestiia*, September 3, 1922. This report was forwarded to the Department of State in Washington; see *NAD, RS,* File No. 861.404/74, September 25, 1922.

Item	Karats	Poods	Pounds	Money
Gold		8	2	
Silver		16,904	37	
Copper		84	38	
Pearls		1	20	
Diamonds and other	166			
Gold rubles				3,265
Silver rubles				19,586

Source: *Izvestiia*, September 3, 1922.

At the same time an article in *Bednota*, September 2, 1922, announced that in view of the termination of the campaign, the People's Commissariat of Finance had instructed the local organs of finance to forward all valuables to Moscow. This signaled the end of the campaign to seize church valuables for famine relief, but by no means meant the end of religious persecution.[21] Indeed, the climax of persecution was in sight.

As to gauging the impact of the plunder on Catholic churches, in some individual cases it is possible to fix the exact amount. For instance, the Roman Catholic church of Ss. Peter and Paul in Moscow, with a membership of 16,343 parishioners in 1904, surrendered 621.87 pounds of gold and silver.[22] The Catholic church in the city of Novgorod, also named Ss. Peter and Paul, lost a "treasure" of 2.5 *zolotniki* of gold and 23 pounds of silver. In Rostov the Catholic church provided 14 pounds of silver.[23]

These were certainly not the only Catholic churches cleared of valuables; in a list of cities and *guberniias* where confiscations had been carried on, thirty-three cities are mentioned in which there were churches and oratories belonging to the archdiocese of Mohylew. In Mińsk the cathedral church of St. Mary was also plundered. Originally built by the Jesuits in 1710, the church had burned but

[21] *Bednota*, September 2, 1922. See also *NAD, RS*, File No. 861.404/74, September 25, 1922.
[22] A. A. Valentinov, *Chernaia Kniga* (Paris, 1925), pp. 261–286, presents a statistical table of church valuables seized in Orthodox and non-Orthodox churches in Moscow; the church of Ss. Peter and Paul is mentioned on p. 263. For the membership of the church see *Elenchus omnium ecclesiarum et universi cleri archidioeceseos Mohyloviensis et dioec. Minscensis pro anno domini 1904 conscriptus*, p. 190.
[23] Valentinov, *op. cit.*, pp. 276–277; *Elenchus omnium . . .* (1904), p. 188.

been rebuilt by Bishop Dederko in 1796. The Polish plenipotentiary in Mińsk, John Białopiotrowicz, reported that for two days Bolshevik troops surrounded the cathedral while the pillaging was going on: the silver embossings from the picture of the Mother of God and the ornaments from the tomb of St. Felician were removed. In the meantime, the clergy were held under arrest. Białopiotrowicz himself had been arrested by the *Cheka,* but released after interrogation.[24]

The government's attack on religion in general and on the Roman Catholic Church in particular was not to go unnoticed at the Vatican. On April 10, 1922, Archbishop Cieplak managed to send a letter to the papal secretary of state, Cardinal Gasparri. He described the perilous condition of the Church in fullest detail. The troubles between the Catholic Church and the Soviets arose from the government's arbitrary action. The government had seized church goods and property, even to the smallest items, and had distributed them to those who were hostile to the Church. The use of the nationalized churches created more friction. The government had renewed its demands for the signature of contracts for the use of these churches. Earlier some parishes, acting without advice from ecclesiastical authorities but with the best of intentions, had signed the agreements; others had attached conditions in order to render the agreements more conformable to canon law; still others had absolutely refused to sign them. For a while the government had "forgotten" about the contracts, but now it had embarked on a program of enforcing their signature. Seeing that the government was constantly adding new and harsh conditions to the "pacts," the archbishop wrote that he had ordered all his priests to refuse to sign the agreements.

Furthermore, wrote the archbishop, the government had even seized cemeteries; everything of value had been seized for sale, while wooden crosses or monuments and hedges were simply burned. Then the government offered to rent the cemetery grounds to the party that would pay the highest price.

In addition, the seizure of the Theological Academy, the seminary,

[24] *BA,* letter of W. Z. Białopiotrowicz to the commissar of foreign affairs, April 29, 1923; letter of W. Z. Białopiotrowicz to the minister of foreign affairs, May 3, 1922.

and the Catholic elementary schools, long supported by the generosity of the Catholics in Russia, had robbed the church of a fundamental means of carrying on its work. Still, the archbishop reported, a secret seminary had been opened, in which students, dressed in civilian clothes and working for the State so as to be free from military service, prepared for the Catholic ministry. The prohibition of religious teaching to anyone under eighteen years of age, the obligatory censorship of sermons, the demand for all church records—all these were thorns in the side of the Church. Moreover, because of the law against any religious associations or congregations, there were no religious orders to carry on their work publicly. The number of priests was very low: together with Archbishop Ropp, sixty-eight priests had been forced to leave Russia for various reasons, allegedly political; but even now when the war had ended, they were not permitted to return.

Finally, the latest move—the seizure of the church valuables under the pretext of famine relief—was providing a new means, if new means were needed, for an attack on the Church. On April 9, 1922, for instance, the church of St. John the Baptist in Petrograd had been stripped of all its sacred vessels. The same thing had already happened in Moscow. As great as the destruction had been in the archdiocese of Mohylew, even greater damage had been done in the dioceses of Łuck-Żytomierz, Mińsk, and worst of all in Tiraspol.

The archbishop also stated frankly that whenever the Polish government's representatives in Moscow protested to the Soviet government against the persecution of the Church, the Soviets replied: "The pope is silent; hence, he has nothing against us."[25]

In addition to writing, the archbishop sent a telegram to the pope to the effect that the "State authorities in Petrograd insist on the surrender of the sacred and valuable articles of worship in order that the money from the sale of them may be devoted to famine relief." Monsignor Pizzardo informed Chicherin, who was at Genoa, by telegram on May 14, 1922, that "the Holy Father is ready to buy these sacred and valuable objects, and to deposit them with Archbishop Cieplak. The price agreed on will be immediately paid to

[25] *CA*, letter of Archbishop Cieplak to Cardinal Gasparri, April 10, 1922. This archive is in the Polish Roman Catholic Museum, Chicago, Illinois.

Your Excellency or to any other whom the government may nominate."[26] These efforts failed.

While the archbishop laid complaints before the supreme authorities of his church, the Polish government had also taken action to protect Polish nationals and Catholics in Russia. The Polish *chargé d' affaires* lodged a protest on April 27, 1922, against the confiscations. The protest pointed out that the Russian government's demands for contracts for the use of nationalized churches were a violation of Article Seven of the Treaty of Riga. As to the demand for church valuables, the protest branded this a violation of the right of property in the Treaty of Riga, of the Soviet constitution, and of canon law. The memorandum pointed, too, to the excesses of the Soviet agents in their confiscations. For instance, the seizure of church valuables extended even to the very impoverished church on Mala Gruzinskaya, which netted two and three-fourths pounds of silver objects for the raiders. As for the censorship of sermons, the *chargé* pointed out that even the tsars had not gone so far. Hoping to make the Soviet authorities more amenable, the protest suggested that perhaps the executive organs of the Soviet government had not understood the guarantees implied in Article Seven of the Treaty of Riga, which had guaranteed self-government to the churches. However, in a reply of July 22, 1922, Chicherin declared that Church and State relations were an internal matter and that Article Seven could only be operative within the framework of Soviet law. Still the Polish government had not given up. On July 18, it had protested against the desecration of the relics of St. Andrew Bobola as a violation of the Treaty of Riga. In spite of the fact that these relics were a Polish historical as well as religious monument, the Russian government rejected this protest in a note of August 15, stating that Poland should cease persecuting the Orthodox population in Poland. This incident illustrated rather well the futility of protest diplomacy with the Bolsheviks.[27]

[26] This telegram and Chicherin's reply are given in Walsh, *op. cit.*, pp. 182–183.

[27] *Mezhdunarodnaia politika RSFSR v 1922 g.* (Moscow, 1923), pp. 46–47; McCullagh, *op. cit.*, p. 110, mistakenly dates the first Soviet reply as June 22, 1922. Information was got to the Polish government by Monsignor Budkiewicz through Bishop Szelążek; see *BA*, letter of Bishop Szelążek to Budkiewicz, June 2, 1922: "Przedstawiłem Ministrowi." See also *BA*, letter of Bishop

As the archbishop's letter to the papal secretary of state pointed out, the conflict with the Soviet government was not limited to the question of the seizure of church valuables for famine relief. The actual plundering of churches had in fact solved that problem. In the course of the year 1922, the Soviet government determined to enforce upon the Catholics the acceptance of a Church-State system that would have subjected the Church to control and oppression by a hostile government. The lengths to which the government was prepared to go underlines its determination to achieve either complete subjection or complete destruction. The parochial committees that had signed contracts for the use of the churches decided that these contracts could no longer be honored; these "pacts" had been made in the expectation of the early fall of the regime. On its side, the Bolshevik government now felt that it had every right to demand the signature of new agreements in order to bring Church and State relations into accord with the law. During August 1922, therefore, the government demanded a new registration of all religious associations.[28]

The Catholic position, however, had remained unchanged. Taking their stand on Archbishop Cieplak's circular of January 3, 1922, the Catholic clergy, especially those in Petrograd, refused to sign the agreements and resisted as much as they could any attempts to inventory church property. Needless to say, serious conflicts developed with the government.[29]

The most feared blow fell on December 5, 1922. Communist militia surrounded the Catholic churches in Petrograd, closed and sealed them. Hoping to have the churches reopened and to forestall further closures, the archbishop turned to the Papal Relief Mission and informed its head, Father Walsh, of the desperate situation of the Catholic Church in Russia. He reported that the Soviet govern-

---

Szelążek to Budkiewicz, April 4, 1922. The Polish *chargé d' affaires* in Moscow, Tomasz Morawski, acted in Moscow; see *BA*, correspondence of Morawski with Budkiewicz in the summer and fall of 1922.

[28] . . .," *Izvestiia*, August 12, 1922, the text of the Instruction. See *NAD, RS*, File No. 861.404/146, June 14, 1923, for an American report on this.

[29] Milich, "Protsess . . .," *op. cit.*, p. 104; McCullagh, *op. cit.*, pp. 154–171, gives the official statement of the accusation, in which the circular is described from the government's point of view (p. 163). However, McCullagh has confused the dates of some events, e.g., pp. 164–174.

ment, seeing the determined resistance to signing agreements, had substituted "receipts" for the formal contracts, but these receipts were in fact disguised forms of the old contracts. Hence, the Catholics had refused to sign them. On December 5 the churches had been closed. The archbishop asked Father Walsh to inform the Holy See and to seek instructions on what course to follow; he felt that the Catholics' only hope lay in papal intervention.[30] In fact, the Bolsheviks had closed the pro-cathedral of the Assumption; the churches of St. Stanislas, St. Francis, St. Casimir, St. Catherine, St. Boniface, the Immaculate Conception, and the Sacred Heart; the Maltese church; the chapel of the Sacred Heart of Mary, and fourteen other chapels.[31] The Catholic clergy of Petrograd tried to circumvent these acts of violence by holding church services in private locations;[32] but these were only temporary expedients.

The Catholic leaders turned their attention to solving the thorny problem of the closed churches. A study of the legal problem, probably prepared by Monsignor Budkiewicz, developed the position which Catholic leaders were taking. The closing of churches, the study argued, was an illegal act, because no such procedure had been provided for in the law, no time limit had been set on the signing of the contracts, and among the closed churches were some that had not as yet given any answer to the question of signing the new contracts. To the archbishop's and the Catholics' protest against the illegality of the action by the Petrograd officials, Krassikov, in charge of religious affairs, declared that the action was completely legal. He declared, the study reported, that the government had closed the churches in order to put pressure on the Apostolic See for an early answer on the matter of the contracts.

[30] *CA*, letter of Archbishop Cieplak to the Papal Relief Mission, December 6, 1922.

[31] Milich, "Protsess . . .," *op. cit.*, pp. 110–111, where the closures and related incidents are described. See also McCullagh, *op. cit.*, pp. 164–167, where the seizures of the churches of the Assumption, St. Casimir, St. Stanislas, St. Catherine, and the Blessed Virgin in Viborg are described. For a list of the chapels closed see *Elenchus cleri et ecclesiarum archidioeceseos Mohiloviensis in Russia in diem 1 Januarii 1926* (Warsaw, 1926), p. 10. See also *CA*, letter of M. Amoudrou, O.P., to the Papal Relief Mission, January 17, 1923.

[32] Milich, "Protsess . . .," *op. cit.*, p. 104. See also *BA*, letter of Monsignor Budkiewicz to Lorenzo Lauri, apostolic nuncio in Warsaw, undated, but after December 5, 1922: "So far divine service has been conducted in private places, at which great crowds of faithful congregate."

The Catholic delegates had presented a formula that would be acceptable to them; but church authorities decided that even this formula should not be signed, for they felt that the Soviet government would present Rome with a *fait accompli.*[33]

Moreover, the Commission for the Defense of Ecclesiastical Property had several times discussed the best means to deal with the sorry business. Some among them felt that Article Seven of the Treaty of Riga established a Polish protectorate over the Catholic Church in Russia, because the church there was overwhelmingly Polish in membership; this protectorate was thought to resemble the one France exercised over the Catholics in the Near East. Poland's rights over the Catholics in Russia might even serve as a base from which to extend her political influence in Russia. However, an inquiry with the members of the Polish Delegation assured the members of the defense commission that this was not the case— that, in fact, the article did not provide any specific protection for Catholics. Nevertheless, the commission decided that in order to protect church property, an appeal would have to be made not only to canon law, on which the clergy had mostly based their position hitherto, but also to Article Seven. The commission decided to demand the return, more especially, of the Theological Academy and the seminary, the churches of St. Petersburg, and churches in its vicinity. Finally, it resolved to open the Catholic schools in Petrograd without seeking the previous consent of the authorities; the authorities were to be merely informed of the fact. The action would be based on an appeal to Article Seven of the treaty.[34]

According to three documents prepared by Monsignor Budkiewicz for the nuncio in Warsaw, the Catholics were to insist upon the illegality of the closing of churches. The reasoning behind this position was that the closing of churches was an arbitrary action by the local authorities in Petrograd and that it was against the laws of the Soviet state. Just at the moment, the monsignor pointed out, the Soviet government was making a great effort to show the world that its work was one of reconstruction; part of this effort was the publication of a code of laws and the establishment of orderly

[33] *BA,* Status questionis iuridicus, undated, but after December 5, 1922.

[34] *BA,* Protokóły komisji obrony i rewindykacji mienia kościelnego przy kurji arcybiskupiej.

juridical procedure. Hence, it was important to impress upon the central Soviet authorities that the closing of churches was a brutal and illegal action and that the impression on the outside world was the worst possible.[35] Moreover, a model of the protest to be sent to the central authorities by the parishioners emphasized that the action violated Soviet law and regulations. According to the instruction for implementing the decree on the separation of Church and State, if no one arrived with the signed contracts to take over the churches, the local Soviet is obliged to announce the fact in the local newspapers three times as well as attach such an announcement to the doors of the churches. Then, if no one came forward in a week, the local authorities were to inform the Commissariat of Public Instruction. The protest pointed out that the parishioners had not been given the prescribed period in which to act and that their failure to present themselves was due to technical reasons beyond their control.[36]

In the third document, the monsignor worked out in detail what he considered the best legal position for the Catholics to take in the whole problem of relations between the Catholic Church and the Soviet government. For negotiations with the government to issue successfully, the monsignor insisted, there must be a thorough knowledge of the details of Soviet law on Church-State relations. In particular, an understanding of three phases of Soviet law was necessary: the articles of the Soviet constitution on the subject of Church-State relations, the decree on the separation of Church and State issued January 23, 1918, and the instruction on the implementation of the decree.

The decree on the separation of Church and State and the other laws dealing with that subject were aimed at, and could only be aimed at, the Orthodox Church, which alone had been united with the government of imperial Russia. The Catholic Church was not

[35] *BA*, La Fermeture des églises catholiques à Petrograd: "Les églises de Petrograd et de ses environs ayant étés illegalement fermées, une plainte contre le comité executif du gouvernement de Petrograd devrait être portée au procoureur par les paroissiens de chaque église en particulière...."

[36] *BA*, Au Procoureur de la Republique au Kremlin: "... nous soussignés, representants la paroisse de l'église catholique de ... à Petrograd, portons plainte contre l'action illegale du comité executif de gouv. de Petrograd et requiérons qu'un ordre soit donné pour l'ouverture immediate des nos églises...."

united in any way with the imperial Russian state, but was in fact regarded as an alien confession and religion. Relations between the Catholic Church and the imperial government had been governed by a concordat with Rome. Once the imperial regime had fallen, the concordat was to be considered abrogated and the formal connection between the Catholics and the regime considered interrupted.

Moreover, the statement goes on to say, this juridical position extends to the material possessions of the Catholic Church in Russia. The decree had proclaimed that the property of all religious or religious associations was the property of the people. This view was based on the popular origin of the goods and properties of the Orthodox Church; these properties and goods could with justice be acclaimed as the property of the Russian people. On the other hand, the property of the Catholic churches and associations could not in any way be classified as Russian in origin, and were rather foreign property and not the national heritage of the Russian people. The literal application of this article of the decree would be an act of brigandage. The special position of the Catholics in Russia demanded special treatment and arrangements.

As to the Russian view that the laws of the State could not be changed just to suit the Catholics' desires, the monsignor suggested that it was the instruction rather than the constitution and the decree which created problems, since both the constitution and the laws left adequate room for an adjustment with the Catholics in Russia.[37]

In spite of the great danger that threatened the Church from external forces, not all was well within the Catholic community either. There were those who found Archbishop Cieplak too timid and weak for his post; some of his own clergy thought so.[38] Councils were confused by the intervention of Archbishop Ropp, who from

[37] BA, Les negotiations avec le gouvernement sovietiste: "L'Eglise Catholique n'a jamais été liée avec l'Etat; ses relations avec le gouvernement russe furent fixées sous le régime impérial par un traité ou concordat conclu entre le gouvernement russe et Le Saint Siège Apostolique, et abrogé par le fait de la chute du régime impérial."

[38] BA, letter of Monsignor Budkiewicz to Archbishop Lauri, undated; see also Jan Ostrowski, Z za Kulis Kurji biskupiej w Leningradzie (Moscow, 1929), pp. 221, 252; letter of John Troigo to Archbishop Ropp, July 1, 1922; letter of Archbishop Ropp to Troigo, no date.

his distant exile in Warsaw tried to give directions to Archbishop Cieplak on what position to take in the matter of church valuables and the signing of contracts. Archbishop Ropp felt, too, that the Treaty of Riga was exceedingly stupid and would not help the Catholics in Russia.[39] Against Archbishop Ropp were arrayed those who felt he was the victim of bad advice.[40] Finally, there were quarrels between the Latin rite priests and the new Russian Catholic clergy of Eastern rite, led by Exarch Fedorov and Father Abrikosov. These squabbles dealt with such things as whether the Julian or Gregorian calendar should be followed; or whether, as Fedorov demanded, all converts in Russia must join the Eastern rite Catholic Church that he headed. To some Latin clergy all this was quite illegal and tainted with fanaticism.[41]

This strife was, of course, a sign of demoralization that was affecting not only the clergy but the laity as well. The clergy voiced dissatisfaction with the moral condition of the laity; others were not too confident about the moral stature of some of the clergy.[42] Nearly as discouraging was the continuing deterioration of ecclesiastical property. For instance, the famed murals of St. Catherine's parish church were in danger of complete ruin; the organ was in disrepair since the failure of the steam heating system in the church.[43] All these seemed to be signs of impending defeat.

Even such measures as closing churches, however, did not break the resistance of the Catholic clergy and their parishioners. They still refused to sign the contracts for the use of the nationalized

[39] *Ostrowski, op. cit.,* pp. 274, 307; letter of Archbishop Ropp to Archbishop Cieplak, 1919; letter of Archbishop Ropp to Archbishop Cieplak, 1921.

[40] Memoir of Father Walerjan Płoskiewicz, unpublished. The original is in the possession of Monsignor Bronislas Ussas, Warsaw.

[41] James J. Zatko, "A Contemporary Report on the Condition of the Catholic Church in Russia, 1922," *The Harvard Theological Review,* LIII (October 1960), 292–293; Ostrowski, *op. cit.,* pp. 228–229; letter of John Troigo to Archbishop Ropp, July 21, 1921.

[42] *BA,* Protokóły komisji obrony i rewindykacji mienia kościelnego przy kurji arcybiskupiej. See also Ostrowski, *op. cit.,* p. 239.

[43] *BA,* report of Monsignor Budkiewicz to the archdiocesan curia, in reply to a communication of October 19, 1922: "At this time the church and the buildings are in lamentable condition. For lack of fuel the church is not being heated; consequently, moisture has developed, and the central steam heating system has been damaged. The roof is in very bad condition . . . in many places water has penetrated around the windows and in some places has ruined the murals. The organ . . . has also been damaged by moisture."

churches. The government, therefore, proceeded to extreme measures. In November 1922, Archbishop Cieplak was served with a statement of charges against him and informed that he would be tried for antigovernment propaganda, inciting Catholics to work for the overthrow of the Bolshevik government, and using religious prejudice to arouse counterrevolution. The trial was set for November 17, 1922, but a delegation of Catholics from Petrograd managed to have it postponed until November 27. Even so, the trial was again postponed in order to extend the accusations as well as the number of persons being charged. The policy of closing churches had provoked resistance by the clergy and their parishioners, who were also to be tried.[44]

Once again, Archbishop Cieplak and Monsignor Budkiewicz turned to the nuncio in Warsaw in hopes that the Vatican would take action. Both men tried to impress on the papal diplomat the urgency of the matter. The archbishop wrote that he had given everything for famine relief, except the church vessels, but even this had not satisfied the government. He pointed out to the nuncio that he had been threatened with prison and that he had reason even to fear for his life, since several members of the Orthodox Church had been executed for "counterrevolutionary" crimes, the very thing with which he was being charged. The monsignor, too, pointed out that the situation had deteriorated and that it would be much more difficult now to solve than had at first appeared.[45]

By December 19, 1922, the archbishop was cheered to learn that the Vatican had assigned or intended to assign Father Walsh to negotiate with the Soviets the settlement of the Catholics' legal problems. The very first of all problems, wrote the archbishop to Father Walsh, was the reopening of churches, for the Catholics were growing weary of the existing situation. If this problem were

[44] McCullagh, *op. cit.*, pp. 112–113; see also Rutkowski, *op. cit.*, pp. 219–222 for details of the persecution.
[45] *BA*, letter of Archbishop Cieplak to the apostolic nuncio in Warsaw, undated: "I am writing what is perhaps my last letter to Your Excellency, for unless I do what is now demanded of me, I shall be jailed and judged by the Revolutionary Tribunal." See *BA*, letter of Monsignor Budkiewicz to the apostolic nuncio in Warsaw, undated: "Moreover, the archbishop and almost all the priests of St. Petersburg have been summoned before the prosecutor, who accuses us of various crimes of 'counterrevolution.'"

solved, then the legal processes rising from the Catholics' resistance might be halted. Moreover, continued opposition by Catholics might so exasperate the government that it might seize all the sacred vessels in the sealed churches. However, if Father Walsh's credentials did not arrive in time, the archbishop inquired whether it might not be possible to sign the contracts in the form presented by the Catholic delegation to Krassikov, but with the changes demanded by the government. The text was, after all, a simple declaration of what the parishioners would do with the churches and of their obligations of maintenance; and the text did not speak of the churches as the property of the State or the people. The pastor of the parish would also be allowed to sign the document with his parochial committee. Finally, this declaration was but a temporary measure, to be suspended or changed after an agreement had been negotiated between the Vatican and the Soviet government.[46]

In the meantime, Archbishop Ropp had written to Archbishop Cieplak, advising him to sign the agreements. Archbishop Ropp felt that the lack of time made it impossible to wait for Rome's permission and that the critical situation of the church demanded immediate action. Indeed, Catholics outside Russia would understand the desperate situation; and Archbishop Lauri, the nuncio, himself would not oppose the action. As a matter of fact, however, the Catholics inside Russia had decided not to sign the new agreements.

While all this correspondence demanding action had been going on, the case against the archbishop and his clergy was being prepared for transmission to Moscow. The archbishop hastened to inform Father Walsh that intervention by the Vatican must come at the latest by January 2, 1923, for the dossier against him was to be forwarded to Moscow on January 3.[47]

By January 16, 1923, the archbishop frankly confessed his uneasiness to Father Walsh, both over the case pending against him and the problem of the closed churches. For his attorney's use he

[46] *CA,* letter of Archbishop Cieplak to the Papal Relief Mission, December 19, 1922.

[47] *CA,* letter of Archbishop Cieplak to the Papal Relief Mission, December 31, 1922.

requested exact information about the Papal Relief Mission's charitable work.[48] Just a few days later the archbishop appeared more cheerful, feeling that perhaps the entire case might be dropped; but Monsignor Budkiewicz did not feel so confident about the matter.[49]

Convinced that a final crisis had arrived, the archbishop wrote a statement about the charges made against him and the clergy and gave it to a Mr. Preston, the British representative in Petrograd. Rejecting all the charges categorically, the archbishop declared that no Catholic counterrevolutionary organization had ever existed, that the conferences held by the clergy were purely private and religious and in no way political, and that both the Catholic priests and the laity were loyal Soviet citizens.[50]

In spite of all his efforts to have the Vatican settle the problem of relations with the Soviets, the archbishop was still waiting for a reply from Rome, as he remarked pointedly in a letter of February 5, 1923, to Father Walsh. The Soviet authorities had refused to have anything to do with the Catholic clergy; hence, all arrangements with the government would have to be made through Father Walsh.[51] At long last, however, and really much too late, the archbishop received a telegram from Father Walsh on February 12, authorizing the signature of the agreements "for the present"—a phrase over which the somewhat hesitant archbishop puzzled, wondering whether the phrase was meant to restrict the agreement to the matter of the closed churches. Since this was hardly a time to dally over such niceties, on February 16 a delegation went to the Smolny to make arrangements with the Petrograd authorities for the "technical" operation of the churches after they were opened.[52] While one phase of the archbishop's problems was at last open to settlement, the other, and personally more dangerous, refused to be

[48] *CA*, letter of Archbishop Cieplak to the Papal Relief Mission, mistakenly dated as December 16, 1923, certainly must be January 16, 1923, for a postscript reads January 17, 1923.
[49] *CA*, letter of Archbishop Cieplak to the Papal Relief Mission, January 20, 1923.
[50] McCullagh, *op. cit.*, pp. 113–114, where the statement is quoted.
[51] *CA*, letter of Archbishop Cieplak to the Papal Relief Mission, February 5, 1923.
[52] *CA*, letter of Archbishop Cieplak to the Papal Relief Mission, February 15, 1923.

solved so easily, as Monsignor Budkiewicz had so wisely remarked.

The question of the case pending against him and his clergy now became more prominent. It was felt that every means had to be used in this now desperate situation. The archbishop felt that an appeal should be made to all the embassies likely to be friendly. Already in December he had suggested approaching the diplomatic representatives of nations who had Catholic nationals in Russia, e.g., German, Lithuanian, and Latvian; he said that the English consul had been most active. He had hoped at the time to present memoranda to all these consulates or embassies, perhaps even to the Italian. Monsignor Budkiewicz felt that the Polish government and the Warsaw Society in Warsaw, composed of distinguished and able Poles, might be most helpful.[53]

All efforts were unavailing. On the night of March 2–3, 1923, all the priests of Petrograd were summoned to appear on March 5, 1923, before the Supreme Revolutionary Tribunal in Moscow. Thither the archbishop and his clergy traveled on March 4, without having had time to settle even the most urgent ecclesiastical or personal business. On their arrival in Moscow, the archbishop and the priests stayed at the parish of Ss. Peter and Paul, where Father Peter Zieliński was the pastor.[54]

As to the Bolshevik motive for this frontal assault on the clergy, Captain Francis McCullagh, an eyewitness to these events, surmised that the driving force was Gregory Zinoviev, who was all-powerful in Petrograd; he was assisted in this by N. B. Krylenko, the public prosecutor of the Supreme Revolutionary Tribunal. Among the leading Bolsheviks, according to the same author, L. B. Kamenev, Leon Trotskii, F. E. Dzierżyński, and N. Bukharin supported Zinoviev and Krylenko, while those Bolsheviks who had to deal with foreigners, and therefore feared the impact on public opinion, e.g., M. I. Kalinin, Maxim Litvinov, George Chicherin, and Leonid Krassin, opposed the trial. McCullagh thought that if Lenin had been well, there would have been no trial.[55]

---

[53] *BA*, letter of Archbishop Cieplak to Monsignor Budkiewicz, December 10, 1922; *BA*, letter of Monsignor Budkiewicz to the apostolic nuncio in Warsaw, undated: "The Warsaw Society, made up of men skilled in political matters and possessing maturity, can help our cause very much."
[54] McCullagh, *op. cit.*, p. 114.   [55] *Ibid.*, p. 117.

However, Father Walsh construed the events somewhat differently. His idea was that the whole attack on the Catholics was a deliberate step on the part of a fanatical left wing group to test whether the same tactics could be applied to other "foreign" religions. Walter Duranty, the *New York Times'* correspondent, misunderstanding events—as did other correspondents in later times —denied that this was so and declared that only a few hotheads entertained such ideas. Christian A. Herter, in the United States Department of Commerce, transmitted a confidential report to the United States Department of State, in which an unknown author felt that Father Walsh had been just a bit too irritated at the time of his statement, that is, after the trial of the clergy, to be very sound. The author of the report, like so many others, looked on the New Economic Policy quite optimistically and tended to construe events in the light of his own optimism.[56]

Whatever the many speculations on this problem, Monsignor Budkiewicz underscored in his letter to the nuncio in Warsaw what was undoubtedly the ultimate motive. From a long experience of Russian government, both the tsarist and the Bolshevik, the monsignor judged well when he said, "Our persecutors use every effort to terrorize us and to subject us to their will." Moreover, from his repeated negotiations with the communists he had developed certain ideas, which he expressed in one of his last letters to the nuncio in Warsaw. "Although the Ministry of Foreign Affairs has informed you that the Soviet government has given up its decision to proceed to trial, you are not to believe their words, but you must demand that whatever is arrived at in discussion, and decided or promised, must be put in writing, because in their conduct of affairs Soviet officials operate with falsehood and delay." Thus many years ago the monsignor who perished at the hands of the Bolsheviks defined

[56] *NAD, RS,* File No. 861.404/124, April 12, 1923, which is an extensive report on conversations with Father Walsh and Walter Duranty. How ill-informed Duranty was is suggested by his statement that the "most eminent of the priests on trial was Monsignor Buchkevisch," in Walter Duranty, *I Write as I Please* (New York, 1935), p. 202. He does not even mention Archbishop Cieplak; however, as a credit to Duranty's honesty, it must be added that he admitted he had mishandled the whole trial, and he had been convinced that it was a merely formal affair.

their conduct in terms of tyranny and duplicity; perhaps he showed only too naive a faith in the written word.[57]

Having thus stated the general motivation behind the Soviet action, Monsignor Budkiewicz saw also another factor entering into the arrest of the Roman Catholic clergy. In a statement prepared for the nuncio in Warsaw, he wrote: "In order to justify in a certain measure the illegal closing of the churches of Petrograd and to inspire fear in the clergy, the Soviet government has organized a political process and placed Archbishop Cieplak and thirteen priests under the threat of an accusation for crimes...." Thus, the desire to justify its acts in public opinion and to terrorize unite in one action.[58]

Whatever the rumors in the ministries of foreign affairs, it was clear that the archbishop and the clergy were going to stand trial. March 14 was set as the trial date. Once more before the trial, on March 9, the security police questioned the archbishop. When asked what his relations with Rome were and whether he had appointed a successor, the archbishop replied that he had not thought it necessary to appoint a successor, since as yet no court had passed sentence on him. In the course of the examination the archbishop declared his friendly feeling for the Russian Catholic Church in Russia and emphasized that both Byzantine and Roman Catholics were members of one church. Questioned about Warsaw, he denied any dependence on Warsaw and affirmed that he owed obedience only to Rome in ecclesiastical matters. He reminded his inquisitors that he had been exiled for two years by the tsarist regime and had already spent two weeks in a communist prison.[59]

[57] *BA*, letter of Monsignor Budkiewicz to the apostolic nuncio in Warsaw, undated: "Persecutores nostri omnem conatum adhibent, ut nos terrore afficiant suoque arbitrio subiiciant.... Quamquam Tibi, Reverendissime, in officio Rerum Externarum dictum est gubernium sovieticum consilium iudicandi abiecisse, non est verbis credendum, sed postulandum ut omnia, ad quae in discussione perventum est et quae statuta vel promissa sunt, in scripto declarentur, quia officiales sovietici omnibus negotiis mendacio et tergiversatione operantur."

[58] *BA*, Le proces du clerge catholique a Petrograd: "Le Gouvernement sovietiste, desireux de justifier dans une certaine mesure la fermeture illegale des églises à Petrograd et de faire peur au clergé. . . ."

[59] *CA*, letter of Archbishop Cieplak to the Papal Relief Mission, March 9, 1923.

In a letter of March 9 he also informed Father Walsh that he and his priests had received a summons to appear before the tribunal to hear the charges lodged against them. The archbishop thanked Father Walsh and through him the pope for their monetary assistance, which, he assured Father Walsh, would be spent to defray the costs of their defense.[60]

On March 10, 1923, the archbishop and his clergy were conveyed through the streets of Moscow in an open truck to appear before the Revolutionary Tribunal.

[60] *Ibid.*

IX

The Trial: Its Significance
and Aftermath

Perhaps no aspect of the Bolshevik regime so reveals its reactionary nature as its judicial procedures. During the very first days of their rule the Bolsheviks rejected the decades of progress made during the tsarist regime after the court reforms of 1864. On November 24, 1917, Decree One on Courts abolished all courts and the office of public prosecutor. To replace the tsarist system of 1864 the Bolsheviks established local courts "elected on a democratic basis" and Worker's and Peasant's Revolutionary Tribunals. These tribunals became the chief instruments in the dispensing of revolutionary justice during the period up to the new criminal code which went into effect in 1924.

These tribunals differed from the dread *Cheka* only by the fact that the hearings were public. There were no provisions to protect the rights of the accused. The tribunals were free to use any measures to combat counterrevolution and sabotage; they were also free to summon witnesses or to admit counsel if they chose to, and they were not bound by any form of judicial procedure.[1] In fact, brute force ruled the proceedings in these tribunals, which acted as

[1] V. Gsovski and K. Grzybowski, *Government, Law and Courts in the Soviet Union and Eastern Europe*, I (New York, 1959), 511–516; for the constitutional structure at this time, see Merle Fainsod, *How Russia is Ruled* (Cambridge, 1954), pp. 291–326, 354–389, a work characterized by the most thorough kind of research and a profound understanding of the Bolshevik system of government.

though there had not been hundreds of years of effort in the creation of systems to provide for justice.

The trial of Archbishop Cieplak and his clergy took place in a former Club of the Nobility, transformed into the House of the Red Labor Unions. The hall selected for the trial was the Blue Room, a large rectangular room with light blue walls and a frieze near the ceiling representing dancing girls and naked cupids. This was hardly a decor suited to the tragedy that was about to occur in this playroom of the old aristocracy.

The clergy summoned before the High Court of the Russian Socialist Federated Soviet Republic were: Archbishop Cieplak (the administrator-archbishop of Mohylew and titular archbishop of Ochrid, Exarch Fedorov (of the Catholic Byzantine rite in Russia), Monsignori Malecki and Budkiewicz, and Fathers Wasilewski, Janukowicz, Ejsmont, Juniewicz, Matulanis, Chwiecko, Troigo, Chodniewicz, Ivanov, Rutkowski, and Pronckietis. Besides the clergy, James Sharnas, a layman and music student at the Petrograd Conservatory, was included in the trial because of his violent attitude during the closing of the churches in Petrograd.[2]

The charges lodged against the prisoners were of the most serious nature. Archbishop Cieplak, Exarch Fedorov, Monsignor Malecki, Monsignor Budkiewicz, Father Wasilewski, Father Janukowicz, Father Ejsmont, Father Juniewicz, Father Matulanis, Father Chwiecko, Father Troigo, Father Chodniewicz, and Father Ivanov were charged with having conspired together to found a counterrevolutionary organization having as its object a revolt against the laws and orders of the Soviet state regulating the relations between Church and State. These crimes were indictable under Articles 63 and 119 of the Criminal Code. Article 63 of the Code provided that all members of any organization which either opposed or utilized the normal functioning of the Soviet institutions and enterprises for counterrevolutionary purposes were liable to the extreme

[2] *OZ*, p. 56, lists the names and addresses of all those indicted; Fathers Baltrushis and Chaevskii had died in the meantime, see p. 58; see also Franciszek Rutkowski, *Arcybiskup Jan Cieplak* (Warsaw, 1934), p. 265. The *New York Times*, March 22, 1923, reported incorrectly that Archbishop Cieplak and *sixteen* priests were put on trial; *Izvestiia*, March 11, 1923, announced the trial of the Catholic clergy.

penalty and the sequestration of property. In case of extenuating circumstances, the penalty might be commuted to five years' solitary confinement and the sequestration of property. However, if the member accused acted in ignorance of the final goal of the organization, he was to be punished by a three years' minimum term. Article 119 provided for punishment by solitary confinement for a minimum of three years to anyone who utilized the religious prejudices of the masses in order to plot against the government or to instigate opposition to the decrees of the Soviet government. In time of war or popular risings, these crimes could be punished by the ultimate penalty.[3]

Archbishop Cieplak was further charged with participation in civil disorders, which constituted a definite act of disobedience to the legal demands of the civil authorities, and with hindering the authorities in the fulfillment of their official duties. The basis for these charges was the archbishop's circular of January 23, 1922, in which he protested against the illegal seizures of church valuables, along with his telegram to Father Rutkowski, declaring the government's demands illegal. This "crime" against Article 77 of the Code was punishable in the case of agitators, leaders and organizers by a minimum term of two years' solitary confinement; other convicted persons were to be punished by an imprisonment for a minimum six months' term.[4]

Father Chodniewicz was also accused specifically of using the religious superstitions of the masses to instigate resistance against the government; hence he was also specifically indicted under Article 119 of the Code.[5]

Father Juniewicz, having resisted the seizure of church valuables, was likewise accused individually under Article 62, which fell upon all members of any organization that attempted to incite the popula-

---

[3] *OZ*, pp. 52–55, gives a detailed statement of the charges. See *Pravda*, March 22, 23, 1923; *Izvestiia*, March 22, 23, 1923. See also Francis McCullagh, *The Bolshevik Persecution of Christianity* (New York, 1924), pp. 169–170; Rutkowski, *op. cit.*, p. 224.

[4] *OZ*, pp. 52–53; *Pravda*, March 22, 1923; *Izvestiia*, March 22, 23, 1923; *KW*, March 22, 1923; McCullagh, *op. cit.*, pp. 169–170; Rutkowski, *op. cit.*, pp. 230–231.

[5] *OZ*, pp. 54, 56; *Pravda*, March 22, 1923; *Izvestiia*, March 22, 23, 1923; McCullagh, *op. cit.*, pp. 170–171, 357.

tion to insurrection, to induce the people to refuse to pay taxes or perform their duties as citizens, or that by any means whatsoever attacked the dictatorship of the proletariat.[6]

Finally, Fathers Rutkowski and Pronckietis were charged with offenses indictable under Article 119 of the Code, namely, for resisting the seizure of church valuables. James Sharnas, the only layman in the groups, was indicted under Article 77, paragraph 2, which makes a nonleader liable to a minimum term of six months.[7]

While the Criminal Code and the articles involved in the indictment seem almost gauged to the trial of the Roman Catholic clergy in Russia, the whole court process against the Catholics, according to the report of F. W. B. Coleman, of the American legation in Riga, justified the structure of the revolutionary courts in Bolshevik Russia. N. V. Krylenko, according to Coleman, candidly admitted that the courts were designed to protect the rights of the toiling masses and to defend the dictatorship of the proletariat; moreover, if this required the courts to trample on the rights of the other classes, the courts would not hesitate to do so. Coleman, pointing to a significant element in the judicial system, called attention to the fact that the appeal from the courts was an appeal to political bodies, that is, from the Provincial Court to the Provincial Executive Committee, and from the Supreme Court to the All-Russian Central Executive Committee. Subsequently, wrote Coleman, the trial of the Roman Catholic clergy had fully justified the confidence of the government in the new courts, for the conduct of the case by Krylenko presented the court with a ready-made verdict.[8]

The cast of characters, in addition to the prisoners, included the judges. The chief judge was A. V. Galkin, a man of about forty-five, who had already distinguished himself as a person full of hatred for religion. His colleagues on the bench were Nemtsov, a workman judge, and Chelyshev, supposedly a peasant judge. These judges did not maintain the impartiality which is associated with the task

[6] *OZ*, pp. 53, 56; *Pravda*, March 22, 1923; *Izvestiia*, March 22, 23, 1923; McCullagh, *op. cit.*, pp. 171, 356.

[7] *OZ*, pp. 54, 56; *Pravda*, March 22, 1923; *Izvestiia*, March 22, 23, 1923; McCullagh, *op. cit.*, pp. 171, 356.

[8] *NAD, RS*, File No. 861.404/123, April 13, 1923. A group of Polish communists added an element of betrayal by meeting to vote anti-Cieplak resolutions, *Izvestiia*, March 28, 1923, and *Pravda*, March 21, 1923.

of a judge, but intervened to assist the prosecution when the need arose.

The prosecutor was N. V. Krylenko, whose conduct is described by Captain McCullagh as violent and overbearing.

The chief defense attorney was Bobrishchev-Pushkin, a very distinguished lawyer of the old regime, with a reputation for fearlessness, integrity, and ability; but he was unable to cope with the vagaries of a revolutionary tribunal that disregarded traditional rules of court conduct and evidence. Captain McCullagh characterized his conduct of the case as apologetic and mild, but perhaps this was the wiser manner in which to handle witnesses of the prosecution. Bobrishchev-Pushkin was ably seconded by a young and courageous lawyer, Kommodov, who had been arrested when a few weeks before the trial he had gone to Petrograd to see the archbishop.[9]

The witnesses for the prosecution were Petrograd officials: Miss Sapunova, the secretary of the Basil Island Executive Committee; Comrade Smirnov, the administrative director of the Moscow-Narva district in Petrograd; Kolesnikov, the representative of the Commission for the Requisition of Church Valuables; Koenig, the president of the church board in the Moscow-Narva district; and finally a Guedix.[10]

On Wednesday, March 21, 1923, the great trial opened. Judge Galkin declared the court of the Supreme Tribunal to be open, and the prosecutor, Krylenko, proceeded. The burden of his opening questions was the decree on the seizure of the church valuables for famine relief. The priests' answers to these questions all had the same tenor: like Father Rutkowski who was questioned by Krylenko, they delared that they had no right to allow the government to conduct inventories of the church valuables. Monsignor Malecki, frank and without guile, confounded the prosecutor when describing the treasures in his private room—a bed, priedieu, table, crucifix, and a portable altar, presumably used to help serve the poorest of

---

[9] McCullagh, *op. cit.*, pp. 142–143, who is a little too severe on the defense attorneys; after all, they had an extremely difficult, if not impossible, task; Rutkowski, *op. cit.*, pp. 229–230, also gives a description of the judges. On the low level of education among the judiciary, see Gsovski, *op. cit.*, p. 517.

[10] *OZ*, pp. 56–57, lists seventeen witnesses; McCullagh, *op. cit.*, p. 176, mistakenly gives one witness' name as Sapinova, but the correct form is Rykunova, as given in the *OZ*, and in Rutkowski, *op. cit.*, p. 243.

the poor. To the prosecutor's questions about religious instruction being given to persons under eighteen years of age, the priests answered that they had instructed such persons and would continue to do so, appealing to a higher law than the Soviet law—a position which the prosecutor found intolerable, and which he condemned by saying that there was to be no discussion of the law, but simply obedience to the Soviet law. Finally, on this first day of the trial, a great to-do was made of the "resistance" offered the government officials when they came to seize the church valuables or to close the Catholic churches in Petrograd in connection with their program. Father Rutkowski, who was accused of "demonstratively" falling on his knees when the militia entered the church of the Assumption, declared that inasmuch as he was unable to prevent the seizure, he fell to praying; Krylenko solemnly proclaimed in the court, "That was a counterrevolutionary act." The interrogation of the first day ended on a solemn note, as the prosecutor declaimed to the accused that they must make a choice between the laws of the Soviet republic and that "other" law; to this a young priest, unidentified by name, declared that in a conflict between the two laws, he would ever follow the law of God and the Church.[11]

The second day of the trial was spent in further cross-examination of the prisoners with regard to the decree of the separation of Church and State—more specifically the conferences held by the clergy with a view to making the decree more acceptable to the Catholics in Russia. The reports in *Izvestiia* and the *Pravda* of March 22, 1923, make clear the construction that the government tried to impose on the conduct of the Catholic clergy during those years. Insisting that their conduct was political rather than purely religious, the prosecution declared that the Roman Catholic clergy in its conference went beyond religious propaganda and even agitation against the Soviet state and had established a formally religious but actually political organization with numerous branches, whose object was to resist the enforcement of the decree on separation of

[11] *Izvestiia*, March 24, 1923; *NAD, RS*, File No. 861.041/19, April 13, 1923, Enclosure No. 9; McCullagh, *op. cit.*, pp. 175–188, where the whole chapter is devoted to the first day; Rutkowski, *op. cit.*, pp. 228–266, describes the whole trial in one chapter, and since he himself was on trial, his testimony is especially valuable, but he concentrates almost exclusively on Archbishop Cieplak. See also *KW*, March 22, 1923.

Church and State. That the archdiocesan central committee and the local committees had been spoken of as organized to last until a strong legal order was established in Russia, was construed as "until the overthrow of the Soviet power." Furthermore, the open "resistance" in connection with the enforcement of the decree of February 23, 1922, concerning the confiscation of church valuables, clearly illustrated the open resistance to the orders of the Soviet government. The disclosure of the various details in the "criminal" activities constituted the substance of the judicial investigation, according to the report.[12]

On the third day of the trial, March 23, 1923, Krylenko resumed an extensive interrogation of Archbishop Cieplak, whom he had begun to examine very late at night on the previous day. In questioning the archbishop, Krylenko used the following documents: the archbishop's circular letter of January 3, 1922; the archbishop's circular of March 20, 1922, appealing to parents to teach their children religion; a letter of Archbishop Ropp dealing with the question of church goods and with the problem of entering into agreements with the Soviet government (a letter which illustrated the position of Archbishop Ropp, who was actually opposed by his fellow-priests in Russia, e.g., Monsignor Budkiewicz, etc., as to the policy he followed); a letter of Archbishop Cieplak, dated September 12, 1919, declaring that church property belongs to the church; a few private letters; the "minutes" of the clerical conferences held from 1918–1920; and several notes by Monsignor Budkiewicz to the effect that the baptismal registers as well as marriage and burial records should not be handed over to the government. Besides two reports by Monsignor Budkiewicz—one about signing the agreements for use of the Catholic churches and the other containing some historical notes about the separation of Church and State—and a few private letters, there was a telegram of congratulations to the Regency Council in Warsaw, dated July 18, 1918.[13] That this telegram was

[12] *OZ*, pp. 54–55; *Izvestiia*, March 22, 23, 1923, and *Pravda*, March 22, 23, 1923.

[13] Monsignor Budkiewicz's survey on the separation of Church and State in Bolshevik Russia is reproduced in the *OZ*, pp. 11–13; for examples of the correspondence between Monsignor Budkiewicz and the nuncio, Archbishop Lauri, in Warsaw, see James J. Zatko, "The Letters of Archbishop Lauri, Apostolic Nuncio in Warsaw, to Monsignor Constantine Budkiewicz of St.

included in the documents certainly served as a warning of what was in store.

After the archbishop admitted that he had sent the circular on the church property, and after defending his action as a religious one, Krylenko's questions took a turn that was ominous, for he began attempting to connect the archbishop with Poland, thus hoping to identify the Catholic clergy on trial with Polish political questions; how dangerous this was, the event proved. But Krylenko failed to make much headway with the archbishop. Hoping to entrap the archbishop in a falsehood, he demanded knowing whether the archbishop in any way depended on Warsaw; when this was denied, Krylenko produced a letter addressed to the archbishop and written by Monsignor Lorenzo Lauri, apostolic nuncio at Warsaw. After the archbishop admitted the authenticity of the letter, Krylenko triumphantly pointed to the letter, reading "the Polish Nunciature, Warsaw." Quickly but courteously the archbishop corrected him, indicating that the correct reading was "Apostolic" and not "Polish." Since Krylenko felt, then, that he had lost this point, he tried to establish the manner in which the archbishop corresponded with the nuncio; but the archbishop declared that he had written directly to the pope, and that the answer had come through the nuncio in Warsaw, for reasons unknown to the archbishop. As to the manner of communicating with Rome, the archbishop testified that he had sent his letter through a private channel with the permission of Peter Krassikov, the head of the religious affairs department in the Comissariat of Justice. Sometimes, added the archbishop, he sent his letters by ordinary post, a comment that provoked much merriment from the prosecutor, who, undoubtedly, felt that very little mail going through the ordinary post could escape the inspection of the Bolshevik authorities or agents.[14]

Catherine's, St. Petersburg, 1922–1923," *The Polish Review,* IV (1959), 127–131; Zatko, "A Contemporary Report on the Catholic Church in Russia, 1922," *The Harvard Theological Review,* LIII (October 1960), 277–295. Other correspondence is cited throughout the present work; this correspondence was used as evidence in the trial. See furthermore, McCullagh, *op. cit.,* p. 199; Rutkowski, *op. cit.,* pp. 235–236.

[14] *KW,* March 24, 25, 1923, as well as *Izvestiia,* March 24, 1923; *NAD, RS,* File No. 861.041/19, April 13, 1923, Enclosure No. 9; McCullagh, *op. cit.,* pp. 196–198; Rutkowski, *op. cit.,* pp. 246–248.

During further cross-examination, the archbishop emphasized his duty of teaching religion to children, while Krylenko insisted that teaching religion to the ignorant was terrorization, a definitely political act. To Krylenko's further inquiry as to why the archbishop opposed the committees of twenty which were to take over church property, the archbishop declared first that the "twenties" were not chosen from the believers and that they violated the rights of the Catholics and of the pastor, as the proper executors of canonical law. These "twenties," according to the archbishop, destroyed the unity of the Church, just as they had effectively destroyed the unity of the Orthodox Church.[15]

The afternoon of the third day of trial was spent in cross-examining Monsignor Budkiewicz, and in the course of the questioning it gradually became clear in what direction the prosecutor was moving. Indeed, the matter of relations with Poland was not even mentioned in the statement of charges, but in Monsignor Budkiewicz's examination this element moved to the fore of the trial. After trying to show from the letters of Archbishop Ropp, who was not on trial, that the monsignor had advocated a policy of resistance— a statement that the monsignor explained, saying that he meant legal resistance by presenting petitions—the prosecutor further attempted to prove that the prisoner had shown pro-Polish tendencies and had followed a pro-Polish policy in his conduct. Thus, the ill-fated telegram of congratulations sent to the Polish government was presented by Krylenko as proof of criminal communication with a foreign government.[16]

Furthermore, the prosecutor tried to establish that Monsignor Budkiewicz's opposition to the signing of the agreements, which the monsignor characterized as fictitious, and the monsignor's policy of resistance were really an organized plan to oppose the direct orders of the government. This the monsignor vigorously denied, insisting that his whole program consisted of trying to find a *modus vivendi* that would be acceptable from the religious and canonical viewpoint. Krylenko, then, returned once more to the question of

[15] Rutkowski, *op. cit.*, pp. 242–243; McCullagh, *op. cit.*, p. 202.
[16] *Izvestiia*, March 25, 1923; *Pravda*, March 25, 1923; *NAD, RS*, File No. 861.041/19, April 13, 1923, Enclosure No. 10; McCullagh, *op. cit.*, pp. 206–208.

relations with the Polish government, more especially to alleged efforts of the monsignor to get a letter of protection for his church from the Danish Red Cross and from the Polish Mission in Moscow. Moreover, Monsignor Budkiewicz's draft of a letter to a member of the Polish Mission in Moscow—a letter that the monsignor denied he actually sent—was used against him. In this letter the monsignor suggested that the Polish government guarantee a loan in the amount of 400,000 rubles which the church of St. Catherine had had to borrow. This was interpreted as an illegal communication with the agents of a foreign government.[17]

On this note the third day of trial ended. Once again, it was the Soviet press that published the official interpretation of the significant aspects of the trial. In reference to Archbishop Cieplak's inquiry to Rome about the church property agreements, Krylenko reportedly asked the archbishop whether he had made inquiries with the Polish government about the agreements; the paper represented the archbishop as giving a hesitant answer, though, of course, the paper did not report Krylenko's mistake in reading "Polish" for "Apostolic." The newspaper report in *Izvestiia*, March 24, 1923, declared that "it became obvious that in addition to maintenance of communications with the Vatican and Poland through official channels (the People's Commissariat of Foreign Affairs), Cieplak also had private channels, which fact he was compelled to admit." Moreover, the paper promised that the judicial investigation would disclose all the details of the underground network of the Catholic clergy during the period 1918–1922.[18]

Izvestiia of March 25, 1923, reported on the cross-examination of both the archbishop and Monsignor Budkiewicz. Significant were the statements made in the report about Monsignor Budkiewicz's contact with the Polish government. Pointing out that the Monsignor was a Russian citizen, the report declared that he had approached the Polish government with a request to take steps towards the return of the confiscated houses, churches, and confiscated church property generally. The ill-omened telegram, too,

---

[17] McCullagh, *op. cit.*, pp. 212–213, where the letter is reproduced.
[18] *Izvestiia*, March 24, 1923, where the report speaks of Archbishop Lauri as Archbishop Lawrence. See also *NAD, RS*, File No. 861.041/19, April 13, 1923, Enclosure No. 9.

was referred to as expressing the patriotic feeling of the Poles in Moscow—a telegram signed by Monsignor Budkiewicz, who was, as the paper pointed out again, a Russian citizen.[19]

The fourth day of the trial opened with a most important statement from Archbishop Cieplak to the effect that he had received information sometime ago that the Vatican had given its permission for the signing of agreements in a form communicated to Vorovskii, the Soviet representative in Rome, with whom the Vatican had negotiated indirectly. The archbishop had communicated this information to the Petrograd Executive Committee; inasmuch as this had been done three weeks before the trial, that aspect of the conflict between the Catholics and the Soviet government could be considered solved. Father Walsh, head of the papal relief mission, had received no less than three letters from Krassikov, discussing the permission to sign—which had been granted by the Vatican in a telegram from Cardinal Gasparri. After Father Walsh had shown this telegram to Krassikov, he suggested that Father Walsh proceed to Petrograd to inform the archbishop; but at Petrograd the local Soviet apparently did not now want the archbishop to sign, much to Father Walsh's surprise. All this took place three or four weeks before the trial.

After this statement to the court by the archbishop, the court inquired of Krassikov's department whether the Commissariat of Justice knew anything about the Vatican's action; to this Krassikov blandly replied, in the evening, that the commissariat knew nothing about this matter "officially." Consequently, Krylenko refused to take cognizance of the event, and it was ignored by the court during the remainder of the trial.[20]

The attitude of the prosecution on this matter was revealed by Krylenko when he declared that from the statement of the archbishop it might be thought that that phase of the question was closed; and, indeed, according to Krylenko, from the viewpoint of the accused it did close it, for they explained their resistance by an

[19] *Izvestiia*, March 25, 1923; *Pravda*, March 25, 1923; *NAD*, *RS*, File No. 861.041/19, April 13, 1923, Enclosure No. 10.
[20] *NAD*, *RS*, File No. 861.041/19, April 19, 1923, Enclosure No. 10; N. V. Krylenko, *Sudebnye rechi, 1922–1930* (Moscow, 1931), p. 3; McCullagh, *op. cit.*, pp. 215–217.

appeal to the canons of their church. Nevertheless, the object of the prosecution, remarked Krylenko with some wit, was not to study canon law, but to examine the activities of the accused, to determine whether they violated the laws of the Soviet government, and to fix the responsibility for the violations; hence, the prosecution could not consider any canons or dogmas which had not been confirmed by the Soviet government.[21]

On this day of the trial, Exarch Fedorov was also extensively examined as to a memorandum he had written on Church-State relations. Exarch Fedorov acquitted himself ably, pointing out that Archbishop Ropp and he had been invited by the fifth section of the Commissariat of Justice to co-operate in drawing up a plan for the application of the decree of separation of Church and State; they had been assured that no explanations or regulations would be issued without their co-operation, but this promise was broken by the appearance of the August instruction on the decree. As to the seizure of the church valuables, he declared that he protested their seizure only because he did not have the authority to dispose of them; for his own part, he felt that the valuables should have been handed over for famine relief, but he also demanded that there should be no sacrilegious violation of churches.[22]

According to Captain McCullagh, the court resumed its sitting at 6:00 P.M., after an interval of three hours; the resumption was signalized by activity on the platform which provided the stage for the trial, on which the judges, lawyers, prisoners and witnesses were clearly visible. Two women, official court stenographers, took their places in order to record the speeches of the prosecuting attorney, the defense lawyers, and the prisoners, who were to plead for their lives and liberty. The president of the court, Galkin, declared that the arguments of the case were concluded and that the prosecutor, Krylenko, had the ear and attention of the court.

[21] *Izvestiia*, March 25, 1923; *Pravda*, March 25, 1923. The entire text of Krylenko's speech can be found in Krylenko, *op. cit.* See also *NAD, RS,* File No. 861.041/19, April 13, 1923, Enclosure No. 10.

[22] *OZ*, pp. 49–51, where the evidence against Fedorov is stated and Fedorov's answers are made to P. Lopatinskii, the investigator. Among other things, Fedorov reports that Krassikov had told him that the Soviets expected to model their separation of Church and State on the system used in the United States (p. 50). See also McCullagh, *op. cit.*, pp. 218–220.

Krylenko, beginning a two-hour speech at 6:10 P.M., rejected any effort to eliminate from the trial the problem of signing agreements with the Catholics in the light of the Vatican's consent. To emphasize the reactionary character of the Church and the clergy as well as to support his position on the counterrevolutionary attitude of the clergy, Krylenko referred to the Soviet constitution which disfranchised clergy and religious together with the former exploiting classes. Pointing out that no religious organization had any political rights or legal status in the republic, he declared that he spat on the religion of the prisoners, as he did on all religions—Orthodox, Mohammedan, Jewish, Lutheran, and all the rest. The church organization was designed to influence the minds of men and thus reduce them to spiritual slavery; it is, therefore, and always was, a powerful instrument for the enslavement of the masses.

As to the conduct of the priests, they claimed that the pope controlled all the church property, but, according to Krylenko, their conduct proved that they owned the property. Moreover, their resistance to government decrees could not be construed as purely religious, for it was clearly political, in object as well as in method. They belonged to a political organization, whose object was political action, i.e., resistance to government orders. Archbishop Cieplak resisted the operation of the law, as his circular proved; Monsignor Budkiewicz had even approached the Polish government not only for guarantees, but to express his fidelity. The clergy, therefore, had created an organization outside the State and opposed to the State. Archbishop Cieplak was the guiding intelligence of this organization and Monsignor Budkiewicz its actual leader, its organizer, and the agent of a foreign state, Poland.

Krylenko then proceeded to demand the supreme penalty for Archbishop Cieplak and for Monsignor Budkiewicz as the leaders of a counterrevolutionary organization. He also demanded the death penalty for Fathers Ejsmont and Chwiecko, as confirmed enemies of the Soviet government, who declared openly that they had broken the law and would continue to do so. The punishment of Fathers Chodniewicz and Juniewicz he left to the discretion of the court; it might be possible, he thought, to give them only ten years' imprisonment. Exarch Fedorov was considered worthy of ten years in

prison, whereas Monsignor Malecki and Fathers Wasilewski, Troigo, Matulanis, Janukowicz, and Ivanov were to receive five years. Fathers Rutkowski and Pronckietis were to be punished to the extent of three years. The lone layman, James Sharnas, who was under age, was to get a sentence of no more than six months.[23]

After the loud applause that had greeted the speech of Krylenko, the defense attorneys had their opportunity to speak, as did Exarch Fedorov, who was conducting his own defense. Kommodov emphasized the purely religious mentality of the clergy and their training in obedience; to require them to change quickly was to demand the superhuman. Since all the leading Catholic clergy approved the decree separating Church and State, he defended the clerical conferences by denying that the priests had any counterrevolutionary character. Moreover, they would all have signed the agreements, if only they had the permission of the Vatican. This certainly was not counterrevolution.[24]

Such was the import of the argument by the defense counsel, Kommodov. His colleague, Bobrishchev-Pushkin, followed the same line of argument, pointing out that the actions of the accused did not constitute counterrevolution. To prove counterrevolution the prosecution had to show that the prisoners were animated by a set purpose to overthrow the Soviet government. The second thesis of the defense attorney, Bobrishchev-Pushkin, as McCullagh notices, was that the actions imputed to the accused were merely individual violations of the government's decrees or administrative orders, but not part of a general conspiracy against the government. He also protested against the death sentence that the prosecution had demanded, for it was much too severe; he urged that the accused should be sentenced to deportation.[25]

[23] Krylenko, *op. cit.*, pp. 3–24. *Izvestiia,* March 25, 1923, and *Pravda,* March 25, 1923, omit the crude outburst about spitting on all religions, and report that only for Archbishop Cieplak and Monsignor Budkiewicz did Krylenko demand the death penalty. The texts in McCullagh, *op. cit.*, p. 232, and Krylenko, *op. cit.*, p. 23, show that he demanded it also for Fathers Ejsmont and Chwiecko.

[24] *NAD, RS,* File No. 861.041/19, April 13, 1923, Enclosure No. 11; *Izvestiia,* March 27, 1923.

[25] *NAD, RS,* File No. 861.041/19, April 13, 1923, Enclosure No. 11; *Izvestiia,* March 27, 1923; Rutkowski, *op. cit.*, pp. 254–257; McCullagh, *op. cit.*, pp. 234–237. Rutkowski considers Bobrishchev-Pushkin's speech convincing (p. 254), whereas McCullagh felt it was weak (p. 235).

Captain McCullagh thought that the appeal by Bobrishchev-Pushkin was feeble; but perhaps the attorney felt that the best he could do was save the lives of the men who were in danger of the death penalty and so concentrated his effort on this objective. Undoubtedly, the distinguished St. Petersburg lawyer knew his court and his opponents. Besides this, he had to endure the sneers of Krylenko as well as Krylenko's attempts to distract the court from the pleas which he was making for the accused.

After the speeches by the defense attorneys, Krylenko had his opportunity to reply; this he did by repeating with even greater bitterness the charges of counterrevolution and conspiracy compounded with crimes against the law and government.[26] One more speech for the defense remained after Krylenko's bitter discourse—the address by Exarch Fedorov, who was conducting his own defense. The exarch spoke with great dignity and conviction. His whole life, he said, had been governed by two principles, love for his church and love for his country. His work had been directed to convincing the Russian government that Russian Catholics were as loyal as other Russians. In tsarist times Catholicism brought upon them, the Russian Catholics, persecution and exile; hence, all Catholics in Russia breathed a sigh of relief when the October revolution came, but the Russian Catholics especially felt happy for it was only the Soviet regime that placed the "Greek Catholic" Church on a footing of equality with the others. When the Soviet government issued the decree of separation of Church and State, the Catholics received the news with joy; if more attention had been paid to the views of Catholics in this question after the issuance of the decree, the exarch declared, they would not now be prisoners on trial before the court, some of them for their lives.

Denying that there was any secret organization and saying that even the Provisional Government referred the affairs of the Catholics to the Department of Foreign Religions, Exarch Fedorov emphasized the terrible conflict imposed on Catholics by the laws of the Soviet republic, which required them to act against their most

[26] Krylenko, *op. cit.*, pp. 24–34; *Izvestiia*, March 27, 1923; McCullagh, *op. cit.*, pp. 237–238; Rutkowski, *op. cit.*, pp. 257–258; *NAD, RS*, File No. 861.041/19, April 13, 1923, Enclosure No. 11.

sacred convictions, for instance, against their duty to teach children religion and the law of God.[27]

This day of the trial ended with another speech by Krylenko, in which he rejected all the arguments of the defense and renewed the charges of counterrevolution and conspiracy. As to the possibility of deportation, this he said was but to throw the fish back into the water. With a greater irony than he knew he told the accused that they had now to carry their cross.[28] The defense again made brief statements on their position, and so the case rested for the day.

The last day of the trial, March 25, 1923, fell on Palm Sunday, thus adding a dramatic touch to the events for those who perceived in the trial an analogy to another, and more famous, trial. On this last day, the prisoners were allowed to make their statements or reaffirm their testimony, and they did so with great dignity. Archbishop Cieplak, declaring that he and his fellow Catholics welcomed the October revolution with joy, denied for himself and for his companions that they had formed any secret conspiratorial or counterrevolutionary organization. Expressing his realization that he might soon stand before the judgment seat of God, he hoped that the earthly tribunal before which he stood would show him justice, as surely as he trusted that his heavenly Judge would show him mercy.[29]

Monsignor Budkiewicz, too, expressed himself with gravity and distinction, denying that he had had any political objective in his conduct toward the Soviet government and its decrees. He, too, denied that he was plotting against the government, but asserted that he had opposed the signature of fictitious agreements in hopes that a real settlement might be made with the Soviet government, a settlement which would not violate the basic principles of the

[27] The *New York Times*, March 26, 1923; McCullagh, *op. cit.*, pp. 238–241. For a survey of the life of Fedorov see Paul Mailleux, "The Catholic Church in Russia and the Exarch Fedorov," *Religion in Russia: A Collection of Essays Read at the Cambridge Summer School of Russian Studies* (London, 1940), p. 45.

[28] McCullagh, *op. cit.*, pp. 243–246.

[29] *NAD, RS*, File No. 861.041/19, April 13, 1923, Enclosure No. 11; *Izvestiia*, March 27, 1923; McCullagh, *op. cit.*, pp. 254–255; Rutkowski, *op. cit.*, pp. 259–260.

Catholic Church. This would require time and energetic action together with negotiations between the Vatican and the Soviet government. He insisted, too, that he could not sign without the consent of the Vatican, for to a Catholic excommunication is not a meaningless weapon.[30]

The other prisoners, too, made their statements to the court in the same vein; but when Krylenko concluded the proceedings, not a dent had been made in his position for he still demanded the same penalties for the prisoners. When the summations came to an end at 4:00 P.M., the court withdrew to consider the fate of the prisoners, among whom was the head of the Roman Catholics in Russia. It was, indeed, a fateful hour for the Catholic Church in Russia.

At the stroke of midnight, the prisoners began to file out onto the stage; in a minute or so, the judges followed. The president of the court, Galkin, indicated that Nemtsov, his fellow judge, was to read the long sentence which the court imposed: Archbishop Cieplak and Monsignor Budkiewicz were found guilty of being with full intent and purpose the leaders of counterrevolutionary conspiracy; of organizing the Roman Catholic clergy in Petrograd for resistance to the Soviet government; of undermining the dictatorship of the proletariat; of attempting to re-establish the Church's former rights of property; and of inciting the body of citizens to active resistance to the Soviet government. They were therefore sentenced to be shot.

Fathers Ejsmont, Juniewicz, Chwiecko, Chodniewicz, and Exarch Fedorov were found guilty of active participation in the counterrevolutionary organization; they were, therefore, condemned to imprisonment for a term of ten years with strict solitary confinement and the deprivation of civil rights.

Monsignor Malecki and Fathers Wasilewski, Janukowicz, Matulanis, Troigo, Ivanov, Rutkowski, and Pronckietis were found guilty of acting as accomplices in the crimes of Archbishop Cieplak and Monsignor Budkiewicz; hence, they were sentenced to imprisonment for a term of three years without strict solitary confinement, but with the deprivation of civil rights. The young layman, James

[30] *NAD, RS,* File No. 861.041/19, April 13, 1923, Enclosure No. 11; *Izvestiia,* March 27, 1923; *KW,* March 27, 1923; McCullagh, *op. cit.,* pp. 257–261; Rutkowski, *op. cit.,* p. 260.

Sharnas, found guilty of insulting behavior toward the Soviet authorities, was sentenced to six months' imprisonment conditionally, and with deprivation of civil rights.[31]

With this the tragedy and travesty of justice were over. A few of the Polish Catholic women present in the court uttered cries of anguish and fell upon their knees; other Polish women fell to the floor in hysterics. The prisoners still stood upon the platform where they had undergone their hour of humiliation as well as their hour of glory, for, indeed, none could ever again achieve the greatness they had reached, except by going through the selfsame ordeal again. The archbishop had turned towards the women and raised his hand in blessing—"Benedicat vos omnipotens Deus"—but the soldiers closed in on the prisoners and hurried them from the court. In a few moments a truck arrived, and the prisoners were thus conveyed to that house of horrors, the Butyrka prison.[32]

An analysis of the proceedings once again reveals the profoundly reactionary nature of the regime. The government was obsessed with an almost hysterical fear of revolutions: the slightest criticism or question was seen as a threat to the permanence of the government; the parochial committees, whose minds were full of worry rather than plots, were looked upon as conspiratorial revolutionary organizations. The Bolsheviks persisted in viewing religion as a supporter of the old regime; however, the Catholics who had suffered so much from the tsarist regime for almost a century and a half could hardly be accused of wishing to restore that system of government. Moreover, the Catholics were but a tiny minority in the Russian sea and it does not seem likely that they posed so serious a threat to the regime.

The execution of the sentence by the Bolshevik court against Archbishop Cieplak and Monsignor Budkiewicz, certain to provoke a world-wide reaction, was postponed until reviewed by the president

[31] *NAD, RS*, File No. 861.041/19, April 23, 1923, Enclosure No. 11; *Izvestiia*, March 27, 1923; *Pravda*, March 27, 1923; McCullagh, *op. cit.*, pp. 364–365, who errs, however, in saying that Chelyshev read the sentence (p. 275); Rutkowski, who was on trial, says that Nemtsov read the sentence (p. 266); *KW*, March 26, 1923; *New York Times*, March 27, 1923. X. J. Eudin and H.H. Fisher, *Soviet Russia and the West, 1920–1927* (Stanford, 1957), p. 227, mistakenly place the trial in July 1922; see also Edmund Walsh, *The Last Stand* (Boston, 1931), pp. 183–184.
[32] McCullagh, *op. cit.*, pp. 275–276.

of the Central Executive Committee.[33] This allowed time for diplomatic action. Without doubt, the external party most interested in the outcome of the trial was the Vatican itself, where for weeks intense efforts were being made by the papal secretariat of state, under the direction of Cardinal Gasparri, to prevent the trial, or, failing that, to insure its safe outcome for the prisoners. While it is sometimes asserted that the Vatican made use of the influence of other powers,[34] the *Osservatore Romano* of March 28, 1923, declared that in the matter of the trial of the Roman Catholic clergy, the Holy See preferred to act on its own, separately from the action of the powers, treating the matter as a simple defense of the hierarchy, in the same manner as it had in the case of Archbishop Ropp, whom it was able to free as a subject of the pope, in 1919.[35]

While Father Walsh tried to deal with the Soviet government in Moscow, Cardinal Gasparri undertook to negotiate with the Soviet state through its representative in Rome, Vorovskii. Cardinal Gasparri, somewhat naively, allowed Vorovskii to convince him that no mortal danger really threatened the prisoners; the papal secretary of state believed that the Soviet government merely wished to expel a few of the priests from Russia, thus further disorganizing the Catholic Church there. He, therefore, followed a policy aimed at keeping the Roman Catholic clergy in Russia on the same basis as that before the trial. Thus, while the cardinal directed his action toward this goal, the Soviet government was actually following a policy of complete destruction.[36]

In mid-March, the cardinal took the very unusual step of meeting personally with the Soviet representative, with whom he had until then negotiated through Monsignor Pizzardo. In his conversation with Vorovskii, the secretary of state impressed upon him that

[33] *NAD, RS,* File No. 861.041/19, April 13, 1923, Enclosure No. 12; *Izvestiia,* March 27, 1923; *Pravda,* March 27, 1923.

[34] Rutkowski, *op. cit.,* pp. 267–268.

[35] *OR,* March 29, 1923; *KW,* April 5, 1923, where Monsignor Około-Kułak takes the same position.

[36] The Gasparri-Vorovskii negotiations are described in detail by Rutkowski, *op. cit.,* pp. 267–270. See also *AAS,* XV, 250–252. The official publication, *V Let Vlasti Sovetov* (Moscow, 1922), pp. 291–292, expressly described the confiscation of church valuables as being a blow aimed at the complete disorganization of religion as well as a relief measure, e.g., p. 292, where it describes the program as the "final blow."

should the trial prove "unfortunate," the Holy See would certainly raise its voice publicly against the conduct of the Soviets; he even indicated the likely contents of the papal declaration. In addition, he defended the position of Archbishop Cieplak, particularly on the basis of the pope's offer to buy all the church treasures, a proposal whose issue, the archbishop rightly awaited. Vorovskii, on his side, reassured the cardinal that the archbishop and priests would either be completely freed by the court or that the sentence would not be carried out. Fearing perhaps that this reply did not satisfy the veteran papal diplomat, Vorovskii insisted that any open action by the Holy Father would be a challenge to the Soviet government that would leave them no recourse but to execute the most severe sentences upon the accused clergy. They would be, if not put to death, then most certainly exiled—and thus Catholics of the Bolshevik state were deprived of any spiritual care.[37]

On March 20, 1923, Monsignor Pizzardo, at the request of Cardinal Gasparri, once again contacted Vorovskii about the Cieplak affair; and the Soviet representative assured him that no danger threatened the archbishop and his companions. Again, on March 31, 1923, Monsignor Pizzardo informed Vorovskii that Cardinal Gasparri would send a telegram to Kalinin and Chicherin, in which he would request the commutation of the death sentence for Archbishop Cieplak and Monsignor Budkiewicz, the freeing of the prisoners and sending them to Rome. Such a message was certainly sent either on March 31, 1923, or April 1, 1923.[38]

Nor had the Holy See limited itself to petitions and protests to the Soviet government. The Vatican had demanded that the Roman Catholic clergy under accusation be submitted to trial by the pope himself, the Soviet government providing the proofs; the pope assured the hostile government that justice would be done, but the Soviets rejected this plan.[39]

Besides the Vatican, the neighboring Polish state took a very intense interest in the welfare of the priests who were on trial. The humanitarian interest involving religious freedom, the religious interest in the Catholics of Russia, and finally concern for the

[37] Rutkowski, *op. cit.*, pp. 268–269.   [38] *Ibid.*, p. 270.
[39] *AAS*, XV, 251, "Gratuli nobis est," May 23, 1923.

Polish national minority in the Soviet state prompted the Polish government to follow the events in Moscow with the closest attention. In spite of the Poles' interest in the welfare of their coreligionists and fellow Poles, the possibilities for action were complicated by political considerations of every kind. Rumors were rife that the Polish government would use a French loan to launch a war against the Soviet state, with the Cieplak case serving as a pretext. Therefore, Polish diplomatic representatives in Paris, London, Brussels, Rome, the Vatican, Berlin, Stockholm, Prague, Vienna and Bucharest were instructed on March 27, 1923, to deny categorically any rumors that connected the French loan and the Cieplak affair with any warlike intentions on the part of the Polish government. The same instruction declared that any rumors of a diplomatic break between Warsaw and Moscow were without foundation.[40] Finally, as a complicating factor, any action by Poland might be construed as interference in the internal affairs of Russia.

These considerations, of course, made any action by the Polish government one that had to be delicate in the utmost, if it were not to jeopardize the lives of the prisoners as well as involve Poland in an unwanted diplomatic furor. The Polish representative in Moscow, Roman Knoll, informed the Commissariat of Foreign Affairs that Prince Leonid Obolenski, the Russian ambassador in Warsaw, had assured the Polish government that the sentence would not be carried out and that the matter was to be negotiated diplomatically. Undoubtedly, not feeling certain about the value of the ambassador's pledge, the Polish government permitted Knoll on March 27 to offer the Soviet government an exchange of prisoners, a step which the Polish government was loathe to take, for it exposed it to future blackmail operations by the Bolsheviks any time one of their agents was arrested in Poland. Nevertheless, the government felt it necessary to take this drastic action in order to save the lives of Archbishop Cieplak and Monsignor Budkiewicz.[41]

In order to clarify Poland's position and to indicate the steps which his government had taken, the prime minister of the Polish

---

[40] Rutkowski, *op. cit.*, p. 271.

[41] Rutkowski, *op. cit.*, p. 274. However, Hugh Gibson's report states that Sikorski was inclined to believe that the sentence would not be carried out. See *NAD, RS,* File No. 860c.00/179, March 29, 1923.

government, Ladislas Sikorski, spoke in the senate on March 31, 1923. Since the now celebrated trial involved problems of religion rather than politics, the Polish government, declared the prime minister, turned to the Apostolic See, waiting upon the papal action in the Moscow trial. Recalling his conversations with the Russian ambassador, Sikorski emphasized that Prince Obolenski assured him the sentence would not be carried out; besides this statement of the ambassador, the government's information from Russia also emphasized this as the position of the Russian government. The prime minister concluded by pointing out the interest which the affair had for the whole West, above all, for the Holy See at Rome; he emphasized, too, that it could not possibly be construed as a political affair and the subject of political struggles.[42]

The final Polish effort was made by the Polish representative in Moscow to have Monsignor Budkiewicz deported to Poland or to arrange an exchange of prisoners; but both these efforts failed.[43]

While the Polish government tried to tread the narrow ground between intervention in Russian internal affairs and more aggressive action, in the Warsaw diplomatic corps, too, rumors complicated an already complex situation, so that the truth was frequently obscured. One report had the United States' ambassador, Hugh Gibson, presenting a protest to Prince Obolenski; however, in a confidential report to his government the ambassador denied that he had taken any such action, and, in fact, denied that there had been any discussion of such a step by the diplomatic corps in Warsaw.[44] On the other hand, the German ambassador to Warsaw, Ulrich Rauscher, called on Prince Obolenski on March 28 and discussed the advisability of carrying out the sentence; he told him that Germany had a distinct interest in avoiding any action that would further prejudice the civilized world against Russia. According to the German ambassador, the proposed execution would, indeed, be

[42] *KW*, March 28, 1923. Prime Minister Sikorski's entire speech is contained in *Sprawozdanie stenograficzne 17 posiedzenia Senatu Rzeczpospolitej z dn. 27 marca, 1923 r.*, XVII (Warsaw, 1923), 2–4. The text of the speech was also transmitted to the United States Department of State, *NAD, RS*, File No. 860c.00/179, March 29, 1923.

[43] Rutkowski, *op. cit.*, p. 274.

[44] Rutkowski, *op. cit.*, pp. 274–275, says that Gibson and Archbishop Lauri made such a protest to Obolenski; but see Gibson's confidential report, where he denies it, *NAD, RS*, File No. 860c.00/179, March 29, 1923.

a gross act of stupidity on the part of the Russian government, nor would there be any compensating element in it. The prince, on his part, suggested that the speech and conduct of Prime Minister Sikorski had been so emphatic and offensive to the Russians, that the Soviet government was in a very difficult position, inasmuch as it could not yield under a Polish "threat." However, in justice to the Polish prime minister, it must be said that all his efforts had been directed to avoiding threats or offense, lest he prejudice the case of the unfortunate victims; nor did Prince Obolenski advert to the fact that the difficult position of the Soviet government was largely of its own making. Prince Obolenski further intimated to the German ambassador that although the Soviet government was not prepared to yield to Poland, yet it would find it less difficult to comply with a direct request from the Vatican and that representations from that quarter would not be unwelcome. The papal nuncio, Monsignor Lauri, had, however, already informed the American ambassador that such steps had been taken. With what effect, the sequel would show.[45]

In view of the publicity given the speech of the Polish prime minister, the Soviet Commissariat of Foreign Affairs could hardly fail to reply. On March 30, 1923, it sent a note to Prince Obolenski, accusing the Polish government of interfering in the domestic affairs of the Russian state and of unfriendly acts toward the Russian government. Furthermore, it rejected very sharply the "claim" of the Polish government to play the role of protector for Russian citizens of Polish origin. In order to divert attention from its own problem, the Soviet note reminded the Polish government of the millions of Ukrainians and Belorussians living in Poland, "with respect to which the Polish government violates the elementary principles, guaranteeing the existence of national minorities." Finally, the Russian note made a declaration that boded ill for the victims of the trial; it denied that the representatives of the Soviet government had told the Polish minister in Moscow, or anyone whatsoever, that this trial was a mere formality that would not have any serious results.[46] This

[45] *NAD, RS,* File No. 860c.00/179, March 29, 1923.
[46] *NAD, RS,* File No. 860c.00/179, March 29, 1923. The text of the statement was published in *Izvestiia,* April 3, 1923, and *Pravda,* April 3, 1923.

statement, of course, should have warned all interested parties that the danger was greater than they had hitherto surmised.

The interest of the American government in the case went beyond the reports that the ambassador from Warsaw forwarded to the Department of State. The Federal Council of Churches of Christ in America on March 29, 1923, sent a cablegram to Chicherin, the commissar of foreign affairs. It asked the Russian government, in the interest of humanity and religious liberty, to reconsider its decision to execute Roman Catholic and Eastern church officials. Robert E. Speer, the president, and John M. Moore, chairman of the Administrative Committee, signed the cablegram.[47] In addition, the National Catholic Welfare Council, through its chairman of the administrative committee, Archbishop Edward A. Hanna of San Francisco, appealed to the president of the United States, Warren G. Harding, to protest to the Soviet government against the sentence of death it had so unjustly passed on Archbishop Cieplak and Monsignor Budkiewicz.[48] On March 29, 1923, the Episcopalian bishop of New York, William T. Manning, appealed to the United States government to exert every possible effort toward preventing the execution of the barbarous sentence of death against Archbishop Cieplak and Monsignor Budkiewicz. Charles Evans Hughes, the secretary of state, assured the bishop that the Department of State had taken steps to express the humanitarian interest of the American people and their earnest hope that the lives of the Roman Catholic ecclesiastics would be spared.[49] In addition to this domestic pressure from religious groups, the United States government was approached by Cardinal Mercier, the archbishop of Malines and world-famous scholar, through the Belgian ambassador on March 27, 1923. The Belgian ambassador, Baron de Cartier de Marchienne, advised the undersecretary of state, William Phillips, that he had received a telegram from Cardinal Mercier, in which the cardinal asked whether the United States government would take any action on behalf of Archbishop Cieplak, who had been condemned to death. The undersecretary told the ambassador that it was very

---

[47] *NAD, RS,* File No. 861.404/91, March 29, 1923.

[48] *NAD, RS,* File No. 861.404/97, March 28, 1923.

[49] See *NAD, RS,* File No. 861.404/94, March 29, 1923, for Bishop Manning's telegram, and April 19, 1923, for Secretary Hughes' reply.

doubtful whether the government of the United States could do anything, because it had no representative to the Soviet government, and the members of the American Relief Mission were pledged not to engage in politics. However, he added, even if the United States had some means of approach to the Soviet government, any action would probably do more harm than good to the cause of the archbishop.[50] In addition to using the Belgian ambassador in Washington, Cardinal Mercier used the United States legation in Brussels to telegraph an urgent message to President Harding, expressing the earnest hope that something would be done to save the Roman Catholic prelates.[51]

In response to these pressures, the secretary of state, Charles E. Hughes, suggested to President Harding on March 28, 1923, the possibility of instructing the American representative in Berlin, Alanson B. Houghton, ambassador extraordinary and plenipotentiary, to make known to the Soviet ambassador in Berlin how deeply the action against the ecclesiastics had stirred public opinion in the United States.[52] President Harding, replying the same day, felt it could do no harm and might be helpful to convey through Houghton an expression of American sentiment in opposition to the death sentence and ordered Secretary Hughes to instruct the American ambassador in Berlin.[53] Accordingly, that same day, March 28, the secretary sent an urgent instruction to the American Embassy in Berlin, advising the ambassador to communicate informally with the Soviet representative in Berlin. He was instructed to inform him of how much the public mind had been stirred in the United States by the death sentence; the United States' effort was only the part of friendliness to let him know the extent and intensity of the feeling which had been aroused and to express the earnest hope in the interest of humanity that the lives of the ecclesiastics might be spared. The problem of communicating with the Soviets was com-

[50] *NAD, RS,* File No. 861.404/96, March 29, 1923, memorandum of conversation with the Belgian ambassador. See also *OR,* March 20, 1923, where Hughes' action is announced, as well as the *New York Times,* March 29, 1923.

[51] *NAD, RS,* File No. 861.404/88a, March 28, 1923, Secretary Hughes' telegram to President Harding, who was in St. Augustine, Florida, at the time.

[52] *NAD, RS,* File No. 861.404/88a, March 28, 1923; *U.S. Foreign Relations,* II, 815–816.

[53] *NAD, RS,* File No. 861.404/89, March 28, 1923, the reply of President Harding to the secretary of state; *U.S. Foreign Relations,* II, 816.

plicated by the lack of recognition and official intercourse; but the Department of State left it to the discretion of the ambassador to determine the form and manner of communication, but this was to involve no formal official representation.[54]

Houghton, the American ambassador in Germany, decided to reach the Russians by using Ludwig Stein, a newspaper correspondent for the *Vossische Zeitung*, as a go-between. Stein saw the Russian ambassador, N. M. Khrestinskii, who agreed to meet Houghton at Stein's apartment. Later, however, the Russian ambassador read in a Reuter dispatch from Washington that the United States secretary of state had instructed Houghton to make representations to him about the Cieplak trial. He sent word to Stein that since the executions had been delayed, the matter was not urgent, and also that he could not at that time meet the American ambassador informally without instructions from Moscow because he knew that the American intended to lay before him a purely domestic matter. Finally, Khrestinskii himself had reportedly forwarded the Reuter dispatch to Moscow. Houghton suggested in his telegram to Secretary Hughes that in view of the developments, he was disinclined to meet Khrestinskii; and if any contact with him would be necessary, it should be through a secretary of the embassy.[55] Secretary Hughes, replying on March 31, 1923, accepted the suggestion of the American ambassador in Berlin, especially since the Russian government had been sufficiently informed about the sentiment of the American government in the matter. He did, however, permit further contact through an embassy secretary, if the ambassador were approached by the Russian representative.[56]

On the United States' side a more effective means of action was found by revoking the entrance visa for Madame Catherine Kalinin, the wife of the president of the Soviet government. She had intended to come to the United States for the purpose of a tour in the interest of Russian relief, as had been suggested by the American Committee for the Relief of Russian Children. The Department of State, with

[54] *NAD, RS,* File No. 861.404/91a, March 28, 1923, Secretary Hughes' instructions to the United States ambassador in Berlin; *U.S. Foreign Relations,* II, 816.

[55] *U.S. Foreign Relations,* II, 817, the ambassador in Germany to the secretary of state, March 30, 1923.

[56] *Ibid.,* II, 817, the secretary of state to the ambassador in Germany, March 31, 1923.

the consent of President Harding, had advised its consular representatives in Riga to grant a visa; but in the light of the Soviet government's action in sentencing Archbishop Cieplak and in executing
Monsignor Budkiewicz, Secretary Hughes now felt that this original
decision to grant a visa was of doubtful wisdom, and a reversal of
this decision would act as a protest against the action of the Soviet
authorities in connection with the condemnation of the Roman
Catholic clergy.[57] With the consent of President Harding,[58] Secretary Hughes instructed the American minister in Latvia, Coleman, to
inform the American consuls in Riga and Reval that the authorization for a visa had been withdrawn. Her presence, he declared, was
wholly undesirable in the United States because of the public
feeling which had been aroused by the execution of Monsignor
Budkiewicz.[59]

In Berlin, meanwhile, after delaying some days before again
approaching the Soviet ambassador, the counsel of the American
embassy, Warren D. Robbins, called on the Russian ambassador on
April 7. When Robbins inquired if Khrestinskii had received instructions with regard to the message communicated to him by Ludwig
Stein, Khrestinskii replied that the United States embassy had been
mistaken and that though he had spoken with Stein about the
United States' message, he did not consider that he could take this
message until it was delivered by a secretary. Robbins then, having
been told by the Russian ambassador that he would take the message from Robbins, went over the whole matter again. Whereupon
Khrestinskii replied that since the message had been presented in a
friendly and informal manner, he would be glad to transmit it to his
government; but, he added, had the note been presented in an
official manner, he would have had to reject it officially, for it was
a protest which solely concerned the internal administration in
Russia.[60] With this the United States government ended its efforts

[57] *Ibid.*, II, 818–819, the secretary of state to President Harding, April 9,
1923.

[58] *Ibid.*, II, 819, President Harding to the secretary of state, April 9, 1923.

[59] *Ibid.*, II, 819–820, the secretary of state to the minister in Latvia (Coleman), April 10, 1923.

[60] *Ibid.*, II, 821–822, the counselor of the embassy in Germany (Robbins) to
the chief of the Division of Russian Affairs, Department of State (Poole),
April 16, 1923. This report speaks inaccurately of "one of the bishops" having
already been executed.

in the Cieplak affair; but it had taken a firm stand in favor of religious liberty, to the extent of canceling the visa authorization for Madame Kalinin.

Even more dramatic were the events involved in the protest of the English government made by its representative in Russia, R. M. Hodgson. On Friday, March 30, 1923, in accordance with the instructions of the British secretary for foreign affairs, the Marquess Curzon of Kedleston, Hodgson lodged a final and earnest appeal against the death sentence which had remained in force against Monsignor Budkiewicz. The message, addressed to Chicherin, pointed out that the execution would cause in the entire civilized world feelings of horror and indignation which would be undesirable for the Russian government, even from the standpoint of its economic interests. Undoubtedly this was an allusion to the economic mission then negotiating in London and headed by Leonid Krassin.[61] To this polite note, G. Weinstein gave an extremely violent reply, dated March 31, 1923, in which the Russian government rejected all British representations. It declared that Russia, as an independent and sovereign state, had an indisputable right to pass verdicts in accordance with its own laws in the cases of persons who violate the law of the country, and every external attempt to interfere and to protect spies and traitors was regarded as an unfriendly act. Furthermore, the note went on, Chicherin had received a telegram from the representative of the Irish republic in France concerning the same matter, asking that the sentence of Archbishop Cieplak be commuted and stating that he did this in spite of the hypocritical interference on the part of Great Britain, which is responsible for the cold-blooded murder of political prisoners in Ireland. These facts and similar incidents in India and Egypt made it difficult, the note declared, to consider "the appeal of the British government in the name of humanity and the sacredness of human life sufficiently convincing."[62] Here a note of humor is interjected into this grim drama. An amusing reason appeared for the fact that "little Weinstein," as the report called him, signed the English note. The Soviet

[61] *Izvestiia*, April 1, 1923. This was also reported to the United States Department of State from Riga, *NAD, RS*, File No. 861.041/19, April 13, 1923.
[62] *NAD, RS*, File No. 861.041/19, April 13, 1923; *Izvestiia*, April 1, 1923.

trade delegation in London insisted that it should be permitted to deal directly with the foreign secretary, but the English government refused and ordered the Russians to deal with the chief of the Northern Department. This apparently aroused the ire of the Bolsheviks, who therefore refused to let Hodgson see or deal directly with Chicherin. Hodgson is reported to have said about the Soviet note: "Its matter was Radek's, its style Chicherin's, and its signature Weinstein's."[63]

The note which the Russian government through its agent Weinstein tried to present to the British government was refused by the British representative, Hodgson; and in the following exchange of notes, the main issue, that is, the preservation of the life of Monsignor Budkiewicz, was lost sight of in a quarrel over mutual dignity, a result that perhaps the Soviet diplomats had in mind when they wrote their first insulting note to the British government.[64]

While thus the world expressed its disapproval,[65] the Soviet government went its own way. The All-Russian Central Executive Committee, reviewing the sentence passed by the court, on March 29, 1923, commuted the sentence of Archbishop Cieplak from death to ten years of solitary confinement. The reason that the Executive Committee gave for the commutation was that Archbishop Cieplak was, after all, the leader of a religious group that had suffered persecution in the times of the tsars and, consequently, the execution of the sentence would cause the Catholic masses to consider the act as an attack on the Catholic religion. With regard to Monsignor Budkiewicz, the All-Russian Central Executive Committee rejected his petition for clemency on the score that his "criminal" activities had been closely connected with direct and open acts of counterrevolu-

[63] *NAD, RS,* File No. 861.404/124, April 12, 1923, contains a letter from an unidentified American in Moscow.

[64] This exchange was published in the Soviet press, *Pravda,* April 1, 12, 1923, and *Izvestiia,* April 11, 1923. The debate on the problem in the English Parliament appears in 53 H. L. Deb. 5s., II, 454–463; 161 H. C. Deb. 5s., II, 1756–1757; 162 H. C. Deb. 5s., III, 269–270, 466–467. The *New York Times,* March 28, 1923, and *KW,* March 17, 1923, also notice the clash in the House of Commons. See also *OR,* March 22, 1923, which reports Lord Curzon as believing that the Cieplak trial was intended to provide an anti-Christian demonstration for Easter and to prepare the process against Patriarch Tikhon.

[65] *OR,* March 30, 31, 1923, mentions protests from Warsaw, Washington, Brussels, Paris, Rome, Sweden, Brazil, as well as from Cardinal Adolph Bertram of Breslau. See also *New York Times,* March 28, 1923.

tion and with a foreign bourgeois power hostile to the Soviet republic, a reference to Poland. The decree was signed by M. Kalinin, the president of the Committee, and by T. Sapronov, its secretary.[66]

Then on April 3, 1923, *Izvestiia* announced that on March 31, 1923, Monsignor Budkiewicz had been executed in accordance with the sentence passed at the trial.[67] Fortunately, the details of his last days are known because of the statements of his fellow prisoners. They declared that the few days from March 25 till March 30 the monsignor passed as though nothing important hung over his head. On Good Friday, March 30, when the monsignor was not in the cell, his fellow prisoners read in the newspapers about the commutation of the sentence of Archbishop Cieplak and the rejection of the monsignor's appeal for clemency. When he returned, the prisoners did not at first inform him about the failure of the appeal; but after a while they felt they had to tell him, and showed him the paper. He assured them that they need not hide the news from him, for he was prepared for every eventuality. When Monsignor Malecki suggested in a private conversation with him that it might be well to prepare for death, Monsignor Budkiewicz assured him that he was completely at peace and prepared for everything. Few, he declared, really understood him and that God alone saw his sacrifice for all his sins. Tears filled his eyes, for certainly it is no small matter to die, and to die as a condemned criminal does not make death any easier. On Holy Saturday, March 31, 1923, about 10:00 A.M., Monsignor Budkiewicz was removed from the cell he had shared with his fellow priests and lodged alone in Cell 42. He bade farewell to all, certain, no doubt, that he would not see them again. That same evening he returned a Russian book to them that he had taken with him; in it he had noted that he was alone in Cell 42 and that it was clean and warm. One of the prisoners who was lodged in the same corridor with the monsignor reported that at 11:30 P.M., March 31,

[66] *NAD, RS*, File No. 861.041/19, April 13, 1923, Enclosure No. 13; *Izvestiia*, March 30, 1923; *Pravda*, March 30, 1923. The text is given in English in McCullagh, *op. cit.*, pp. 365–366, and in Polish in Rutkowski, *op. cit.*, pp. 282–283. The Executive Committee's decision was also published in the Polish press, e.g., *KW*, March 30, 1923.

[67] *Izvestiia*, April 3, 1923; *NAD, RS*, File No. 861.041/19, April 13, 1923, Enclosure No. 12; *KW*, April 3, 1923. Monsignor Około-Kułak wrote a brief survey of the monsignor's life in *KW*, April 4, 1923.

1923, two men came and ordered him to take his belongings, and then led him away to an automobile. Thus, the monsignor was executed during the night of March 31 to April 1, 1923, that is, the night of Holy Saturday and dawn of Easter.[68]

The real motives for the Bolshevik action may perhaps remain shrouded in mystery forever; but several explanations were advanced. Walter Duranty's explanation was that the Bolsheviks at first planned clemency, but were driven into executing the priest by the protests—"undiplomatically worded"—of the Poles and the British. However, the texts of the original protests were far from undiplomatic in their wording; rather they disclaimed all interference in Soviet internal affairs and emphasized the humanitarian interests of the case. If any notes were "undiplomatically" worded, the replies of the Russian Commissariat of Foreign Affairs to the Polish and British governments were insulting in the extreme, as the texts show.[69] On the other hand, Father Walsh was certain that the monsignor had been executed on the morning of March 30, 1923, before the Russian government received the British protest, a conclusion drawn from the horrible telephone calls he had received during the early morning hours. However, the testimony of the fellow prisoners now shows Father Walsh's conclusion to have been false. As to the motives for the execution, Father Walsh's idea was that this attack on the Catholics was a deliberate step on the part of a fanatical left wing group as a sort of test to determine whether they could do the same thing to the foreign religions. Further, he explained, the Bolsheviks roughly had five fronts on which they meant to put their ideas across: the political, economic, religious, social, and intellectual. He felt that they had had to back down on the political and economic fronts; and he argued that the expulsion of professors in the previous fall, that is, 1922, was an action on the intellectual front.

[68] Rutkowski, *op. cit.*, pp. 283–284. This corrects the surmisal of McCullagh, *op. cit.*, pp. 279–280, that the monsignor had been shot before this; McCullagh based his surmisal on the telephone calls made after midnight on the morning of March 30, 1923, to Father Walsh, who took the calls only to be answered by coarse laughter. Father Walsh's acquaintances assured him that this was a technique used by the Cheka when executing a person. Father Walsh repeats this version in *The Last Stand* (see fn. 31), p. 184. The same information is contained in a State Department report in *NAD, RS,* File No. 861.404/124, April 12, 1923. An unreliable description was published in *KW*, April 11, 1923.
[69] *NAD, RS*, File No. 861.404/124, April 12, 1923.

The execution of Monsignor Budkiewicz was part of the religious phase of the program. Walter Duranty, who was not always the best informed man on this case, checked that idea with his "sources," and concluded that it was not the correct explanation, except for a few leaders such as Krylenko. Duranty reported too that the "big guns" were extremely sorry about the shooting of the priest, because they felt they were in hot water and did not know what to do about it. The report surmised that Patriarch Tikhon's case was postponed indefinitely, because the "big guns" were afraid to kill him. If this is so, then the death of the monsignor did an unnoticed service to the Orthodox Church and its patriarch. Father Walsh felt that the Bolsheviks did not shoot Archbishop Cieplak because they were afraid to shoot so important an official—afraid to see in the foreign press the words "Archbishop Shot."[70]

All these statements are surmisals at best, worth only as much as the information their authors had. The general Catholic reaction was that the shooting was but one incident in the general campaign against all religion and against Catholicism in particular.

[70] *Ibid.*, where a letter of F. W. B. Coleman, the United States Legation, Riga, July 11, 1923, mentions the monsignor's death as a moderating factor in Soviet conduct.

X

The Epilogue

The heavy blow had fallen; the hierarchical organization of the Roman Catholic Church in Russia was destroyed. A pall of silence settled over the once agitated battle arena; and underneath it somehow or other the Church attempted to live on. The great lack of information about life in Russia, especially about Catholic life, makes assessment of the damage very difficult; but some assessment must be made.

Archbishop Ropp, head the vast archdiocese of Mohylew, lived in exile in Warsaw. Archbishop Cieplak was in prison. As of May 12, 1925, there were 1,007,150 Catholics in Russia, 411 churches, and 330 chapels. In the territories of Łuck-Żytomierz and Kamieniec-Podolski, there were 710,300 Catholics, 237 churches, and 143 chapels. Of the 245 priests who served these dioceses in 1914, only about 70 were left by 1925.[1]

With regard to the archdiocese of Mohylew, there is more adequate information. Before the revolution, the archdiocese had numbered about 1,160,000 Catholics, 331 parishes, and 400 priests. The establishment of the sees and vicariates of Mińsk, Riga, Vladivostok, Siberia and Finland had reduced the number of Catholics in the archdioceses from 690,000 to 227,000. Two hundred thousand are unaccounted for—flight, exile, and death during the fearful years

[1] *CA*, memorandum of the Polish Executive Committee, presented to Archbishop Cieplak, May 12, 1925.

of war, civil war, and persecution suggest what happened to them:

The Archdiocese of Mohylew, 1925

Catholics	227,504
Parish churches and chapels	119
Oratories and chapels with care of souls	204
Latin rite priests in the archdiocese	88
Latin rite priests in prison in Russia	6
Latin rite priests in exile	151
Priests and clerics engaged in study	19

Source: *Elenchus cleri, . . . 1926*

This drastic reduction in the number of Catholics saw an even greater reduction in the number of priests serving the Catholics of the vast archdiocese. There was one priest available for every 2,774 Catholics. Indeed, there were more priests of the archdiocese in exile than there were in Russia. This shortage of priests was aggravated by the large distances in the archdiocese, which made almost hopeless the task of some 80 priests in the archdiocese.

The situation created by the shortage of priests is vividly illustrated in the deanery of Smoleńsk, where Father Adolph Lassatowicz administered the parish church of Smoleńsk (5,000 members), the parish of Mazalcewo (1,000 members), and the parish of Wiazma, for which there are no figures. In the deanery of Samara Father Ladislas Kunda served the parish of Samara (2,000 members), the chapels of Hoffenthal and Reinsfeld, and the parish church of Orenburg (1,000 members).[2] Hence, among the results of the events from 1917 to 1924 was this drastic lessening of the number of priests available for parochial work in Russia.

The effect of the war and revolution can be even more accurately considered in Petrograd. The clergy of the city had been arrested and tried; its two most prominent clergymen, Archbishop Cieplak and Monsignor Budkiewicz, had been eliminated. Moreover, the decline in the parochial membership in Petrograd is even more startling. St. Catherine's parish, which in 1904 served 29,000 mem-

[2] *Elenchus cleri et ecclesiarum archidioeceseos Mohiloviensis in Russia in diem 1 Januarii 1926* (Warsaw, 1926), pp. 9–22.

bers, now had only 8,000; St. Stanislas' parish church, which had 17,000 members in 1904, now numbered only 3,000.[3]

The material losses of the churches in Petrograd because of nationalization were also considerable. For instance, the church buildings on Nevsky Prospect were seized on October 10, 1919; even earlier in 1918, the *gymnasia* for boys and girls had been seized. The properties owned by St. Catherine's had produced in 1917 an income of 285,000 rubles. After deducting 15 per cent for repairs, and so forth, Monsignor Budkiewicz estimated the losses in income for the parish from 1919 to the end of 1920 at about 500,000 tsarist or gold rubles.[4]

The losses in St. Petersburg included the Theological Academy, transferred there from Wilno in 1842, as well as the seminary whose origin went back to Archbishop Siestrzencewicz himself, the first archbishop of Mohylew. In 1917 the Theological Academy had 17 faculty members; its rector was Father Ignatius Radziszewski, who was later to become the first rector of the Catholic University of Lublin. The Academy had 83 students pursuing higher theological studies; in the same year the seminary numbered 102 theological students preparing for ordination.[5]

From an organizational viewpoint, the greatest loss was the elimination of the hierarchical leadership. Archbishop Cieplak was languishing in a Bolshevik prison, the Butyrka, in Moscow. The details of the archbishop's way of life in prison are known from a letter by Father Peter Zieliński, pastor of the church of Ss. Peter and Paul in Moscow, who for a while was the archbishop's companion in prison. Writing on August 27, 1923, to a dear friend of Archbishop Cieplak's, Bishop Anthony Nowowiejski of Płock, Father Zieliński described

[3] *Ibid., p. 9; Elenchus omnium ecclesiarum et universi cleri archidioeceseos Mohyloviensis et dioec. Minscensis pro anno domini 1904 conscriptus* (St. Petersburg, 1904), pp. 184, 185.

[4] *BA*, reply to Archdiocesan Communication, October 19, 1922: "The buildings brought in . . . in 1917 over 285,000 rubles. After subtracting 15 per cent for the repair and equipment of the buildings, etc. (about 40,000 rubles), as a result of the seizures the church lost about 225,000 rubles yearly. Reckoning from October 1919 to the end of 1921, more than 500,000 tsarist rubles or gold rubles."

[5] Antoni Około-Kułak, "Kościół w Rosji dawniej, obecnie i w przyszłości," (Cracow, 1928), pp. 9–10.

the archbishop's cell as being six feet in width and eighteen feet in length. Daylight penetrated through one small window, which, of course, had a grate; for the evening and night there was but one small lamp in the room. A small wooden table with a bench and an iron bed with an old straw mattress provided the furniture. The iron door opened but three times a day, at six in the morning, at twelve noon, and at six in the evening. The archbishop usually rose at seven and retired at ten. For exercise he strolled about the prison yard, surrounded by high prison walls, for about an hour every day. He passed the time by reading his breviary, saying his rosary, and performing his other customary spiritual exercises; beyond this, he read books from the prison library and newspapers which it was possible to obtain through the prison authorities. In order to occupy his mind and to do something useful, the archbishop undertook the study of Italian, and so spent hours pacing back and forth in his cell, memorizing the words of that language. The prison fare was far from attractive: a daily ration of three fourths of a pound of black bread; boiling water three times a day; at noon some meat soup; and at six in the evening a millet gruel, rarely of buckwheat or corn. Besides the food supplied by the prison, a prisoner was allowed to receive packages once a week; however, by way of special indulgence, the archbishop was permitted to receive packages twice a week. When out of prison, Father Zieliński took upon himself the task of providing the packages for the archbishop as well as he could. Mrs. Catherine Pieszko, representative of the Polish Red Cross, and Father Walsh, head of the Papal Relief Mission, were permitted to visit the archbishop. In addition to these visitors, there were the Bolshevik guards, whom Father Zieliński speaks of ironically as Bolshevik "angels." The archbishop was not able to see anyone else; this isolation and the uncertainty of the future were the greatest torment. Father Zieliński added in his letter that, besides the archbishop, he had to take care of twenty priests who were being held in various prisons in Moscow at that time.[6]

Father Walsh succeeded in visiting the archbishop on Friday, May 11, 1923, in the Butyrka prison in Moscow; the visit, of course,

---

[6] Franciszek Rutkowski, *Arcybiskup Jan Cieplak* (Warsaw, 1934), pp. 291–292, where the entire text of the letter is published.

took place in the offices of the prison. Father Walsh, on seeing the archbishop, kissed the prelate's hand and saw that he was not wearing his episcopal ring. Father Walsh delivered a message from Pius XI, assuring the archbishop of his continuing care, prayers, and support. His eyes filling with tears, the archbishop expressed his gratitude and added that he would always do his best to satisfy the wishes of the Holy See. As to his own condition, the archbishop said that he suffered from a cough, especially at night, and that his cell was on the third floor of the prison, a cell that he was sharing at that time with Father Zieliński; he was permitted one hour a day in the prison yard. Father Walsh then gave him some packages, mostly meat and fruit, and a number of books—among them an Italian grammar.[7] The visit lasted exactly half an hour; their conversation was in French.

Besides these contacts with the outside world, it was permissible to correspond by letter with one's fellow prisoners, a means of communication that both the archbishop and the imprisoned priests used to lighten their hours. For instance, the priests sent the archbishop greetings for his name day, June 24, 1923, the feast of St. John the Baptist. All this correspondence was, of course, censored by the prison authorities.[8]

About the middle of March, 1924, Archbishop Cieplak was removed from the Butyrka prison and transferred to the infamous prison of Lubianka. He did not realize that steps had been taken to secure his release. For on March 22, 1924, the All-Russian Central Committee in a secret vote had decided to free the archbishop and to expel him from Russia. Already, on March 24, the papal secretary of state, Cardinal Gasparri, had been unofficially informed of the decision. Perhaps the Soviet government feared that Pope Pius XI would revive the Cieplak case in his speech to the consistory, and, at any rate may have wished to weaken the impression of the pope's statement by freeing the archbishop.[9]

On April 9, 1924, the archbishop was completely unaware of the

[7] *OR*, June 6, 1923; Rutkowski, *op. cit.*, p. 289.

[8] Several of these letters were published in Rutkowski, *op. cit.*, pp. 287–288, 289–290, 292–294.

[9] *OR*, March 24, 25, 1923; *AAS*, XVI (1924), 123, "Amplissimum consensum vestrum." March 24, 1924; Rutkowski, *op. cit.*, p. 295.

turn of events when guards came to his cell in Lubianka and ordered
him to an automobile. He did not know whether this was a transfer
to a new prison or whether he was being taken out for execution;
but his guards and he boarded a train that eventually took them to
the Latvian frontier, where they handed him an identification card,
a herring and a piece of bread, and turned him free. The archbishop
boarded the train for Riga; and when the conductor came to take
his ticket, the archbishop explained that he had just been freed from
a Bolshevik prison and did not have any money. In the course of
their discussion, the archbishop told the conductor his name, which
was well known in Latvia. The conductor, a Pole, with his own funds
bought the archbishop a ticket for Riga; thus, the archbishop's first
stage on his journey to freedom after Russia was provided by a
Polish conductor who remains nameless, in the best tradition of
charity.

In Riga, the archbishop made his way to the church of St. Francis
and to the pastor, Father Alexander Jodowlakis, who failed at first
to recognize Archbishop Cieplak in the bearded, white-haired priest
clothed in a torn priestly gown. That same day, the episcopal chancery, after having been informed, quickly passed the news to the
Polish Minister Ładoś in Latvia. The minister, in his turn, rushed
the information to the Ministry of Foreign Affairs in Warsaw. Thus
began what became a triumphal procession for the archbishop,
who was greeted by all, of whatever nationality, as a hero. To the
Polish people he was, of course, a hero of the nation as well as a
hero of the Church; to Catholics, who thronged his way, he was a
martyr. Although everywhere the welcome was great, the cities of
Wilno and Warsaw outdid themselves. His arrival in Warsaw on
April 12, 1924, was the signal for a national celebration: Cardinal
Alexander Kakowski; the apostolic nuncio, Archbishop Lauri; the
Warsaw governor, Ladislas Sołtan; and Senator Baliński were among
the dignitaries present to welcome the archbishop. Having stayed
in Warsaw about two weeks, the archbishop departed for Rome to
thank the Holy Father for the assistance given him and to inform
the Vatican of the situation of the Church in Russia, but he found
time to visit the great national shrine of the Mother of God at
Częstochowa, where he also wished to express his thanks to the

great patroness of the Catholic Church in Poland and of the Polish nation.[10]

At last, on May 8, 1924, the archbishop arrived in Rome, where he was welcomed by Cardinal Gasparri himself, Ladislas Skrzyński, the Polish ambassador to the Vatican, and August Zaleski, the Polish ambassador to the Quirinal, with other representatives of the diplomatic and ecclesiastical worlds that meet in the Eternal City.[11] At ten-thirty that same morning, May 8, the feast of St. Stanislas, the patron of Poland, Archbishop Cieplak celebrated mass in the church of St. Stanislas. On that same day, too, the archbishop was summoned by Pius XI, who sent his own carriage for him; the two met in an audience that lasted about forty-five minutes. Both the archbishop and pope, moved to tears, could hardly speak; but after the first emotions died away, the pope had the archbishop sit beside him and discussed with him the condition of his fellow-prisoners, the situation of the Church in Russia, his own liberation, and the journey to the free world.[12]

Although the archbishop was acclaimed everywhere as a martyr for his faith and as a hero of his nation, he himself was most careful in his statements not to give offense to the Soviet government. Undoubtedly, the reasons behind his attitude included solicitude for his fellow prisoners and for the Catholics in Russia who had to continue living under a regime that was still hostile; but beyond this lay his own desire to return to Russia, if this were possible.[13] Nor was such caution unwise; for at a reception the Soviet ambassador to the Quirinal, Jurenev, remarked to the Polish Ambassador Zaleski that Archbishop Cieplak was acting very tactfully with regard to the Soviet government, especially by not criticizing it. He expressed himself sympathetically about the archbishop and his problems. Zaleski, of course, informed the archbishop of his conversation with the Soviet ambassador; thereupon, the archbishop, after receiving the permission of the Vatican, arranged for a visit to the Russian ambassador. The Vatican consented only on the condition that the archbishop state to Jurenev that the visit was purely a

[10] *OR*, April 13, 14, 15, 1924, and May 3, 7, 1924; Rutkowski, *op. cit.*, pp. 297–308.

[11] *OR*, May 9, 1924.

[12] Rutkowski, *op. cit.*, p. 312.   [13] *Ibid.*, pp. 334, 335.

private one and on the archbishop's initiative. Jurenev received the archbishop very graciously, listened to his pleas on behalf of the prisoners in Russia, and promised to do what was possible for them. The conversation then drifted to the problem of Soviet relations with the Vatican, and the ambassador suggested that it would undoubtedly be a factor in the matter of the prisoners if the Holy See would take the first step in reopening negotiations. He added that the Soviet government would not demand recognition *de iure*. If the Holy See should be inclined to open negotiations, he himself would write to Moscow, which would then send a special representative to deal with the Vatican. After the visit, the archbishop submitted a written report of the conversation to Cardinal Gasparri, with the knowledge and consent of Jurenev; but apparently no answer was given.[14]

While the archbishop was in Rome, he was also privileged to participate in the celebrations that accompanied the arrival in Rome of the relics of the then Blessed Andrew Bobola,[15] the very relics that he had so heroically defended against Bolshevik desecration while he was in Russia. These relics were interred in the Jesuit Church of the Gesu in Rome.[16]

The archbishop remained in Rome eighteen months, after which he went on a journey to the United States, where again a hero's welcome awaited him from the Catholic Americans of Polish descent. While on this tour he was named the archbishop of Wilno, a great see that was indeed worthy of so great a prelate. This was done at a secret consistory held on December 14, 1925.[17] However, the archbishop did not live to take possession of his see, for he was struck with pneumonia on his journey in the United States; he died the night of February 17, 1926, in St. Mary's Hospital, Passaic, New Jersey.

While Archbishop Cieplak found his way to freedom from the "darkness at noon" of the Russian prisons, there was among the number of imprisoned priests and Catholics another important figure in the life of the Russian Catholic Church, Leonid Fedorov, the exarch of the Byzantine Rite Catholic Church in Russia. He,

[14] *Ibid.*, pp. 334–335.
[16] *OR*, May 19, 20, 1924.
[15] He was canonized in 1938.
[17] *AAS*, XVII, 647.

too, had been tried with the archbishop, and had been sentenced to ten years' imprisonment—a long term, indeed. However, neither he nor the Catholics of Eastern rite, particularly the Russians among them, were forgotten, and continual efforts were being made for their liberation from prison, even at the cost of expulsion from Russia.

Although the charge is sometimes made that the Russian and Bolshevik hatred against the Catholic Church is motivated largely by a hatred and fear of Polonism, which they associate with the Catholic Church, certainly this explanation does not suffice to explain the attack of the Bolsheviks against the Byzantine rite Catholics who were ethnically Russians and did all in their power to dissociate their church from any form of that vague phantom, Polonism. Indeed, this movement in the Russian Catholic community did not associate itself with the Union of Brest of 1596, although its superior was Metropolitan Szeptycki. The Russian Catholics did not adopt Latin usages; rather, they tried to preserve everything that was typically Russian. However, this did not enable them to escape the fury of Bolshevik persecution. Strange as it may seem, there are grounds for suspecting that the so-called communistic Red priests of the Russian Orthodox Church, collaborating as they were with the Bolsheviks, were responsible in some degree for the arrests of the Catholics of Eastern rite in Petrograd and Moscow. Whatever the reasons for their hatred of the Eastern rite Catholics, the Church's seeming attraction for the Russians had frightened the "Red" clergy. The attack had begun by the expulsion of Vladimir Abrikosov from Russia—a layman who along with his wife had adhered to Eastern rite Catholicism. Soon after they joined that rite, Abrikosov was ordained a priest and entered the Dominican Order; his wife, too, had resolved to become a religious. Together they converted their flat in Moscow into the home of the first Russian Dominican Community, of which the wife of Abrikosov was the foundress and mother superior. The Community consisted of eighteen sisters, all Russian but one; its work, which began after the revolution of 1917, was primarily educational and confined to the slums of Moscow. Father Abrikosov opened a church and school in Moscow and was making considerable headway when the Bolshevik authorities closed both the church and the school; he was expelled from Russia in September 1922. Still the work went on, for Exarch Fedorov himself continued Father Abrikosov's endeavor; but the exarch too was arrested, put on trial with Archbishop Cieplak, and condemned to ten years imprisonment. A Father Nicholas Alexandrov was the only priest left in this mission.[18]

In the winter of 1923–1924, the Russian Catholics of the Byzantine rite were arrested in Moscow and in Petrograd—among them priests, nuns, and lay men and women—to be sentenced to various terms in prison or exile. Thus, by the end of that winter, four priests were under arrest or imprisoned: Exarch Fedorov; Father Alexandrov, dean of Moscow, pastor of the church of the Nativity of the Blessed Virgin in Moscow, and chaplain of the Dominican community in Moscow; Father Epiphan Akulov, vicar of the church of the Holy Spirit in Petrograd; and Father John Deibner, priest of Petrograd imprisoned at Suzdal. All 18 of the Dominican sisters were arrested; and the mother superior, Anna Abrikosova, was detained in a prison at Tobolsk. Sister Julia Danzas, superior of the Order of Saint Basil in Petrograd, was also under detention. Fifteen Russian laymen were under arrest as well; to this number must be added two foreign women: one a Czech, Anna Posseipal, and a Polish woman identified only as Żukowska. Thus, 39 Russian Catholics were either under arrest or in exile; and the two non-Russian women made the total 41. The place of detention of the majority was unknown, as well as the gravity and extent of their punishment.[19]

A letter from the superior of the Dominican nuns, Anna Abrikosova, written on August 15, 1925, from a prison in Tobolsk in Siberia, informed the unknown recipient (perhaps Monsignor Około-Kułak, exiled in Warsaw and serving as advisor to Archbishop Ropp) who

[18] *The Messenger of the Sacred Heart*, No. 471 (1924), 86–87; Francis McCullagh, *The Bolshevik Persecution of Christianity* (New York, 1924), pp. 308–309.

[19] *CA*, memorandum to the Commission of Russian Affairs at the Congregation for the Oriental Church, December 6, 1925, by Vladimir Abrikosov. The text is in Italian. *CA*, list of Russian Eastern Catholics held in prisons or exiled by the Soviets (winter, 1923–1924), attached to a letter by Monsignor Około-Kułak, November 17, 1924. For Father Walsh's account of the arrest see *NAD, RS*, File No. 861.404/172, included in a letter of Coleman to the secretary of state, December 7, 1923. See Paul Mailleux, *Exarch Leon Fedorov* (New York, 1964), pp. 193–219.

concerned himself especially with the liberation of these suffering Catholics that she had regular news of the sisters, that they were in good health and full of courage, although they were in a difficult situation financially.[20] A letter of Monsignor Około-Kułak's, dated August 21, 1925, indicated that there was no change in the condition or number of the prisoners, and that the subsidies provided for them had to be permanent.[21]

The formal efforts to provide for the prisoners and, if possible, secure their liberation were suggested by Monsignor Około-Kulak in a letter of November 17, 1924, to Father Abrikosov in Rome.[22] In spite of an agreement made with the Polish government, the Soviet government kept placing obstacles in the path of a "personal" exchange of prisoners; in fact, the Soviet government excluded from the possibility of exchange Anna Abrikosova, Julia Danzas, as well as the two non-Russian women, Anna Posseipal and Żukowska. Besides excluding these women, religious and lay, it excluded from a possible exchange Exarch Fedorov, and Fathers Alexandrov, Akulov, and Deibner. While, according to the convention with Poland, the Bolsheviks had no right to exclude anyone from the exchange, they did not hesitate to do so—on the score that to release Russian citizens was an insult to the Russian state. The situation seemed so hopeless that the Polish government had to consider abandoning the project of liberating the Russian citizens, for a large part of the prisoners who were to be subject to exchange— some 220—were in danger; that the danger was not a mere fiction was clear from the fact that even while negotiations were being carried on, seven of them had been shot.

With the negotiations between Poland and Russia thus not coming to a successful issue, Monsignor Około-Kułak reported to Father Abrikosov that the Soviet government would not under any conditions release Russian citizens to Poland, but might be disposed to do so at the request of the Vatican. The unnamed person who so informed Około-Kułak had the monsignor's confidence; the monsignor, therefore, suggested to Father Abrikosov that he should try

[20] *CA*, extract from a letter of Anna Abrikosova, August 15, 1925, Tobolsk.
[21] *CA*, extract from a letter of Monsignor Około-Kułak, August 21, 1924.
[22] *CA*, letter of Monsignor Około-Kułak to Father Abrikosov, November 17, 1924.

to have the Vatican initiate negotiations with Jurenev, the Soviet representative at the Quirinal.[23]

Father Abrikosov, acting in his capacity of procurator in Rome for the exarch of the Russian Catholics, drew up a memorandum to be presented to the Commission for Russian Affairs attached to the Congregation for the Oriental Church. In it he presented a detailed plan of what could and should be done to aid the Russian Catholics who were imprisoned. After pointing out the possibility of negotiations between the Vatican and the Soviets, but not neglecting the difficulties of that course, the memorandum suggested the means needed to assist the Russian Catholic prisoners and exiles. If $12.50 were provided monthly for each prisoner and $17.50 for each exile, the total amount needed per month would be $667.50; but if this large sum were not available, a smaller sum would at least relieve the greatest needs and would be distributed proportionally. Monsignor Około-Kułak, the vice-president of the Society for Aid to the Famine-Stricken in Russia, in immediate contact with the Polish Red Cross, would be able to transmit any available aid by the safest possible means.[24]

But all the efforts to free these Russian Catholics were unsuccessful. In spite of this, the Polish government did obtain the release of a number of the priests who had been tried and imprisoned; but they spent the rest of their lives outside Russia, even though they hoped and prayed that they might somehow return to work in the old harvest fields and vineyards. All their hopes proved of no avail, for what had been accomplished in the few years from the Bolshevik revolution was the destruction of the Catholic Church in Russia, the Roman or Latin church as well as the newly organized Byzantine rite for Russian Catholics. Of the Byzantine rite, the exarch and his few priests were imprisoned; and the sisters were also in prison. Hence, the Russian Catholics of Eastern rite were without the ritual aid of their own priests; fortunately, they could go to the Latin rite priests who gladly took care of them. The archdiocese of Mohy-

---

[23] *CA*, memorandum on the liberation of Russian Catholics held by the Soviet government, November 25, 1924, presented by Father Abrikosov to the papal secretary of state.

[24] *CA*, memorandum on the liberation of Russian Catholics, October 6, 1925, presented to the Commission for Russian Affairs, Congregation for the Oriental Church.

lew, that immense territory only recently broken into smaller units, was without a bishop to head it; indeed, by 1924 only the aged Bishop Zerr of Tiraspol remained in Russia for all the Catholics there. According to a list drawn up by Father Xavier Klimaszewski, on August 31, 1924, there were only 127 Roman Catholic priests left in Russia at that time—16 were in prisons, and 111 were at their clerical posts.[25]

Neither had Archbishop Ropp forgotten the problems of the Catholics in Russia. Unfortunately for all, the government of the diocese had remained divided. Archbishop Ropp continued trying to govern from Warsaw; in Petrograd itself a skeleton administration continued to function. The treasurer of the archdiocese, Monsignor Około-Kułak, lived in exile in Poland and played a controversial role in the subsequent history of the archdiocese. The metropolitan curia, made up of vicar general, chancellor, and vice-chancellor, also continued to function in Petrograd, as did a metropolitan court of a *vice-officialis*, three judges, a defender of the matrimonial bond, and a notary. Father Anthony Wasilewski, honorary canon of the cathedral and administrator of St. Catherine's parish, was the *vice-officialis* of the court; and one of the judges was Father Boleslas Sloskan, at present the administrator of the archdiocese and in exile in Belgium.[26]

The existence of these ecclesiastical institutions shows that the skeleton of an organized church life remained in Russia even after the expulsion of the hierarchy.

However, superimposed on this structure was Archbishop Ropp's secretariat, located first at Mazowiecka 11/31, Warsaw. The archbishop himself resided at Piękna 24. His vicar general was Monsignor Około-Kułak, into whose hands the actual administration of affairs fell. Besides this secretariat, there was also a metropolitan ecclesiastical court of the archdiocese of Mohylew, but resident in Warsaw (Mazowiecka 11/31). Of this court, Monsignor Około-Kułak was *officialis*, a position that gave him added power and influence.

[25] *CA*, list of priests outside Russia for a variety of reasons, August 31, 1924, drawn up by Father Xavier Klimaszewski. See Edmund Walsh, *The Last Stand* (Boston, 1931), pp. 184–187, for a list of prisoners for the years 1924–1928. The list was compiled in 1930.

[26] *Elenchus cleri . . . 1926*, pp. 24–27.

Moreover, Archbishop Ropp had established at Lublin and associated with the Catholic University a mission institute to educate priests for work in eastern Europe and especially in Russia. In 1925 there were 11 students. In other parts of the world, there were 18 priests and clerics pursuing studies outside the boundaries of the archdiocese of Mohylew, among them the distinguished historian, Alexei Petrani, now a member of the faculty of the Catholic University of Lublin.[27]

According to the archbishop, the object of the secretariat was to keep united the 151 priests who were in exile and to keep them in readiness to return to Russia, when the opportunity came. These priests were distributed throughout various dioceses: Poznań, Cracow, Warsaw, Łomża, Kielce, Sandomierz, Łódź, Lublin, Katowice, Podlasie, Włocławek, Wilno, and Pińsk. There were also priests from the archdiocese working in Sejny and Samogitia in Lithuania, in Riga in Latvia, and in the United States. Warsaw had 20; Samogitia, 22; and Wilno, 30.[28]

Through the secretariat, the archbishop undertook not only to keep his priests united by days of recollection and retreats, but also undertook to govern them and to tax them.[29] He insisted that they must remain incardinated in the archdiocese of Mohylew and thus prevented them from joining dioceses where they were actually working. The local diocesan authorities could not give parishes to priests from another diocese. Hence, a disproportionate number of priests, some of them ordained twenty years, were given such tasks as teaching religion to school boys. From this many of them could hardly make an adequate living wage.[30]

From the small income of his priests the archbishop demanded a 3 per cent income tax.[31] Beyond this, the secretariat began to send out appeals for mass stipends, no matter how small.[32] Other steps of the secretariat seemed more fantastic. By a decree of May 8, 1931, it created a decoration, a memorial cross, *Pro fide et Ecclesia in*

---

[27] *Ibid.*, pp. 23–24; Około-Kułak, *op. cit.*, p. 38.

[28] *Elenchus cleri . . . 1926*, pp. 28–32.

[29] *KU*, April 1, 1931; see also W. Płoskiewicz, memoirs, in manuscript form, made available to this writer by Monsignor Bronislas Ussas.

[30] See *Elenchus cleri . . . 1926*, pp. 28–32, where the positions of these priests are listed.

[31] *KU*, June 1, 1931.   [32] *KU*, July 9, 1931, and August 20, 1931.

Russia Merito, which was to be given to clergy and laity who distinguished themselves in work for the faith and the Church in Russia.[33] This seemed, in fact, to recall to mind the old tsarist decorations and orders; but above all it seemed a way to extract more funds. The reception the priests of the archdiocese gave to this financial program can be judged from the fact that not one mass stipend was sent, in spite of the appeals of the archbishop's vicar general, Około-Kułak.[34]

Besides these financial problems, the secretariat badgered the clergy with questionnaires about their *curriculum vitae* since they went into exile and inquiries about their positions; all this seemed unnecessary to many of the clergy, who regarded it as another effort to discover their income, so that it could be taxed.[35]

The result of all this activity was that great ill-feeling developed among the exiled clergy of the archdiocese. Most of this hostility was directed not against the aging archbishop, but against his vicar general in Warsaw, Około-Kułak. There were charges of oppression, allegations of the misuse of funds for personal and family gain. Father W. Płoskiewicz finally appealed to Pope Pius XI himself in a personal audience, in which he explained in detail the difficulties of the exiled clergy and requested papal permission to incardinate in the archdiocese of Warsaw. The pope told Father Płoskiewicz to be patient, because the matter would soon be settled.[36]

In the meantime, the secretariat and the archbishop had been lulled into a false sense of security. The Pontifical Commission *Pro Russia* in a letter of April 22, 1931, had thanked the archbishop for his work on behalf of the Church in Russia, especially for his efforts to organize the exiled clergy of the archdiocese of Mohylew, for his efforts to educate clergy for Russia in the Mission Institute at Lublin, and for his charitable work among the emigrés from Russia.[37] Less expected was the blow which fell at the end of the year.

On December 9, 1931, the nuncio in Warsaw, Archbishop Marmaggi, informed Archbishop Ropp that there was no longer any

[33] *KU,* August 20, 1931.   [34] *KU,* October 1, 1931.
[35] *KU,* April 4, 1931, May 5, 1931, and July 8, 1931.
[36] Płoskiewicz, memoirs, in manuscript form.
[37] *KU,* May 5, 1931.

need for the maintenance of a secretariat of the archdiocese of Mohylew in Warsaw and that as of December 31, 1931, the secretariat was to cease to exist. The archbishop, according to the decision of the Holy See, would remain the archbishop of Mohylew, and the exiled clergy would remain incardinated in the archdiocese of Mohylew; they would be at the disposal of the Holy See for future work in Russia. Moreover, should any one of the priests of the archdiocese wish to be incardinated in the diocese where they work, they were to approach the nuncio in Warsaw, who would then undertake to deal with the Holy See on the matter. In fact, all the significant matters relating to the clergy of the exiled archdiocese of Mohylew were reserved to the Holy See. The archives of the metropolitan curia were to remain at the disposal of the Holy See.[38]

The archbishop himself, in a letter of December 16, 1931, announced the decision to his clergy: "Beloved brethren: This is the last time that I address you as your bishop . . . This then is farewell, like a voice from beyond the grave . . ."[39]

With this the existence of a separate government of the archdiocese ended on December 31, 1931, but the bitterness lasted a long time. The hostility against Monsignor Około-Kułak also persisted, for some of the priests considered him to have been the archbishop's bad angel.

A further complication occurred, due to events in Moscow. There in 1927 Bishop Michael d'Herbigny, a Vatican emissary, consecrated three bishops: the dean of the cathedral chapter and administrator of the archdiocese, Anthony Malecki; the vicar of St. Catherine's church, Boleslas Sloskan; and the pastor of the French church in Moscow, Father E. Neveu. It was hoped to provide a continuing government and administration of the Church in Russia.[40]

The picture that emerges from the sources is one of a church considerably weakened by the loss of leadership and by decrease in numbers, especially in St. Petersburg. In the provincial areas the Catholic population showed considerable stability, in spite of revolution, civil war, and persecution. Finally, we find among the exiled

---

[38] *KU*, December 16, 1931.   [39] *KU*, December 16, 1931.
[40] Jan Wasilewski, *Arcybiskupi i administratorowie archidyecezji mohylowskiej* (Pińsk, 1930), pp. 184–186.

clergy all the disputes of emigrés. These disputes were necessarily ended by the intervention of Rome in a manner that was mercifully quick and decisive. The effect of the years of persecution by the Bolsheviks had left its effect, frightening for loyal Catholics. The resistance of the Catholic element in Belorussia had been seriously weakened: defections among Catholics and adherence to various sects, particularly to the "Stundists," were becoming more and more frequent. Undoubtedly, this bore out the truth of what Archbishop Cieplak had written in 1922 that there was need of haste in making some sort of settlement with the Bolsheviks about the churches, for the faithful would grow weary of resistance, especially without the spiritual strength that comes from association with one another in the church services.[41] Even so esteemed a man as Father Fedukowicz, after being tortured at length by the *Cheka,* signed a letter drawn up by the Soviets against the leaders of the Catholic Church; but on his return to Żytomierz, he died a martyr's death, imploring God to forgive him for what he had done.[42]

More dangerous perhaps than the use of naked force against the people and the clergy were the efforts of the Bolsheviks to organize a schismatic Catholic Church, independent of Rome. These autonomous spiritual units were, of course, to be mastered and controlled by communist or communist collaborators, who would certainly prepare a general apostasy.[43] However, these plans on the part of the Bolsheviks failed of any signal success, particularly with the Latin Catholics, at least at this early date; two decades later they were not completely unsuccessful.

Thus, the work of destruction had come to an end. The Catholic Church in Russia lay prostrate—disorganized and without leadership—before the overwhelming power of the Bolshevik state. Its leading clergy were imprisoned or exiled and the laity deprived of the sacramental support that only ordained priests could provide.

[41] *CA,* letter of Archbishop Cieplak to the Papal Relief Commission, December 19, 1922.

[42] *CA,* memorandum of the Polish Executive Committee in Ruthenia, presented to Archbishop Cieplak, May 12, 1925.

[43] *CA,* memorandum of the Polish Executive Committee, May 12, 1925. See also Edmund Walsh, *Why Pope Pius XI Asked Prayers for Russia on March 19, 1930* (New York, 1930), p. 16.

All the efforts of the Catholic leaders in Russia to make an agreement with the government had failed; further efforts to solve the conflict between the Catholics and the government by diplomatic means had also failed. "Coexistence" had apparently proved impossible, for on the government's terms it meant abject submission to the civil authorities and unlawful interference in the internal activities of the Church.

Appendix

A Contemporary Report on the Condition
of the Catholic Church in Russia, 1922

THIS DOCUMENT is an extremely valuable source. It is a rough draft of a report on the condition of the Catholic Church in Russia in September 1922. Its author was Monsignor Constantine Budkiewicz, pastor of St. Catherine's church in Petrograd and dean of the Petrograd Catholic clergy. He was executed by the Bolsheviks on March 31, 1923, after a sensational trial in which he and Archbishop John Cieplak, administrator of the Archdiocese of Mohylew since the arrest and exile of Edward Ropp, the archbishop of Mohylew, were the most prominent defendants. Monsignor Budkiewicz wrote the report for Lorenzo Lauri, the titular archbishop of Ephesus and papal nuncio in Warsaw. What enhances the value of this document is the fact that the final draft sent to the nuncio most probably perished in Warsaw during the Second World War. So far as the present writer could discover, with the closing of the nunciature in Warsaw after the Polish defeat in 1939, the archives of the nuncio were transferred to the Primate's Palace in Warsaw for safekeeping. Presumably the archives perished when the Primate's Palace was destroyed.

The document was made available to the writer by Monsignor Bronislas Ussas, one of the few remaining priests of the archdiocese of Mohylew and now resident in Warsaw. He had been a member of the Commission for the Revindication of Polish Archives.

The significance of the document, furthermore, consists in this that it sheds light on the life of the St. Petersburg Catholics and their internal problems, as well as on their relations with the Bolshevik government, while they made an effort at some sort of coexistence with Bolshevik communism.

STATUS ECCLESIAE IN RUSSIA

In eunte regimine communistarum in Russia, pietas fidelium non solum non est diminuta, sed etiam aucta. Debiliores sane propter perturbationem rerum et idearum defecerunt, sed hi sunt paucissimi. Communiter autem homines sentientes se omnino in calamitatibus hodiernae vitae et persecutionem patientes nullum aliud refugium vident nisi solum Deum. Quam ob causam fideles nostri in Russia nunquam erant tam religioni addicti quam hos nostro tempore. Cuius rei testimonium est frequens fidelium communio et defensio Ecclesiarum et sacerdotum, aliquando magno cum periculo vitae et libertatis suscepta. Unde certo dici potest nunquam fuisse tam arctam coniunctionem fidelium cum ecclesia quam nunc.

Res temporales Ecclesiae in Russia pessime se habent. Causae huius rei sunt duae. Altera causa est reemigratio fidelium in patriam. Propter calamitiosam conditionem vitae in Russia permulti fideles discesserunt regione multique volunt discedere. Exemplo est paroecia s. Catharinae Petropoli, quae habuit circa 30,000 fidelium, nunc autem habet 5,000. Idem apparet in aliis paroeciis. Sunt quidem paroeciae, quarum numerus parochianorum non excedit 50 fideles. Altera causa inopiae ecclesiarum est status rerum oeconomicarum in Russia ac sic dicta "nationalisatio" bonorum ecclesiasticorum. Decreto de "nationalisatione" ecclesiae privatae sunt paucis reditibus, quos antea habuerunt, oblationes vero fidelium non sunt sufficientes ad honestam sustentationem. Quam ob rem sacerdotes necessitatibus carentes, coguntur paroecias relinquere et in patriam una cum parochianis suis redire, et aliquando contingit, ut ne quidem censuris ecclesiasticis in loco suae residentiae retineri possint. Nunc 30 ecclesiae una cum curia archiepiscopali carent pecunia necessaria. Nisi huic rei consulatur ecclesiae a sacerdotibus relictae in usum prophanum a communistis destinentur, et tali pacto stationes ecclesiasticae, tanto cum studio erectae, peribunt, et missionarii, qui aliquando revenient, non habebunt locum residentiae. Ex dictis patet Ecclesiam in Russia in periculo esse ac auxilio alacri indigere.

Praeterea periculum imminet omnibus ecclesiis nostris ex parte decreti

23 Januarii 1918 anni de separatione ecclesiae a statu, vi cuius omnia bona ecclesiastica declarantur pertinere ad populum Russiae seu ad rempublicam. Qua de causa parochiani, ut ius utendi ecclesia habeant, debent pactum cum gubernio inire, quod omnino discipinae ecclesiasticae adversatur.

Hactenus contingebat fidelibus, ut bono cum successu contra dictum pactum protestarentur. Nunc autem, cum regimen communistarum audacius factum sit, magna cum tenacitate subscriptio pacti a fidelibus expostulatur simulque minatur si fideles resistant, ecclesias clausurum iri. Delegatus archiepiscopi Cieplak impetravit Moscoviae indutias unius mensis, intra quem Archiepiscopus posset a Sede Apostolica responsum accipere. Dubitando decisionem Beatissimi Patris eumque omnino spernentes sic dicti commissarii regiminis de novo conantur dictas subscriptiones fidelibus extorquere et iam unam ecclesiam in oppido Gatschina prope Petropolim clauserunt.

Tali pacto, si nullum nobis auxilium obveniet, ecclesiae nostrae claudentur et exspoliationi exponentur.

Optimum ecclesiis in Russia auxilium posset praestare gubernium polonicum vi Rigensis tractatus. Sed gubernium illud propter causas politicas erga regimen Russiae tam debile se ostendit, ut catholici nostri omnem spem melioris sortis a Polonia provenientis amitterent. Non est dubitandum, quin delegatio reipublicae polonicae bonam voluntatem interveniendi habeat urgendo observationem Rigensis tractatus. At difficultas in eo posita est, quod gubernium Poloniae non magna auctoritate utatur apud gubernium Russiae. Quam ob causam art. VII Rigensis Tractatus hactenus a Russia non observatur, quamquam post suam notam diplomaticam de hac re legatio Poloniae aliquoties verbaliter tractabat. Quod quidem in praesenti apparet, quando gubernium Russiae maxima cum severitate nostras ecclesias opprimit, etiam claudit et reliquias sanctorum prophanat.

Error fanaticus communistarum optime apparuit in prophanatione reliquiarum b. Andreae Bobolae. Momentum rei in eo positum est, ut gubernium adversus decretum suum de separatione ecclesiae a statu, quod inter caetera habet articulum de tolerantia, ingerat se in doctrinam Ecclesiae nostrae appellando cultum reliquiarum superstitionem.

Censebamus gubernium Russiae gratum se praebiturum Sedi Apostolicae pro subsidio famelicis praestito, sed spes nos fefellit. Officiales Russiae tam ephemeridibus quam in colloquio supradictum auxilium parvi pendere student. Maxime vero haec ingrata relatio ad Sanctam Sedem apparuit in rebus sacris redimendis. Ut nobis nunc notum est, Curia Romana, post promulgationem decreti de sic dicta exemptione rerum preciosarum ope telegraphi gubernio Russia proponebat se precium aequivalens pro rebus sacris solvere velle. At gubernium non solum nullum responsum dedit, sed etiam prophanationi dictas res sacras exponere curabat simulque sacerdotes hac in re etiam passive se habentes in custodiam includebat et iudicio tradebat. In hac etiam causa Archiepiscopus J. Cieplak multa perpessus est et adhuc patietur. Ex mandato Archiepiscopi decanus Budkiewicz de redimendis rebus sacris Moscoviae cum gubernio tractabat. Nimirum Archiepiscopus statim post acceptum ab Eminentissimo Cardinali Gasparri de hac re nuncium scripsit ad gubernium epistolam, ubi postulabat, ut, vi conventionis cum Sede Apostolica, res sacrae ultra non eximerentur, iam, exemptae ecclesiis redderentur, et sacerdotes hac in causa in custodiam traditi liberarentur. Cum gubernium nihil responderet, supradictus Budkiewicz in scripto proposuit conditiones emptionis rerum sacrarum, explicans quod tam Archiepiscopus quam sacerdotes hac in re accusati non debent tractari ut animo "contrarevolutionis" gubernio non obedientes, sed solummodo ut secundum ius canonicum agentes, atque vi decreti de tolerantia religiosa nulla poena afficiendos esse. Ad hoc propositum respondit officialis Crassicof gubernium severissimo modo reos iudicaturum et puniturum. Quod vero attinet res sacras auferendas, gubernium non posse suum decretum mutare, sed posse Sedi Apostolicae res iam ablatas vendere, ut vendit mercatoribus, precio maximo.

Responsum hoc mirum videtur, si perpendatur pacifica propositio Sedis Apostolicae emendi res sacras.

Alii delegato Cancelario Trojgo gubernium Russiae respondit se non posse res sacras vendere, quia ignorat, ubi sint.

Causa propter quam gubernium non abstinuit se a prophanatione rerum sacrarum videtur esse haec, quod sperabat se occasione "exemptionis" scissionem in Ecclesia facturum, ut factum est in confessione russica.

Gravissimi momenti est propagatio fidei Catholicae in Russia. Cum Exarcha unitarum Petropoli pro Russia nominatus esset, sine merito sperabatur permultos Russos ad Ecclesiam ritus orientalis conversuros esse. Sed spes illa feffelit. Exemplo esse potest Petropolis. Habitant hic in praesenti praeter exarcham quattuor sacerdotes ritus orientalis, quorum unus manet apud parochiam Sancti Stanislai. Exarch Fiodorof habet in urbe capellam suam, duo manent penes ecclesiam s. Catharinae, unus ad procathedralem ecclesiam. Omnes isti sacerdotes sunt viri pii bonumque exemplum vitae praebent. Nihilominus tamen numerus conversorum in ritum orientalem non excedit 90 personas. E contra ad ritum latinum conversi sunt circa 3,000. Eadem proportio apparet etiam in aliis locis.

Quamquam et sacerdotes ritus latini praedicant in lingua russica, hoc tamen (contra opinionen Exarchae Fiodorof) non impedit, quominus conversi eligant ritum slavonicum. Inter praedicationem Exarchae Fiodorof, et praedicationem aliorum sacerdotum, etiam ritus orientalis, Petropoli hoc est discrimen, quod hi explicant et errores schismatiscorum, pater vero Fiodorof putat hoc esse magnopere noxium propagationi unionis et tolerantiam suam eousque extendit, ut etiam schismaticis nondum conversis in sua capella sacramenta poenitentiae et s. Eucharistiae administret (ut dicit, ex verbali licentia Beatissimi papae Pii X). Iidem schismatici sacramenta suscipiunt tam in capella Exarchae quam in ecclesiis schismaticis. Praeterea Fiodorof eo tendit ut Sedes Apostolica exclusive ipsi soli suisque subditis propagationem fidei catholicae in Russia committat omnesque conversos Russos necessario ritum orientalem complecti. Sacerdotes vero ritus latini ad haec respondent se nullam hucusque hac in re specialem dispositionem Sanctae Sedis accepisse ideoque debere dirigi Jure Canonico et theologia pastorali; quod autem ad ritum attinet—neminem posse vi adtrahi.

Idem Fiodorof opinionem propagat polonos sacerdotes non posse propagatores fidei inter Russos esse propter nationalismum polonorum et invidiam Russorum erga polonos. Unde, ut ait Exarcha Fiodorof, Russi, qui nunc non convertuntur, sed decursu temporis converti possunt, odio erga polonos praedicatores vel missionarios ducti (aucto propter conversionem aliquorum Russorum in ritum latinum) etiam in ritum slavonicum non convertuntur. Opinionem hanc esse erroneam patet ex eo, quod sacerdotes poloni non produnt nationalismi animum, sed e contra sciunt linguam russicam et hac lingua praedicant. Praeterea, parochi poloni videntes inopiam sacerdotum conversorum, hospitio in domus saus illos recerperunt. Insuper in ecclesia s. Catharinae celebratur quavis Dominica specialis missa pro Russis in ritu latino et slavonico—cum praedicatione. Unde ratio propter quam quidam contumaces converti nolunt, omnino ridicula et irrationabilis videtur. Ob eandem rationem displicent Exarchae Fiodorof praelectiones et disputationes de rebus fidei, quae lingua russica quavis hebdomada magno cum concursu Russorum penes ecclesiam s. Catharinae Petropoli locum habent.

Tali pacto res, quae ad mentem Ecclesiae unitis viribus fieri debeat, dividitur in contrarias partes, quarum altera repraesentatur a fanaticis ritus orientalis, Fiodorof Petropoli et Abricosof Moscoviae, altera vero a sacerdotibus latinis et ceteris sacerdotibus ritus orientalis, qui exarchae sui fanaticum errorem non sequuntur.

Adhuc pauca verba de biritualismo, qui dicitur. Persuasione sacerdotum latinorum et nonnullorum orientalium opus propagandae fidei catholicae in Russia maxime promoveretur, si sacerdotes latini et orientales haberent facultatem celebrandi in uno vel altero ritu pro rerum locorumque ratione, quod nostris praesertim temporibus, quando numerus sacerdotum catholicorum in Russia in dies minuitur, omnino necessarium videretur. Biritualismus ideo etiam optandus videtur, quod tunc non oriretur in Russia ista spiritui amoris christiani opposita divisio in duas ecclesias catholicas: latinam et orientalem, quae quidem divisio hic et nunc non existit, sed importuno agendi modo effici potest. Imo, biritualismus perpetuo moneret fideles utriusque ritus unam esse ecclesiam catholicam, quae utrumque ritum eiusdem valoris esse docet et ideo pro rerum necessitate, in uno alterove ritu celebrare permittit. Ex idea biritualismi sua sponte unitas hierarchica sequitur.

Paucitas conversorum in ritum orientalem videtur sequenti ratione explicari posse. Russi, etsi iam natura sua sunt "Deum quaerentes" (russice bogazhatieli), hoc est, veram fidem cognoscere sapientes, maxima ignorantia in rebus fidei laborant. Quam ob causam horum fides fere omnino affectu et animi motibus innititur, non vero ratione, et hoc quidem notatur non solum apud indoctos, sed etiam apud nobiles et cultos homines. Quod quidem omnibus gentibus orientalibus proprium est, quorum animus superstitionem paganorum in religionem christianam transfert. Illo affectu ducti Russi, de veritate in Ecclesia catholica latente persuasi, maxima ex parte tantam aversionem erga schismaticam confessionem sentiunt, ut omnem reminiscentiam eius (ergo et ritum orientalem) vitare curent. At non solum ritus illis schismaticam confessionem in memoriam revocat, sed et ipsi sacerdotes uniti. Qui, etiamsi Catholici iam sint, manent tamen cultura orientali, vel potius defectu culturae, imbuti et habent eundem modum agendi, ac schismatici sacerdotes. Unde neoconversi interrogati ad quem ritum adnumerari velint, respondent se velle omnino Ecclesiae Catholicae adscribi et eligunt ritum latinum. Quamquam enim eis res clare explicatur, maxima tamen ex parte habent quandam Ecclesiam ritus orientalis non omnino catholicam. Quae quidem opinio dominat non solum apud laicos sed etiam apud clerum schismaticum, cui non sunt ignota principia ecclesiasticae disciplinae.

Praeter enumeratas quaestiones, sunt quaedam quae spectant calendarium. Exarcha vi potestatis a metropolita, A. Szeptycki, obtentae, exigit ut sacerdotes ritus orientalis penes ecclesias latinas degentes in celebratione missae tam privatae quam solemnis calendarium veteris styli servent, quod nobis videtur contrarium regulis liturgicis simulque offendit liturgicum ordinem in ecclesiis latinis, et causat quoddam scandalum parochianorum, v.g., si die Paschatis secundum novum stylum celebretur missa quadragesimalis.

Pseudoreformatio confessionis schismaticae, quae nunc fit in Russia, initio videbatur profutura conversioni Russorum. Qui vere orthodoxum animum habent, in sua ecclesia vertitatem erroribus contaminatam videntes, necessario ad catholicam fidem se conversuros. Sed hac in re aliter factum est. Imprimis clerus schismaticus, curae et tutelae gubernii assuetus, sine qua iam illi existere difficile est, curam novi gubernii non detractat. Communistae, a priori omnem religionem negantes, post aliquod tempus intellexerunt se non posse religionem in populo eradicare, sed posse ecclesiam schismaticam in servitutuem sibi redigere. Sane, si clerus schismaticus spiritum ecclesiasticum haberet, hoc illis non contingeret. Sed clerici, praesertim aliqui superiores, protestantismo imbuti, iam ideam puram Ecclesiae amiserunt, et patriarcham suum vi amoverunt. Hoc quidem eo modo factum est, quod gubernium imperatorum timens, ne clerus Russiae aliquid commune cum Ecclesia Catholica habeat, curabat ut, ad veritatem obumbrandam principia protestantismi in scholis ecclesiasticis traderentur. Tali pacto decursu temporis factum est, ut ecclesia schismatica, quae in dogmatibus videbatur parum differre ab Ecclesia Catholica, nunc protestantismum sapiat. Unde facile intelligi potest illud, cur clerus Russiae, olim approbante gubernio, aliquoties cum ecclesia Anglicana et cum sic dictis veteribus Catholicis de fide convenire conatus est. Populus, ut supra dictum, est, quoad fidem omnino rudis et incultus, et gubernium timens, propter inertiam suam, sicut in aliis rebus, ita et in causa religionis, post aliquod tempus pseudoreformatae ecclesiae suae assuescet. Paucissimi solummodo tam laici quam clerici resistere pseudoreformationi conantur, sed hi maxima ex parte in custodiam traduntur. Factum est sane quod sat multi clerici cum laicis, praeside archiepiscopo Antonino, qui initio animo pseudoreformationis novo gubernio obediebat, in comitiis Moscoviae protestabant contra pseudoreformationem et ingerentiam gubernii in res ecclesiae, sed hoc parum confessioni schismaticae prodesse videtur. Gubernium ad hoc respondit sese vi decreti de separatione ecclesiae a statu rebus ecclesiae non ingerere. Fautores autem pseudoreformationis contra Antoninum eiusque asseclas comitia fecerunt et excommunicationem pronuntiaverunt.

Has ob causas ecclesia Russiae, ab imperatoribus captivata et depravata, nunc gubernio Sovietistico subiecta manet. Quod quidem gubernium cautissime curat, ne "viva ecclesia" a quibusdam missionariis aliquid detrimenti capiat. Unde propagatio veritatis a missionariis extraneis omnino impossibilis videtur.

Petropoli die   Septembris 1922 a.

The Condition of the Church in Russia

Since communist rule began in Russia, the piety of the faithful has not only not lessened, but rather has increased. The weaker element has indeed defected because of the confusion of things and ideas, but it is very small. Generally men, perceiving themselves in the midst of calamities and suffering persecution, see no refuge but God alone. For this reason our faithful in Russia have never been more attached to religion than at this time. Evidence is the frequent reception of Holy Communion and the defense of the churches and clergy, sometimes undertaken with danger to life and liberty. Hence, we can certainly say that never has there been such a close bond between the Church and the faithful.

The temporal affairs of the Church are in very bad condition. There are two reasons for this. One is the re-emigration of the faithful to their fatherland. Because of the calamitous conditions of life in Russia, very many of the faithful have departed from this region and many wish to leave. St. Catherine's parish in Petrograd is an example. It had 30,000 members; now it has 5,000. The same is true of other parishes. There are some parishes which do not have 50 parishioners. The other reason for the poverty of the churches is the economic condition of Russia and the so-called nationalization of church property. By the decree of "nationalization" the churches were deprived of the small income which they formerly had; and the offerings of the faithful are not sufficient for a decent existence. Therefore, priests, lacking necessities, are forced to abandon their parishes and to return with their parishioners to their homeland; and sometimes they cannot be kept in their place of residence even by ecclesiastical censures. Now about 30 churches, together with the archiepiscopal *curia*, lack the necessary funds. Unless this situation is remedied, the churches abandoned by priests will be converted to profane uses by the communists, and in this way churches, built with such zeal, will perish. And the missionaries, who will some day return, will have no place of residence. From what I have said it is clear that the Church in Russia is in danger and needs speedy assistance.

Moreover, danger threatens all our churches from the decree of January 23, 1918, on the separation of Church and State. By virtue of this decree, all church property is declared the property of the Russian people or of the republic. Therefore, the parishioners, in order to have the right to use the church, must enter into an agreement with the government. This is altogether contrary to ecclesiastical discipline.

So far the faithful have been able to protest successfully against the above-mentioned pact. Now, however, since the communist regime has grown bolder, it is demanding very persistently from the faithful the signature of the agreement; at the same time it threatens to close the churches, if the faithful resist. Archbishop Cieplak's delegate in Moscow requested a delay of one month, within which the archbishop could obtain a reply from the Apostolic See in this matter. Refusing to await the decision of the Holy Father and altogether spurning him, the so-called commissars of the government are trying anew to force signatures from the faithful and have already closed one church in the village of Gatschina near Petrograd.

If we do not receive help, in this way our churches will be closed and exposed to plunder.

By virtue of the Treaty of Riga, the Polish government would have been able to give the best assistance to the churches in Russia. But that government, because of political factors, shows itself so weak in the face of the Russian government, that our Catholics have lost all hope of an improved situation owing to action by the Polish government. Undoubtedly, the Polish delegation has the good will to intervene by urging the observance of the Treaty of Riga; the difficulty, however, lies in the fact that the Polish government does not enjoy great authority with the Russian government. Therefore, Article Seven of the Treaty of Riga is not being observed by Russia so far, although the Polish legation has dealt with the matter verbally several times after its diplomatic note. This is clear at present, when the Russian government is persecuting our churches with the greatest severity, even closing them and desecrating the relics of the saint.

The communists' fanatical error appears best in the desecration of relics of Blessed Andrew Bobola. It is significant that the government, against its own decree on the separation of the Church and State (which also contains an article on religious toleration) intervenes in Catholic teaching by calling our veneration of relics a superstition.

We had thought that the Russian government would be grateful for the Apostolic See's assistance in the famine, but this hope has deceived us. Russian officials endeavor to discount that aid both in their newspapers and in their conversations. This ungrateful attitude toward the Holy See appeared most strongly in the matter of the purchase of the sacred vessels. As we know now, the Roman Curia, after the decree on the so-called expropriation of valuables, by telegraph offered the Russian government to pay an equivalent price for the sacred objects. But the government not only failed to give an answer, but also designedly exposed the sacred objects to profanation, and at the same time imprisoned and put on trial even priests who maintained a passive attitude in this matter. In this affair, too, Archbishop John Cieplak has already suffered and will suffer more. By order of the archbishop, Dean Budkiewicz negotiated with the government at Moscow with a view to redeeming the sacred objects. Immediately after receiving the information from Cardinal Gasparri, the archbishop had written the government a letter in which he demanded that in virtue of the agreement with the Apostolic See, sacred objects should no longer be seized, those already expropriated be returned to the churches, and the priests arrested over this matter be freed. When the government gave no reply, the aforementioned Budkiewicz in a letter proposed conditions for the purchase of the sacred objects; he explained that the archbishop as well as the priests charged in this matter ought not to be treated as disobeying the government from a spirit of "counter-revolution," but only as acting according to canon law. Hence, by virtue of the decree on religious toleration, they are not to be punished in any way. To this proposal Krassikov, an official in the Commissariat of Justice, replied that the government would judge and punish the guilty parties most severely; with regard to the removal of the sacred objects, the government could not change its decree, but it could sell objects already seized to the Apostolic See at the highest price, just as it was selling them to merchants.

This reply certainly seems marvelous, if one considers the peaceable offer of the Holy See to purchase the sacred objects.

To the other delegate, Chancellor Troigo, the Russian government replied that it cannot sell the sacred objects, because it does not know where they are.

The reason why the government did not restrain itself from the desecration of sacred objects seems to be that it hoped to produce a schism in our Church by the "expropriation," as it did in the Russian confession.

The propagation of the Catholic faith in Russia is of the greatest importance. When a Uniate exarch at St. Petersburg was named for Russia, it was hoped, but without reason, that very many Russians would be converted to the church of the Eastern rite. This hope has proved false. Petrograd can serve as an example. Besides the exarch, four priests of the Eastern rite live here, one of whom stays at the parish of St. Stanislas. Exarch Fedorov has his chapel in the city; two are at St. Catherine's church and one at the procathedral. All these priests are pious men, and they give good example by their lives. Nevertheless, the number of converts to the Eastern rite does not exceed 90 persons. There are, on the contrary, about 3,000 converts to the Latin rite. That same proportion appears in other places.

Although the priests of the Latin rite preach in Russian, this does not (contrary to the opinion of Exarch Fedorov) prevent the converts from choosing the Slavonic rite. Between the preaching of Exarch Fedorov and the preaching of other priests (also of the Eastern rite) at Petrograd there is this difference, that the latter explain the error of the schismatics; Fedorov, however, considers this very injurious to the spread of the Union, and pushes his tolerance so far as to administer the sacraments in his chapel to schismatics who have not as yet been converted. He asserts that he does this by reason of a verbal permission from Pope Pius X. These schismatics receive the sacraments in the exarch's chapel as well as in their own schismatic churches; furthermore, Fedorov declares that the Apostolic See has committed the propagation of the faith in Russia exclusively to him and his subjects, and that all Russian converts must necessarily embrace the Eastern rite. To this the Latin rite priests answer that on this problem they have so far not received any special instructions from the Holy See and that, therefore, they must be directed by canon law and pastoral theology. With regard to rite, they say that no one can be forced to adopt any rite.

Exarch Fedorov is also spreading the opinion that Polish priests cannot be propagators of the faith in Russia because of the nationalism of the Poles and the hatred the Russians feel for the Poles; therefore, says Fedorov, Russians who are not being converted now, but could be converted in the course of time, are not being converted even to the Slavonic rite because of a hatred for the Polish preachers (a hatred increased by the conversion of some Russians to the Latin rite). That this opinion is wrong is obvious, for the Polish priests do not act in the spirit of nationalism but, on the contrary, they know the Russian language and preach in this language. Moreover, the Polish pastors, seeing the poverty of the convert priests, receive them as guests in their homes. Besides, every Sunday a mass in the Slavonic rite and the Latin rite is celebrated for the Russians in St. Catherine's church—together with a sermon. Hence, the reason why certain obstinate persons do not wish to be converted seems altogether ridiculous and irrational. For the same reason, Exarch Fedorov is displeased with the lectures and debates on matters of faith which are held every week in Russian at St. Catherine's church in Petrograd with a large Russian attendance.

In this way a matter which ought to be done with united forces leads to division into two opposite factions. One is represented by the fanatics of the Eastern rite, Fedorov at Petrograd, and Abrikosov at Moscow; the other is represented by the Latin rite priests, and the rest of the Eastern rite clergy, who do not follow their exarch's fanatical error.

Still a few words about so-called biritualism. It is the conviction of the Latin priests and some of the Oriental clergy, that the work of spreading the Catholic faith in Russia would profit greatly if Latin and Oriental priests had permission to celebrate in one or the other rite, depending on the time and place; especially in our times, when the number of Catholic priests is daily decreasing, this seems to be altogether necessary. Biritualism also seems advisable for the reason that then there would not rise in Russia that division into two Catholic churches, Latin and Oriental, a division contrary to the spirit of Christian charity, and one which does not here and now exist, but could be created by an inopportune manner of acting. Furthermore, biritualism would always teach the faithful that there is one Catholic Church which teaches that both rites have the same value. It permits celebration in one or the other rite according to necessity. From the idea of biritualism follows naturally hierarchical unity.

The fewness of converts to the Eastern rite seems explicable from the following reason. Russians, even though they are by their nature already "God-seekers," that is, knowing how to recognize the true faith, are afflicted with a great ignorance in matters of faith. Therefore, the faith of these people rests almost wholly on sentiment and emotional states, and not on reason; and this is true not only of the unlettered but also of noble and educated men. This, indeed, is characteristic of Oriental peoples, whose spirit has transferred pagan superstition into the Christian religion. Led by this sentiment, the Russians, convinced that truth lies hidden in the Catholic Church, for the most part feel such an aversion for the schismatic confession, that they wish to avoid its every memory (hence, also the Eastern rite). But not only does the rite recall to them the schismatic confession, but so do the Uniate priests themselves. Even though these priests are Catholic, they remain imbued with an Oriental culture (or rather a lack of culture), and behave in the same way that the schismatic priests do. Hence, when new converts are asked what rite they wish to belong to, they reply emphatically that they wish to join the Catholic Church and they choose the Latin rite. Although the matter is explained to them clearly, they mostly consider an Eastern rite church as not entirely Catholic. This opinion is dominant not only among layfolk, but also among the schismatic clergy, who are not unacquainted with the principles of ecclesiastical discipline.

Besides these questions already listed, there are some pertaining to the calendar. The exarch, by virtue of power received from Metropolitan Andrew Szeptycki, demands that priests of Eastern rite attached to Latin churches follow the Old Style calendar in the celebration of private as well as solemn mass, which seems to us contrary to liturgical regulations, disturbs the liturgical order in the Latin churches, and somewhat causes scandal among the parishioners, for example, on Easter Day (according to the New Style), they celebrate a lenten mass.

The pseudoreformation of the schismatic confession now going on in Russia seemed first as though it might aid conversion of the Russians. But those who have a truly orthodox spirit, seeing in their church the truth fouled by errors, necessarily will be converted to the Catholic faith. The schismatic clergy, accustomed to the care and protection of the government, does not reject the support of the new government. The communists, *a priori* denying all religion, after a while realized that they cannot eradicate religion in the population, but that they can reduce the schismatic church to slavery. Indeed, if the schismatic clergy had the ecclesiastical spirit, this would not have happened to them. But the clergy, especially some of the higher clergy, imbued with Protestantism, have already lost the pure concept of the Church, and have forcibly removed their patriarch. This was effected in the following manner. The imperial government, fearing lest the Russian clergy have anything in common with the Catholic Church, in order to confuse the truth, undertook to see that the principles of Protestantism were taught in the ecclesiastical schools. Thus in the course of time the schismatic church, which seemed to differ but little from the Catholic Church in dogma, took on a Protestant coloring. Hence, it is easily understood why the Russian clergy, with the approval of the government, tried several times to come to an agreement on matters of faith with the Anglican Church and with the so-called Old Catholics. The people, as I have said above, are altogether illiterate, uneducated, and fearful of the government, and because of its inertia in religion as in other matters will after some time grow accustomed

to their pseudoreformed church. Only very few clergy and laity tried to resist the pseudoreformation, but most of these have been cast into prison. In fact, a considerable number of priests and lay folk, under the leadership of Archbishop Antonin, who at first in the spirit of the pseudoreform obeyed the new government, met in Moscow and protested against the pseudoreform and against government intereference in ecclesiastical matters. However, this seems to benefit the schismatic church but little. The government replied to this that by virtue of the decree on separation of Church and State it does not interefere with ecclesiastical matters. The advocates of the pseudoreform convoked a synod against Antonin and his followers and pronounced a sentence of excommunication.

For these reasons the Russian Church, held captive and corrupted by the emperors, is now subject to the Soviet government. This government takes the greatest care lest the "Living Church" suffer any harm from certain missionaries. Hence, the propagation of the truth by foreign missioners seems completely impossible.

St. Petersburg   September, 1922

BIBLIOGRAPHY

Unpublished Sources (Primary Material)

Budkiewicz Archive. Collection of Bronisław Ussas, Warsaw.
Cieplak Archive. The Archives of the Polish Roman Catholic Union, Chicago, Illinois.
Collection of E. T. Colton. Hoover Library, Stanford University, Stanford, California.
National Archives of the United States. Washington, D.C.: Department of State Decimal File (1910–1929), File Nos. 861.404/16–172.
The Status of Religion in the USSR. Washington, D.C.: Office of Strategic Services, 1944. This secret report, declassified in January 1950, is in the Hoover Library, Stanford University, Stanford, California.
Ussas Archives, Warsaw.
Wykaz alfabetyczny biskupów i kapłanów oraz zakonników polskich przebywających do obecnej chwili na wygnaniu w Syberyi i głębokiej Rosyi, June 1881. Rome: Library of the Pontifical Oriental Institute.

Published Documents (Primary Material)

Acta Apostolicae Sedis. Rome: Vatican Press. Vols. XIII (1921); XV (1923); XVI (1924).
Adamov, E. A. *Diplomatiia Vatikana v nachaluiu epokhu imperializma, 1887–1900.* Moscow: Gosudarstvennoe sotsialno-ekonomicheskoe izdatelstvo, 1931.
Alfavitnyi ukazatel k zhurnalam Vremennogo Pravitelstva za Aprel 1917 goda. Petrograd: Gosudarstvennaia tipografia, 1917.
Bishop, Donald G. *Soviet Foreign Relations: Documents and Readings.* Syracuse: Syracuse University Press, 1952.
Borowski, Stanisław (ed.). *Kodeks Stanisława Augusta Zbiór Dokumentów.* Warsaw: Towarzystwo Prawnicze, 1938.

Bunyan, J. and Fisher, H. H. (eds.). *The Bolshevik Revolution, 1917–1918.* Stanford: Stanford University Press, 1934.

Certain Legislation respecting Religion in Force in the Union of Soviet Socialist Republics. London: His Majesty's Stationery Office, 1930.

A Collection of Reports on Bolshevism in Russia. London: His Majesty's Stationery Office, 1919.

Commissariat du peuple pour les affaires étrangères. *Livre Rouge: Recueil des documents diplomatiques relatifs aux relations entre la Russie et la Pologne, 1918–1920.* Moscow: Commissariat du peuple pour les affaires étrangères, 1920.

Degras, Jane. *Calendar of Soviet Documents on Foreign Policy, 1917–1941.* London: Royal Institute of International Affairs, 1948.

————— (ed.). *Soviet Documents on Foreign Policy.* London: Oxford University Press, 1951.

Documents Officiels émanés de la Secrétairerie d'état du Saint-Siège au sujet de la persécution des Catholiques en Pologne et en Russie et de la rupture des relations avec le gouvernement Russe. Zurich: Imprimerie F. Schulthess, 1878.

Dvenadsatyi Sezd Rossiiskoi Kommunisticheskoi Partii (Bolshevikov): Stenograficheskii otchet. Moscow: Krasnaia, November 1923.

Expositio Documentis Munita Earum Curarum Quas Summus Pontifex Pius IX Assidue Gessit in Eorum Malorum Levamen Quibus in Ditione Russica et Polona Ecclesia Catholica Afflictatur e Latinis Ephemeridibus Excerpta. Rome: Sacred Congregation of the Propaganda Fide, 1870.

Ezovitov, K. *Belorussy i Poliaki: Dokumenty i fakty iz istorii okkupatsii Belorussii Poliakami v 1918 i 1919 godakh.* Kovno: Francis Skoryna Press, 1919.

Elenchus omnium ecclesiarum et universi cleri archidioeceseos Mohyloviensis et dioec. Minscensis pro anno domini 1904 conscriptus. St. Petersburg, 1904.

Elenchus cleri et ecclesiarum archidioeceseos Mohiloviensis in Russia in diem 1 Januarii 1926. Warsaw, 1926.

Eudin, Xenia J. and Fisher, Harold H. *Soviet Russia and the West, 1920–1927: A Documentary Survey.* Stanford: Stanford University Press, 1957.

Filipowicz, Tytus (ed.). *Confidential Correspondence of the British Government respecting the Insurrection in Poland, 1863.* Paris: Librairie H. Le Saudier, 1914.

Główny Urząd Statystyczny Rzeczpospolitej Polskiej. *Pierwszy powszechny spis Rzeczpospolitej Polskiej z dnia 30 września, 1921 roku.* Vol. XXI. Warsaw: Główny Urząd Statystyczny, 1927.

Hansard, *Parliamentary Debates.* Fifth Series. Vol. LIII (1923).

—————. *Parliamentary Debates.* Fifth Series. Vol. CLXI (1923).

—————. *Parliamentary Debates.* Fifth Series. Vol. CLXII (1923).

History of the Communist Party of the Soviet Union (Bolsheviks). New York: International Publishers, 1939.

de Journel, M. J. Rouet. *Nonciatures de Russie d'après les documents authentiques.* 4 vols. Nos. 166 (1952); 167 (1943); 168 (1922); 169 (1927), of Studi e Testi. Vatican: Vatican Library, 1922–1952.

La Legislation soviétique contre la religion. Orientalia Christiana, Vol. V-1 (October 1925). Rome: Pontifical Oriental Institute, 1925.

Makowski, Julian. *Umowy międzynarodowe Polski, 1919–1934.* Warsaw: Drukarnia Wł. Łazarskiego, 1935.

"Materialy dlia istorii prisoedineniia Polshi k Rossii (1772–1815)," *Russkii Arkhiv,* I (1863), 500–599.

Meisel, J. H., and Kozera, E. S. (eds.). *Materials for the Study of the Soviet State System: State and Party Constitutions, Laws, Decrees, Decisions, and Official Statements of the Leaders in Translation.* Ann Arbor: George Mahr Publishing Company, 1950.

Ministerstvo Iustitsii SSSR. *Osnovy sovetskogo gosudarstva i prava.* Moscow: Iuridicheskoe izdatelstvo, 1947.

Narodny Komissariat Iustitsii. *Alfativno-predmetnyi ukazatel a Ianvar 1922 g. k dekretam, postanovleniiam, rasproiazheniiam i prikazam.* Moscow: Izdanie Narodnogo Komissariata Iustitsii, 1922.

_____. *Materialy Narodnogo Komisariata Iustitsii.* Moscow: Izdanie Narodnogo Komissariata Iustitsii, 1918–1922. Vypusk I, II, III, IV, V, VI, VII, VIII, X, XI, XII, XIII, XV.

Narodny Komissariat po delam natsionalnostei. *Otchet Narodnogo Komissariata po delam natsionalnostei za 1921 god.* Moscow: Narodny Komissariat po delam natsionalnostei, 1922.

_____. *Politika Sovetskoi vlasti po natsionalnomu voprosu za tri goda 1917–xi–1920.* Moscow: Gosudarstvennoe izdatelstvo, 1920.

Narodny Komissariat po inostrannym delam. *Genuezskaia konferentsiia: Materialy i dokumenty.* Moscow: Narodny komissariat po inostrannym delam, 1922.

_____.*Mezhdunarodnaia politika R. S. F. S. R. v 1922 g.* Moscow: Narodny Komissariat po innostrannym delam, 1923.

_____. *Rosja Sowiecka a Polska.* Moscow: Narodny Komissariat po inostrannym delam, 1921.

_____. *Sovetskaia Rossiia i Polsha.* Moscow: Narodny Komissariat po inostrannym delam, 1921.

Notes Exchanged on the Russian-Polish Situation by the United States, France, and Poland. No. 155. New York: American Association for International Conciliation, 1920.

Opisanie dokumentov Arkhiva zapadnorussiskikh Uniatskikh mitropolitov, 1701–1839. 2 vols. St. Petersburg: Synodal Press, 1907.

People's Commissariat of Justice. *The First Code of Laws of the Russian Socialistic Federal Soviet Republic.* Petrograd: People's Commissariat of Justice, 1919.

Polish-Soviet Relations, 1918–1943: Official Documents. Washington, D.C.: Polish Embassy, 1943.

Polnoe Sobranie zakonov rossiiskoi imperii. 3 Series. St. Petersburg: Codification Commission, 1825–1916.

Protokoly deviatogo Sezda RKP (b). Moscow: Partiinoe izdatelstvo, 1934.

Rocznik Polityczny i Gospodarczy, 1937. Warsaw: Polska Agencja Telegraficzna, 1934.

Sedmoi sezd Rossiiskoi Kommunisticheskoi Partii: Stenograficheskii otchet. Moscow: Gosudarstvennoe izdatelstvo, 1923.

A *Selection of Papers Dealing with the Relations Between His Majesty's Government and the Soviet Government, 1921–1927*. London: His Majesty's Stationery Office, 1927.

Sprawozdanie stenograficzne z 32 posiedzenia Sejmu Rzeczpospolitej z dn. 12 kwietnia, 1923 r. Vol. XXXII. Warsaw, 1923.

Sprawozdanie stenograficzne z 17 posiedzenia Senatu Rzeczpospolitej z dn. 27 marca, 1923 r. Vol. XVII. Warsaw, 1923.

Sprawozdanie z działalności Komisji Likwidacyjnej do Spraw Królestwa Polskiego za czas od 15-go marca do 1-go sierpnia, 1917 r. Petrograd: Drukarnia Społeczna, 1917.

Svod Zakonov rossiiskoi imperii. St. Petersburg: Codification Commission, 1832–1916.

Trinadsatyi Sezd Rossiiskoi kommunisticheskoi Partii (Bolshevikov): Stenograficheskii otchet. Moscow: Krasnaia, November 1924.

Tsentralnoe statisticheskoe upravlenie. *Biulletin tsentralnogo statisticheskogo upravleniia*. No. 77. August 25, 1923. Moscow: Tsentralnoe statisticheskoe upravlenie, 1923.

————.*Statisticheskii spravochnik SSSR za 1928*. Moscow: Statisticheskoe izdatelstvo, 1929.

U. S. Department of State. *Papers Relating to the Foreign Relations of the United States, 1923*. Vol. II. Washington, D.C.: Government Printing Office, 1938.

Verwaltungsbericht der Militärverwaltung Bialystok-Grodno für die Zeit 10 Oktober 1916 bis 1 April 1917. No. 22. Druckerei der Militärverwaltung Bialystok-Grodno.

Vossoedinenie Ukrainy s Rossiei: Dokumenty i materialy v trekh tomakh. 3 vols. Moscow: Izdatelstvo Akademii Nauk SSSR, 1954.

Vremenoe pravitelstvo, Ministertsvo vnutrennikh del. *Proekty i predpolozheniia Ministerstva*. Petrograd: Gosudarstvennaia Tipografia, 1917.

Welykyj, Athanasius G. (ed.). *Documenta Pontificum Romanorum Historiam Ucrainae Illustrantia (1075–1953)*. Rome: Ukrainian Emigre Press, 1953.

Zhurnal Zasedaniia Vremennogo pravitelstva, 1917 Mart-Mai. Vols. I, II. Petrograd: Gosudarstvennaia Tipografia, 1917.

Memoirs (Primary Material)

Borodicz, Józef. *Pod wozem i na wozie*. Chrzanów: M. Ziembiński Press, 1918.

Buchanan, A. *My Mission to Russia and Other Diplomatic Memories*. 2 vols. Boston: Little, Brown, and Company, 1923.

D'Abernon, Viscount. *The Eighteenth Decisive Battle of the World: Warsaw, 1920*. London: Hodder and Stoughton, 1931.

Feliński, Zygmunt. *Pamiętniki*. 2nd ed. 2 parts. Lwów: Zienkowicz and Chęciński, 1911.

Fortescue, L. M. Anderson. *Seven Months' Residence in Russian Poland*. London: Macmillan and Company, Ltd., 1864.

Francis, David, R. *Russia from the American Embassy: April 1916–November 1918*. New York: Charles Scribners' Sons, 1921.

McCullagh, Francis. *The Bolshevik Persecution of Christianity.* New York: E. P. Dutton and Company, 1924.

Moulens, Joseph. *Mon Ambassade en Russie Soviétique, 1917–1919.* Vol. I. Paris: Librairie Plon, 1933.

Piłsudski, Józef. *Rok 1920. Pisma zbiorowe.* Vol. XII. Warsaw: Instytut Józefa Piłsudskiego, 1937.

Trotsky, Leon. *My Life.* New York: Charles Scribners' Sons, 1930.

"Zapiski Polskogo Episkopa Butkevicha," *Ruskii Arkhiv,* XIV-2 (1876), 321–353.

Zatko, James J. "A Contemporary Report on the Condition of the Catholic Church in Russia, 1922," *The Harvard Theological Review,* LIII (1960), 277–295.

_____. "The Letters of Archbishop Lauri, Apostolic Nuncio in Warsaw, to Monsignor Constantine Budkiewicz of St. Catherine's, St. Petersburg, 1922–1923," *The Polish Review,* IV (1959), 127–131.

Newspapers (Primary Material)

Dziennik Petrogradzki. St. Petersburg, May 16, 1917.

Izvestiia. Moscow, 1918–1923.

Kurjer Polski. Warsaw, 1917–1923.

Kurjer Warszawski. Warsaw, 1917–1923.

Naród i Państwo. Warsaw, 1918.

New York Times. New York City, 1918–1923.

Osservatore Romano. Rome, 1917–1924.

Polska. Warsaw, 1918.

Pravda. Moscow, 1917–1923.

Zhizn Natsionalnostei. Moscow, 1918–1924.

Articles (Primary Material)

Chemko, J. "Pokhozhdeniia metropolita Andreia grafa Sheptitskogo v. Amerike," *Revolutsiia i tserkov,* Nos. 1–3 (1922). p. 60.

"Demokratizatsiia Vatikana," *Revolutsiia i tserkov,* Nos. 3–5 (1919), p. 60.

Edlinskii, Gr. "Uniia s Rimon i mitropolit graf Sheptitskii," *Revolutsiia i tserkov,* Nos. 1–3 (1924), pp. 108–109.

"Epizody polskoi voiny," *Revolutsiia i tserkov,* Nos. 9–12 (1920), pp. 54–55.

Gorev, Mikhail. "Vskrytie moshchei Tikhona Zadonskogo i Mitrofana Voronezhskogo," *Revolutsiia i tserkov,* No. 2 (1919), pp. 9–23.

Halecki, Oscar. "Possevino's Last Statement on Polish-Russian Relations," *Orientalia Christiana Periodica,* XIX (1953), 261–302.

Karewicz, Archbishop F. "Z dziejów pracy unijnej w Rosji," *Kościół katolicki w Rosji: Materiały do jego historji i organizacji,* pp. 43–57. Warsaw: Secretariat of the Archbishop of Mohylow, 1932.

Kolpinskij, Diodor. "Początki katolicyzmu wchodniego obrządku w Rosji," *Kościół katolicki w Rosji: Materiały do jego historji i organizacji,* pp. 24–34. Warsaw: Secretariat of the Archbishop of Mohylew, 1932.

Komorovskii. "Kulturnye dostizheniia Poliakov RSFSR," *Zhizn natsionalnostei* (January 1923), pp. 232–233.

Kremer, D-r. "Vatikan i sovetskoe pravitelstvo," *Revolutsiia i tserkov*, Nos. 1–2 (1924), pp. 9–13.

Loster, Antoni. "Towarzystwo św. Wincentego a Paulo w Rosji," *Kościół katolicki w Rosji: Materiały do jego historji i organizacji*, pp. 87–104. Warsaw: Secretariat of Archbishop of Mohylew, 1932.

Milich, M. "Protsess rimsko-katolicheskogo dukhovenstva," *Revolutsiia i tserkov*, Nos. 1–3 (1923), pp. 102–116.

Orlovskii, E. "Natsionalny vopros v Polshe," *Zhizn natsionalnostei* (1923), pp. 139–146.

Płoskiewicz, Walery. "Władza biskupów rz.-katolickich w świetle prawodawstwa b. Imerjum Rosyjskiego," *Kościół katolicki w Rosji: Materiały do jego historji i organizacji*, pp. 71–79. Warsaw: Secretariat of the Archbishop of Mohylew, 1932.

"Prikhovstni polskich panov," *Revolutsiia i tserkov*, Nos. 6–8 (1920), p. 102.

"Sovetskaia politika v religioznom voprose," *Revolutsiia i tserkov*, No. 1 (1919), pp. 1–5.

Urban, Jan. "Prace Jezuitów w Rosji," *Kościół katolicki w Rosji: Materiały do jego historji i organizacji*, pp. 11–23. Warsaw: Secretariat of the Archbishop of Mohylew, 1932.

Books and Pamphlets (Secondary Material)

Abraham, Władysław. *Powstanie organizacyi kościoła łacińskiego na Rusi*. 2 vols. Lwów: Towarzystwo dla popierania nauki polskiej, 1904.

Almedingen, Martha E. *The Catholic Church in Russia Today*. New York: P. J. Kenedy, 1923.

Ammann, Albert M. *Abriss der Ostslawischen Kirchengeschichte*. Vienna: Thomas Morus Press, 1950.

Anderson, Paul B. *People, Church and State in Modern Russia*. New York: The Macmillan Company, 1944.

Arsenev, Nikolai S. *Pravoslavie, katholichestvo, i protestantizm*. Paris: YMCA Press, 1948.

————. *La Sainte Moscou*. Paris: Cerf, 1948.

Arturov, O. A. *Vatikan i ego politika*. Moscow: Izdatelstvo *Pravda*, 1947.

Aubert, R. *Le Pontificat de Pie IX (1846–1878)*. Vol. XXI of *Histoire de l'Eglise*. Edited by A. Fliche and V. Martin. Paris: Bloud and Gay, 1952.

Bain, Nisbet T. *The Last King of Poland and His Contemporaries*. London: Methuen and Company, 1909.

Barinov, G. P. *Osnovnye voprosy konstitutsii SSSR*. Moscow: Gosudarstvennoe uchebno-pedagogicheskoe izdatelstvo, 1948.

Batiushkov, P. N. *Podoliia: Istoricheskoe opisanie*. St. Petersburg: Obshchestvennaia Polza, 1891.

————. *Volyn: Istoricheskiia sudby iugo-zapadnogo kraia*. St. Petersburg: Obshchestvennaia Polza, 1888.

Baykov, Alexander. *The Development of the Soviet Economic System: An Essay on the Experience of Planning in the U.S.S.R.* New York: The Macmillan Company, 1948.

Bennigsen, George (ed.). *Religion in Russia: A Collection of Essays Read at the Cambridge Summer School of Russian Studies, 1939.* London: Burnes, Oates, and Washbourne, Ltd., 1940.

Berdiaev, N. *The Origin of Russian Communism.* New York: Charles Scribners' Sons, 1937.

_____. *The Russian Idea.* New York: Sheed and Ward, 1948.

Berman, H. J. *Justice in Russia.* Cambridge: Harvard University Press, 1950.

Biernacki, Mikołaj. *Ius "Orthodoxorum" Russorum respectu Iuris Ecclesiae Romano-Catholicae Consideratum.* Poznań: St. Adalbert Society, 1914.

Boudou, Adrien. *Le Saint-Siège et la Russie: Leurs Relations Diplomatiques au XIXe siècle.* 2 vols. Paris: Librairie Plon, 1922.

Brückner, Aleksander. *Tysiąc lat kultury polskiej.* 3rd ed. Vol. I. Paris: Księgarnia Polska, 1955.

Bujak, Francis. *Poland's Economic Development: A Short Sketch.* London: George Allen and Unwin, Ltd., 1926.

Bukharin, N. and Preobrazhensky, E. A. *The ABC of Communism.* Translated by Eden and Cedar Paul. London: The Communist Party of Great Britain, 1922.

Bukharin, Nikolai. *Finance Capital in Papal Robes.* New York: Friends of the Soviet Union, 1930.

Bulatov, Ivan. *Imperialism and the Church Prepare War against the U.S.S.R.* Moscow: Tsentralnoe izdatelstvo, 1931.

Carr, Edward H. *The Bolshevik Revolution, 1917–1923.* 3 vols. London: Macmillan and Company, Ltd., 1950–1953.

_____. *German-Soviet Relations between the Two World Wars, 1919–1939.* Baltimore: Johns Hopkins Press, 1951.

Chamberlin, A. H. *The Russian Revolution, 1917–1921.* 2 vols. New York: The Macmillan Company, 1935.

Cianfarra, Camille M. *The Vatican and the Kremlin.* New York: E. P. Dutton and Company, 1950.

Clark, Colin. *A Critique of Russian Statistics.* London: Macmillan and Company, Ltd., 1939.

Cumming, C. K., and Pettit, W. W. *Russian-American Relations, March 1917–1920.* New York: Harcourt, Brace, and Howe, 1920.

Curtiss, John S. *Church and State in Russia: The Last Years of the Empire, 1900–1917.* New York: Columbia University Press, 1940.

_____. *The Russian Church and the Soviet State, 1917–1950.* Boston: Little, Brown and Company, 1953.

Der Czar und der Nachfolger des heiligen Petrus. Eine Erklärung der papstlichen Darlegung über die schweren Leiden der Katholischen Kirche in Russland and Polen und der damit verbunden Actenstücken für das Katholische Volk. Mainz: Kirchheim, Schott, und Thielmann, 1842.

Czekanowski, Jan. *Stosunki narodowościowo-wyznaniowe na Litwie i Rusi.* Prace geograficzne, Zeszyt I. Lwów: Książnica Polska, 1918.

Dark, Sidney, and Essex, R. S. *The War against God.* New York: The Abingdon Press, 1939.

Dennis, A. L. P. *The Foreign Policies of Soviet Russia.* New York: E. P. Dutton and Company, 1924.

Deutscher, Isaac. *Stalin.* New York: Oxford University Press, 1949.

————. *The Prophet Armed: Trotsky, 1879–1921.* New York: Oxford University Press, 1954.

Diadichenko, A. and Chermak, L. *Statisticheskii spravochnik.* Vypusk I. *Naselenie i zemlevladenie Rossi.* St. Petersburg: Knigoizdatelstvo "Zemlia i Volia," 1906.

Domanski, Francis. *The Great Apostle of Russia, Servant of God, Archbishop Cieplak.* Chicago: (n.p.), 1954.

Duranty, Walter. *I Write as I Please.* New York: Simon and Schuster, 1935.

Dyboski, Roman. *Poland in World Civilization.* New York: J. M. Barrett, 1950.

Emhardt, William. *Religion in Soviet Anarchy.* London: Morehouse Publishing Company, 1929.

Fainsod, Merle. *How Russia Is Ruled.* Cambridge: Harvard University Press, 1954.

Fischer, Harold H. *America and the New Poland.* New York: The Macmillan Company, 1928.

————. *The Famine in Soviet Russia, 1919–1923: The Operations of American Relief Administration.* Stanford: Stanford University Press, 1935.

Fischer, Louis. *The Soviets in World Affairs: A History of the Relations between the Soviet Union and the Rest of the World, 1917–1929.* 2 vols. Princeton: Princeton University Press, 1951.

Frank, S. L. *A Solovyov Anthology.* Translated by Natalie Duddington. New York: Charles Scribners' Sons, 1950.

Genkin, E. B. *Obrazovanie SSSR.* 2nd ed. Moscow: Gosudarstvennoe izdatelstvo politicheskoi literatury, 1947.

Golubinskii, E. E. *Istoriia russkoi tserkvi.* 2 vols. Moscow: University Press, 1900–1901.

Grabski, Stanisław. *The Polish-Soviet Frontier.* New York: Polish Information Center (n.d.).

Grushevskii, Mikhailo. *Istoriia Ukraini-Rusi.* 8 vols. New York: Knigospilka, 1954.

Gsovski, Vladimir. *Church and State behind the Iron Curtain.* New York: Mid-European Studies Center, 1955.

————. *Soviet Civil Law.* Ann Arbor: University of Michigan Press, 1948.

Gudzy, N. K. *History of Early Russian Literature.* Translated by Susan Wilbur Jones. 2nd ed. New York: The Macmillan Company, 1949.

Gulovich, Stephen. *Windows Westward: Rome, Russia, and Reunion.* New York: D. X. McMullen Company, 1947.

Gurian, Waldemar. *Bolshevism: An Introduction to Soviet Communism.* Notre Dame: University of Notre Dame Press, 1952.

Gurvich, G. S. *Osnovy sovietskoi konstitutsii.* 8th ed. Moscow: Gosudarstvennoe izdatelstvo, 1930.

Halecki, Oscar. *Borderlands of Western Civilization: A History of East Central Europe.* New York: The Ronald Press Company, 1952.

Hamel, Alban de Malezieux du. *Le pape et la Société des Nations.* Paris: Editions Albricht Mechelnick, 1932.

d'Herbigny, Michel. *L'aspect religieux de Moscou en Octobre 1925.* Rome: Pontifical Oriental Institute, 1926.

Hrushevsky, Michel. *A History of Ukraine.* Translated by O. J. Frederickson. New Haven: Yale University Press, 1941.

Iaroslavskii, E. *Die Gottlosenbewegung in der Sowjet-Union.* Moscow: Verlagsgenossenschaft äuslandischer Arbeiter, 1933.

_____. *Kratkaia istoriia VKP(b).* Moscow: Gosudarstvennoe izdatelstvo, 1930.

Iswolsky, Helen. *Soul of Russia.* London: Sheed and Ward, 1944.

Ivanov, V. N. *Osnovye prava i obiazatelnosti grazhdan SSSR.* Moscow: Gosudarstvennoe izdatelstvo iuridicheskoi literatury, 1953.

Jasny, Naum. *The Socialized Agriculture of the USSR: Plans and Performance.* Stanford: Stanford University Press, 1949.

Karmanskii, P. *Vatikan-vdokhnovatel mrakobesiia i reaktsii.* Moscow: Gospolizdat, 1953.

Kellerman, Edouard de, duc de Valmy. *Liberté Religieuse: Etude sur la législation de la Russie et de la France en matière de religion.* Paris: Jacques Lecoffre et Cie., 1848.

Kennan, George F. *Russia Leaves the War.* Vol. I of Soviet American Relations, 1917–1920. Princeton: Princeton University Press.

_____. *Siberia and the Exile System.* 2 vols. New York: The Century Company, 1891.

Klein, Fritz. *Die diplomatischen Beziehungen Deutschlands zur Sowjetunion.* Berlin: Rutten und Loenig, 1952.

Klostermann, R. A. *Probleme der Ostkirche: Untersuchungen zum Wesen und zur Geschichte der Griechisch-Orthodoxen Kirche.* Goteborg: Wettergren und Kerbers Forlag, 1955.

Kobliakov, I. K. *Ot Bresta do Rapallo: Ocherki istorii sovetsko-germanskikh otnoshenii s 1918 po 1922 g.* Moscow: Gosudarstvennoe izdatelstvo politicheskoi literatury, 1954.

Kochan, Lionel. *Russia and the Weimar Republic.* New York: Frederick A. Praeder, 1954.

Koialovich, Mikhail I. *Lektsii po istorii zapadnoi Rossii.* Moscow: T. Bakhmetev, 1864.

Kolarz, Walter. *Religion in the Soviet Union.* New York: St. Martin's Press, 1961.

_____. *Russia and Her Colonies.* New York: Frederick A. Praeger, 1952.

Kologrivof, Ivan. *Essai sur la sainteté en Russie.* Bruges: Beyaert, 1953.

Koncevicius, Joseph B. *Russia's Attitude towards Union with Rome (9th–16th centuries).* Washington: Catholic University of America, 1927.

Komu sluzhat tserkovniki i sektanti: sbornik statei. Iaroslavl: Iaroslavskoe oblastnoe izdatelstvo, 1938.

Korzon, Tadeusz. *Wewnętrzne dzieje Polski za Stanisława Augusta (1764–1794).* 2nd ed. 6 vols. Warsaw: Teodor Paprocki i s-ki, 1897.

Kornilov, Aleksander A. *Modern Russian History from the Age of Catherine the Great to the End of the Nineteenth Century.* Translated by Alexander S. Kaun. New York: A. A. Knopf, 1943.

Krakowski, Stefan. *Kościół a Państwo Polski do początków XIV w.* Warsaw: Książka i Wiedza, 1950.

Krasnozhen, M. *Inovertsi na Rusi. Polozhenie nepravoslavnykh khristian.* Vols. X and XI of Uchenyia zapiski imperatorskogo Iurevskogo Universiteta. Iurev: K. Mattisen, 1902–1903.

Krylenko, N. V. *Sudebnye rechi, 1922–1930.* Moscow: Gosudarstvennoe iuridicheskoe izdatelstvo, 1931.

Krylev, I. *Pochemu my boremsia protiv religii?* Moscow: Ogiz, 1940.

Kucharzewski, Jan. *The Origins of Modern Russia.* New York: The Polish Institute of Arts and Sciences in America, 1948.

Kulakov, G. V. *Konstitutsiia SSSR i obrazovanie sezdov sovetov v skhemakh.* 4th ed. Moscow: Gosudarstvennoe izdatelstvo, 1925.

Kulski, W. W. *The Soviet Regime.* Syracuse: Syracuse University Press, 1954.

Kurczewski, Jan. *Biskupstwo Wileńskie.* Wilno: J. Zawadzki, 1912.

Lama, Friedrich. *Papst und Kurie in ihrer Politik nach dem Weltkrieg.* Illertissen: Martinusbuchhandlung, 1925.

Ledit, Joseph, S.J. *Archbishop John Baptist Cieplak.* Montreal: Palm Publishers, 1964.

Lefton, Jean. *La Crise Révolutionnaire, 1789–1846.* Vol. XX of *Histoire de l'Eglise depuis les Origines.* Edited by A. Fliche and V. Martin. Paris: Bloud and Gay, 1949.

Lenin, V. I. *The Letters of Lenin.* Translated and edited by Elizabeth Hill and Doris Mudie. New York: Harcourt, Brace, and Company, 1937.

————. *Materialism and Empirio-Criticism: Critical Comments on a Reactionary Philosophy.* New York: International Publishers, 1927.

————. *O religii.* Gosudarstvennoe politicheskoe izdatelstvo, 1955.

————. *Sochineniia.* 4th ed. 35 vols. Vols. XV, XVI, XX. Moscow: Ogiz, 1947.

Lescoeur, Louis. *L'Eglise Catholique en Pologne sous le gouvernment Russe depuis le premier partage jusqu'à nos jours (1772–1875).* 2nd ed. 2 vols. Paris: E. Plon et Cie., 1876.

Likowski, Eduard. *Die Ruthenisch-römische Kirchenvereinigung genannt Union zu Brest.* Translated by Paul Jedzinik. Freiburg i. B., Herdersche Verlagsbuchhandlung, 1904.

Lorimer, Frank. *The Population of the Soviet Union: History and Prospects.* Geneva: League of Nations, 1946.

Lossky, M. O. *History of Russian Philosophy.* New York: International Universities Press, Inc., 1951.

Lukachevskii, A. T. (ed.). *Antireligioznyi uchebnik.* Moscow: Ogiz, 1933.

Luzhnitskii, Grigor. *Ukrianska tserkva mizh skhodom i zakhodom: Naris istorii ukrainskoi tserkvi.* Philadelphia: Providence Association of Ukrainian Catholics, 1954.

Lyashchenko, Peter I. *History of the National Economy of Russia to the 1917 Revolution.* Translated by L. M. Herman. New York: The Macmillam Company, 1949.

Mailleux, Paul, S.J. *Exarch Leonard Fedorov: Bridgebuilder between Rome and Moscow.* New York: P. J. Kenedy and Sons, 1964.

Maliszewski, Edward. *Białoruś w cyfrach i faktach.* Piotrków: Wiadomości Polskie, 1918.

_____. *Polacy i polskość na Litwie i Rusi*. 2nd ed. Warsaw: Wł. Łazarski, 1916.

Manning, Clarence. *Ukraine under the Soviets*. New York: Bookman Associates, 1953.

Marx, Karl. *Capital: A Critique of Political Economy*. Translated by Samuel Moore and Edward Aveling. New York: The Modern Library, 1906.

Maynard, John. *Russia in Flux*. London: Victor Gollancz, 1946.

Meldin, William K. *Moscow and East Rome: A Political Study of the Relations of Church and State in Muscovite Russia*. Geneva: Librairie E. Droz, 1952.

Melgunov, S. P. *Krasnyi terror v Rossii, 1918–1923*. 2nd ed. Berlin: (n.p.), 1924.

Meysztowicz, Walerian. *De Archivo Nuntiaturae Varsaviensis quod nunc in Archivo Secreto Vaticano Servatur*. Vatican: (n.p.), 1944.

Mikhnevich, D. E. *Ocherki iz istorii katolicheskoi reaktsii*. Moscow: Akademiia nauk SSSR, 1953.

Miliukov, Paul. *La politique exterieure des Soviets*. 2nd ed. Paris: Libraire General de Droit et de Jurisprudence, 1936.

Moore, Barrington, Jr. *Soviet Politics—The Dilemma of Power: The Role of Ideas in Social Change*. Cambridge: Harvard University Press, 1951.

McCabe, Joseph. *Russia and the Roman*. London: Watts and Company, 1941.

Około-Kułak, Antoni. *Kościół w Rosji, dawniej, obecnie, i w przyszłości*. Sprawy misyjne. Series I. No. 8. Cracow: Wydawnictwo Księży Jezuitów, 1928.

Okolski, Szymon. *Biskupów kijowskich i czernichowskich świętego katolicko-rzymskiego kościoła porządek i liczba*. Cracow: Czas, 1853.

Paprocki, S. J. (ed.). *Minority Affairs and Poland: An Informatory Outline*. Warsaw: Nationality Research Institute, 1935.

Pawłowski, Stanisław. *Ludność rzymsko-katolicka w Polsko-Ruskiej części Galicji*. Prace geograficzne, Zeszyt III. Lwów: Książnica Polska, 1919.

Petrani, Aleksy. *Kolegium Duchowne w Petersburgu*. Lublin: Catholic University of Lublin, 1950.

Petrowicz, Gregorio. *L'Unione degli Armeni di Polonia con la Santa Sede (1626–1686)*. Rome: Pontifical Oriental Institute, 1950.

Philaret, Archbishop. *Geschichte der Kirche Russlands*. Translated by Dr. Blumenthal. Frankfurt am Main: Joseph Baer, Sotheran, and Company, 1872.

Pichon, Charles. *The Vatican and Its Role in World Affairs*. Translated by John Misrabi. New York: E. P. Dutton and Company, Inc., 1950.

Pierling, Paul. *La Russie et le Saint-Siège: Etudes Diplomatiques*. 2nd ed. 5 vols. Paris: Librairie Plon, 1906.

Pipes, Richard. *The Formation of the Soviet Union: Communism and Nationalism*. Cambridge: Harvard University Press, 1954.

Piwarski, Kazimierz. *Kuria rzymska a polski ruch narodowowyzwoleńczy, 1794–1863*. Warsaw: Państwowe Wydawnictwo Naukowe, 1955.

Predin, E., and Jarry, E. *Les luttes politiques et doctrinales aux XVIIè and XVIIIè siècles*. Vol. XIX-2 of *Histoire de l'Eglise depuis les Origines*. Edited by A. Fliche and V. Martin. Paris: Bloud and Gay, 1956.

Radek, Karl. *Vneshnaia politika sovetskoi Rossii*. Moscow: Gosudarstvennoe izdatelstvo, 1923.

Reddaway, W. F., Penson, J. J., Halecki, O., and Dyboski, R. (eds.). *The Cambridge History of Poland from Augustus II to Piłsudski (1697-1935)*. Cambridge: Cambridge University Press, 1951.

Reshetar, John S., Jr. *The Ukrainian Revolution, 1917–1920: A Study in Nationalism*. Princeton: Princeton University Press, 1952.

Reyburn, Hugh Y. *The Story of the Russian Church*. London: Andrew Melrose, Ltd., 1924.

Robinson, G. T. *Rural Russia under the Old Regime*. New York: Longman, Green, and Company, 1932.

Romer, Eugene. *Spis ludności na terenach administrowanych przez zarząd cywilny ziem wschodnich (grudzień 1919)*. Prace geograficzne, Zeszyt VII. Lwów: Książnica Polska, 1920.

Rostow, W. W. *The Dynamics of Soviet Society*. New York: Norton, 1953.

Rubakin, N. A. *Rossiia v tsifrakh. Strana. Narod. Sosloviia. Klassy*. St. Petersburg: Izdatelstvo "Vestnik Znaniia," 1912.

Rutkowski, Francis. *Arcybiskup Jan Cieplak (1857–1926): Szkic biograficzny*. Warsaw: Archdiocesan Press, 1934.

Rutkowski, Jan. *Histoire économique de la Pologne avant les Partages*. Paris: Librairie Ancienne Honoré Champion, 1927.

Saint Denis, André. *Pie XI contre les idoles*. Paris: Librairie Plon, 1939.

Schwartz, Harry. *Russia's Soviet Economy*. New York: Prentice-Hall, Inc., 1950.

Schweigl, P. J. *Moskau gegen den Vatikan*. Augsburg: Haas und Grabherr, 1930.

Sheinmann, M. M. *Vatikan mezhdu dvumia mirovymi voinami*. Moscow: Izdatelstvo Akademii Nauk SSSR, 1948.

_____. *Vatikan i Katolitsizm na sluzhbe mezhdunarodnoi reaktsii*. Moscow: Znanie, 1954.

Shibaev, V. P. *Etnicheskii sostav naseleniia evropeiskoi chasti soiuza SSSR*. Leningrad: Isdatelstvo Akademii Nauk SSSR, 1930.

Shmurlo, E. *Le Saint-Siège et L'Orient Orthodoxe Russie, 1609–1654*. Prague: Orbis, 1928.

Shub, D. *Lenin*. New York: Doubleday and Company, 1948.

Shotwell, James, and Laserson, Max M. *Poland and Russia, 1919–1945*. New York: The Carnegie Endowment for International Peace, 1945.

Sochaniewicz, Kazimierz. *Sprawa rewindykacji Archiwów i mienia kulturalnego Polski od Rosji*. Warsaw: Wydawnictwo T-wa Straży Kresowej, 1921.

Spinka, Matthew. *Christianity Confronts Communism*. London: The Religious Book Club, 1938.

_____. *The Church and the Revolution*. New York: The Macmillan Company, 1927.

Spridovich, A. I. *Istoriia bolshevizma v Rossii ot vozniknoveniia do zakhvata vlasti, 1883–1903–1917*. Paris: Franco-Russian Press, 1922.

Stalin, Joseph. *Sbornik Statei*. Moscow: Gosudarstvennoe izdatelstvo, 1920.

Stepanov, I. *The Problems and Methods of Anti-religious Propaganda*. Moscow: Gospolitprosvet, 1923.

Świechowski, M. *Das Polnische Element in den Litauischen Landen*. Cracow: Zentrales Verlagsbureau des Obersten Nationalen Commitees, 1918.

_____. *Population d'après les nationalités et la propriété foncière sur la terre du Grand Duché de Lithuanie*. Cracow: Bureau Central d'édification du Comité Suprême Polonais, 1918.

Szcześniak, B. *The Russian Revolution and Religion.* Notre Dame: University of Notre Dame Press, 1959.

Timasheff, Nicholas S. *The Great Retreat: The Growth and Decline of Communism in Russia.* New York: E. P. Dutton and Company, 1946.

_____. *Religion in the Soviet Russia.* New York: Sheed and Ward, 1942.

Tokarzewski, Marjan. *Przyczynek do historji męczeństwa rzymsko-katolickiego w dyecezjach kamienieckiej i łucko-żytomierskiej, 1863–1930.* Łuck: Drukarnia Kurji Biskupiej, 1931.

Tolstoi, Dmitri. *Romanism in Russia: An Historical Study.* Translated by Mrs. M'Kibbin. 2 vols. London: J. T. Hayes, 1874.

Towster, J. *Political Power in the U.S.S.R., 1917–1947.* New York: Oxford University Press, 1948.

Tyszkiewicz, S. *Sovetskoe Bezbozhie i papstvo.* Rome: (n.p.), 1950.

Umiastowski, R. *Russia and the Polish Republic, 1918–1941.* London: Aquafondata, 1944.

Vakar, Nicholas P. *Belorussia: The Making of a Nation.* Cambridge: Harvard University Press, 1956.

Vaks, Bor. *Ot Oktiabra do Genui. Mezhdunarodnye otnosheniia R. S. F. S. R.: Spravochnik.* Moscow: Izdatelstvo Narodnogo Komissariati po Innostrranym Delam, 1922.

Valentinov, A. A. *The Assault of Heaven: A Collection of Facts and Documents Relating to the Persecution of Religion and Church in Russia Based Mainly upon Official Sources.* Berlin: Max Mattisson Ltd., 1924.

_____. *Chernaia kniga.* Paris: Russian National Student Union, 1925.

Walsh, Edmund A. *The Last Stand: An Interpretation of the Soviet Five-Year Plan.* Boston: Little, Brown and Co., 1931.

_____. *Total Empire: The Roots and Progress of World Communism.* Milwaukee: The Bruce Publishing Company, 1951.

_____. *Why Pope Pius XI Asked Prayers for Russia on March 19, 1930,* New York: The Catholic Near East Welfare Association, 1930.

Wasilewski, Jan. *Arcybiskupi i administratorowie archidyecezji mohylowskiej.* Pińsk, 1930.

Wasilewski, Leon. *Kresy Wschodnie: Litwa i Białoruś. Podlasie i Chełmszczyzna, Galicya Wschodnia. Ukraina.* Warsaw: Towarzystwo Wydawnicze, 1917.

Wetter, Gustav A. *Dialectical Materialism.* New York: Praeger, 1958.

Wolfe, Bertram D. *Three Who Made a Revolution.* Boston: Beacon Press, 1948.

Zaleski, Stanisław. *Jezuici w Polsce.* Cracow: W. L. Anczyc i sp., 1908.

Zenkovsky, V. V. *A History of Russian Philosophy.* 2 vols. New York: Columbia University Press, 1953.

Zuev, F. *Mezhdunarodnyi imperializm—organizator napadeniia panskoi Polshi na Sovetskuiu Rossiiu.* Moscow: Gosudarstvennoe izdatelstvo politicheskoi literatury, 1954.

Articles (Secondary Material)

A. D., " White Russia," *Soviet Russia,* IV (January 8, 1921), 31–32.

Ammann, Albert M. "Mohilev," *Enciclopedia Cattolica,* VIII (1952), 1207–1208.

218   *Descent Into Darkness*

B—in, A. "Russkie katoliki v Moskve v kontse XVII stoletiia," *Istoricheskii vestnik,* XXV (St. Petersburg 1886), 588–599.

Brentano, H. "Zur Geschichte des Katholicismus in Russland," *Die Kultur,* IV (Vienna, 1906), 385–410.

"Church Treasures Used for Famine Relief," *Soviet Russia,* VI (1922), 294–295.

Demianovich, A. "Iezuity v zapadnoi Rossi (v 1569–1772 godakh)," *Zhurnal ministerstva narodnogo prosveshcheniia,* CLVI (St. Petersburg, 1871), 181–236.

Dudon, Paul. "Papes et tsars (1800–1847)," *Etudes,* CLXXII (Paris, 1922), 30–43.

Dziewanowski, M. K. "Piłsudski's Federalist Policy, 1919–1921," *Journal of Central European Affairs,* X (1950), 113–128, 271–287.

Fiedorowicz, J. "Znaczenie Litwy i Białej Ruśi dla Polski," *Świat,* I (1919), 1–3.

Gąsiorowski, Zygmunt J. "Polish-Czechoslovak Relations, 1918–1922," *The Slavonic and East-European Review* XXXV (1956), 172–193.

George, André. "Le Procès de Mgr. Cieplak en Russie," *Correspondent,* CCLXXXXV (Paris, 1924), 532–536.

Gnatowski, J. "Katolicyzm i Państwo Rosyjskie," *Świat,* XII (1917), 1–2.

_____. "Rzym a Rosya," *Świat,* XII (1917), 1–3.

Halecki, Oscar. "Wschodnia granica Polski w świetle historji," *Przegląd dyplomatyczny,* I (Warsaw, 1919), 45–57.

Hanski, Pierre. "La tragédie de l'église Russe," *Etudes,* CLXXII (1922), 295–312.

Hermogen, Archbishop. "Vatikan i krestovye pokhody," *Zhurnal Moskovskoi patriarkhii* (March 1953), pp. 58–64.

Innokentti, Arkhimandrit. "Sviato-Uspensko-Pochaevskaia lavra v borbe katolicyzmom," *Zhurnal Moskovskoi Patriarkhii* (October 1953), pp. 28–32.

Ivanov, A. "Velikii grekh papskoi gordyni," *Zhurnal Moskovskoi Patriarkhii* (January 1954), pp. 51–56.

_____. "Znachenie krestovykh pokhodov v rozvitii vzaimnootnoshenii mezhdu Pravoslavnym Vostokom i katolicheskim Zapadom," *Zhurnal Moskovskoi Patriarkhii* (February 1954), pp. 39–46.

Karpovich, Michael. "Church and State in Russian History," *The Russian Review,* III (1944), 10–20.

Konopczyński, L. "Polish Instruction in Lithuania and Ruthenia," *The Eastern Provinces of Poland* (Paris, Polish Commission of Works preparatory to the Peace Conference, 1919).

Lacko, Michael. "Minsk," *Enciclopedia Cattolica,* VIII (1952), 1057.

Loret, M. "Kościół katolicki w początkach panowania Aleksandra I," *Biblioteka warszawska,* No. 3 (1913), pp. 493–520.

L., J. "Z działalności rosyjskiej konferencji politycznej w Paryżu," *Przegląd dyplomatyczny,* I (1919), 322–330.

Maliszewski, Edward. "Białoruś Sowiecka i jej stosunki narodowościowe," *Sprawy narodowościowe,* I (1927), 509–519.

Meysztowicz, Walerian. "L'église Catholique," *Pologne, 1919–1939,* I (1946), 335–362.

_____. "Kościoły katolickie ob. łac. na obszarach Rosji (1772–1914)," *Sacrum Poloniae Millenium,* II (Rome, 1955), 467–497.

Mikhailov, André. "Les origines anticatholiques du Bolshevisme," *Etudes,* CC (1929), 14–43.

"Mohylewska archidjecezja i prowincja," *Encyklopedja kościelna,* XIV (Warsaw, 1875), 531–558.

Nikanov, V. "Rol pravoslavnoi tserkvi v osvoboditelnoi voine ukrainskogo naroda," *Zhurnal Moskovskoi Patriarkhii* (December 1953), pp. 3–41.

"Obecny stan ludności polskiej na Ukrainie," *Sprawy narodowościowe,* I (1927), 459–462.

Olšr, Giuseppe. "Storia Religiosa," *Enciclopedia Cattolica,* X (1953), 1464–1466.

"O vvedenie russkogo iazyka v katolicheskoe bogosluzhenie (1864–1869)," *Russkii Arkhiv,* XII (1874), 1262–1270.

"Polonja na dalekim wschodzie," *Przegląd powszechny,* CLIX (1932), 281–284.

Palmieri, Aurelio. "Russia," *The Catholic Encyclopedia,* XIII (1912), 231–275.

"Petlura and the Vatican," *Soviet Russia,* III (1920), 214–215.

Poczapowski, Jan. "Z Rozważań nad naszym programem agrarnym," *Naród i Państwo,* July 10, 1918.

"Polacy w powiecie rzeczyckim i homelskim," *Sprawy narodowościowe,* I (1927), 69.

"Polacy na Ukrainie," *Sprawy narodowościowe,* II (1928), 379–392.

"Polityka narodowościowa na Białorusi Sowieckiej," *Sprawy narodowościowe,* I (1927), 18–23.

"Rejon polski w Dolbuszu im. Marchlewskiego," *Sprawy narodowościowe,* I (1927), 314–316.

Reshetar, John S., Jr. "Ukrainian Nationalism and the Orthodox Church," *The American Slavic and East European Review,* X (1951), 38–49.

Rhode, Gotthold. "Die Entstehung der Curzon-Linie," *Osteuropa,* I (1955), 81–92.

——————. "Die Ostgrenze Polens im Mittelalter," *Zeitschrift für Ostforschung,* II (1953), 51–65.

Rimsky, M. J. "L'aide pontificale aux affamés de Russie," *Etudes,* CLXXII (1922), 651–661.

Shchebalski, P. K. "Katolichestvo v Rossii pri Ekaterine i posle neia," *Russkii vestnik,* LII (1864), 62–644.

Shliapkin, J. A. "K istorii polemiki mizhdu moskovskimi i malorusskimi uchenimi v kontse XVII veka," *Zhurnal ministerstva narodnogo prosveshcheniia* (1885), pp. 210–252.

Shmurlo, E. "Russkie katoliki kontsa XVII veka," *Zapiski russkogo nauchnogo instituta v Belgrade,* Vypusk 3 (1931), pp. 1–30.

S. K., "Ukraińska prawosławna Cerkiew," *Sprawy narodowościowe,* I (1927), 63–64.

Slovachevskii, L. "Po uniatskom delu (1873-1875)," *Russkii Arkhiv,* XIII-2 (1875), 355–365.

Stark, T. "Description démographique," *Pologne, 1919–1939,* II (1946), 97–126.

Timasheff, N. S. "The Church in the Soviet Union," *The Russian Review,* I (1941), 20–30.

"Tyraspol," *Podręczna encyklopedya kościoła,* XXXVIII (Cracow, 1913), 334–335.

Vega. "Ottorgnutye nasiliem–vozsoedineny liuboviu," *Katolichaskii vestnik,* III (1933), 1–4.

V. M. "Exposing the Powers of Darkness," *Soviet Russia,* I (July 12, 1919), 16–17.

Volkonsky, P. M. "Obrazovanie russkoi katolicheskoi tserkvi v Rossii," *Katolicheskii vestnik,* XI (Harbin, 1941), 154–159.

Wiercinski, Felix. "Auf den steilen Pfaden zur russischen Union," *Stimmen der Zeit,* III (1926), 278–293.

Zatko, James J. "The Union of Suzdal, 1222–1252," *The Journal of Ecclesiastical History,* III (1957), 33–52.

————. "The Catholic Church and Russian Statistics, 1804–1917," *The Polish Review,* V (1960), 35–52.

————. "The Roman Catholic Church and its Legal Position under the Provisional Government in Russia in 1917," *The Slavonic and East European Review,* XXXVIII (1960), 476–492.

"Zjazd rad mniejszości polskich na Ukrainie," *Sprawy narodowościowe,* I (1927), 194.

"Z ziem wschodnich od Rosji przez okupację odciętych," *Naród i Państwo,* No. 12 (April 13, 1918), 59–66.

"Z życia mniejszości polskiej na Białorusi Sowieckiej," *Sprawy narodowościowe,* I (1927), 317–318.

INDEX